The Mountsberg Heritage

The Mountsberg Historical Society

THE MOUNTSBERG HERITAGE

The
Mountsberg Historical Society

The Mountsberg Heritage
Revised – 3rd Edition

The Mountsberg Historical Society was formed primarily to produce this publication. It no longer exists. The photographs, negatives and much of the research material used to produce this book are now part of the collection of the Flamborough Archives.

In 2014 the book was revised by the Flamborough Heritage Society primarily to enhance the photographs. Aside from correcting a few spelling errors and adding the index which was previously produced as a separate document, no other changes were made. It was only available on CD.

Due to multiple requests for the publication, it is has now been reprinted in book form.

> The Waterdown-East Flamborough Heritage Society
> The Flamborough Archives

August 2015
Waterdown, Ontario

ISBN: 978-0-921592-47-1

Table of Contents

Credits ....(iv)
Bibliography ....(iv)
 Acknowledgements ....(v)

Part I

Pre-Settlement Times 3
Settlers Arrive 5
Early Surveys and Land Grants 6
Topography, Land and Soil Classification 7
Clearing the Forest 8
Farming in Mountsberg from 1840 to 1900 9

Part II

Concession 11 15
Concession 12 (including the Store and the Post Office) 25
Concession 13 63
Concession 14 87

P art III

The Churches 96
The School 110
Council Members 115
The Railway 115
Barn Raising 117
Telephones 119
The Community Park 119
Literary Society 122
Women's Institute 122
4-H 123
Conservation Authority 124

Part IV

Folklore 127

Credits

Mrs. Douglas Cleghorn
The Late Mrs. Frank Coulson
Mrs. Donald Farquharson
The Late Mrs. Albert Hewins
Mrs. Wallace Hopkins
Mrs. Frank Jamieson
Mr. Ernest W. Kerr
Mr. C.C. Laking
Miss Margaret MacPherson

Miss Fanny Mount
Mrs. Patricia Orosz, Typist
Mrs. A. Page
Mrs. Chris Sauer, Typist
Mr. Gordon Stewart
Mr. William Wingrove
The Late Mr. T. Roy Woodhouse
Kind response from everyone

Bibliography

Attendance Record 1840-1966, S.S. No. 6, East Flamborough
County Registry Office, Hamilton Directories-1861, 1865-66, 1867, 1868, 1869, 1871
Dominion of Canada Archives
Hamilton Public Library
Preliminary History of Mountsberg, compiled by G.A. Hewins and Beatrice Woolsey
Statutes of Upper Canada, 1792-1840
WENTWORTH Page Atlas of 1875

Acknowledgements

In 1978, the Mountsberg Historical Society was formed to compile and publish a history of Mountsberg. The work of producing this book, "The Mountsberg Heritage", has truly been a community project. Present residents, past residents and their families and friends have all contributed their part of the story of this community, roughly bounded by the school section for S.S. No. 6, East Flamborough. The result is a very complete account of the Mountsberg heritage for the people who founded the community in the 1830's and those of us who came later, to the 1st of January, 1980.

Seventeen people volunteered as directors, the majority of whom are senior citizens. They were: Gordon A. Hewins, President; Cliff McKay, Vice-President; John D. Campbell, Treasurer; Mrs. David A. Croft, Secretary; Mrs. W.C. Cust; Terence Dempsey; the late Miss Eba Haines; Mr. and Mrs. D.M. Heddle; Mr. A.R. Hewins; Mr. and the late Mrs. Oliver Leslie; Mr. and Mrs. J.K.H. Parry; Mrs. Peter Pawlik and Mr. and Mrs. Oscar Pegg.

The Directors are particularly grateful to the many individuals who went out of their way to search family and community records and to provide photographs so that our writers would have as complete information as possible on which to base this history. On the opposite page we list many of these people and say a very sincere "Thank you" to them and apologize if inadvertently we have overlooked anyone.

In this, as in most organizations, the work load does not fall equally on all participants; and nowhere is this more true than when we recognized the contribution of Mrs. W.C. (Merle Hewins) Cust, who, for over two years has given unstintingly of her time and has done the majority of the writing. Without her, there would not have been "The Mountsberg Heritage".

Mrs. David A. (Jane) Croft, our Secretary, has been an indefatigable worker, not only looking after all the administration, but spending many hours tracking down potential contributors of historical records and photographs, which have provided much of the detail and interest that makes this book a true heritage of Mountsberg.

The material gathered for this book was also used for the Mountsberg Women's Institute Tweedsmuir History, so any additions or corrections can be made at that source.

The Directors express gratitude to the New Horizons Fund of the Department of Health and Welfare, Ottawa, for their financial assistance, without which, publication of this book would not have been possible. Our thanks also to the Flamborough Recreation Committee for the use of the Community Centre.

I

The Coming of the Settlers

Mountsberg Store on Centre Road, 1909. *The late Mrs. Oliver Leslie.*

Pre-settlement Times

Our lands were steeped in history long before the settlers began to arrive in the 1830's. The beginning of the Indian era is lost to time, but about 1500 A.D. this area marked the northerly reaches of the Neutral Nation. In 1648, the Iroquois raided Huronia (near Midland) and, because the Neutrals gave refuge to fleeing Hurons, they, too, were either killed or scattered, never to be known as a nation again. Our vicinity, the first to be reached by the invading Iroquois, must have suffered most severely.

The Iroquois did not remain. Later, the Ojibways came for a while and, still later, the Mississaugas, both members of the Algonquin tribe and noted for wandering.

Indian relics, such as arrowheads and skinning stones, turned up from time to time, in practically every farm in the neighbourhood. The flatlands beside the Twelve-Mile Creek, between the 13th Concession and Mountsberg Road, showed much evidence of Indian presence of the past. According to local legend, two large burial mounds once were evident southwest of the creek, near the 13th Road, on the farm settled by Josiah Mount. And, not far from the little-used 12th Concession, on Lot 7, southwest (present Pawlik property), is a blackened stone 'oven' believed to have been used by Indians.

In past times, Indian encampments, some with palisades, have been discovered in our general area, the nearest being a campsite, excavated more than 100 years ago on Lot 8, Concession 13, not far from Centre Road. Artifacts, indicative of the Neutrals, were unearthed. Mr. Joseph H. Smith, our former teacher and school inspector, told of it in his 'Historical Sketch of the County of Wentworth', published in 1897, saying:

> *"A large camping ground was recently discovered, in which there was a bed of ashes fully five feet in depth. The camping ground was covered with heavy timber and must, therefore, have been a very old resort, which, doubtless, belonged to the Neuter Nation. When this bed of ashes was carefully examined, it was found to contain many valuable relics. Near the top were glass beads, brass kettles, and other evidences of contact with Europeans. Farther down, the relics were of bone and stone or pottery".*

Even after settlers had moved in, groups of Seneca hunters occasionally roved our hills and woodlands. It was their custom to stop at a spring at the home of Pioneer John Haines, on Lot 2, northwest, Concession 12.

Flamboro East, West of 10th Con.

Flamborough East, Concessions 11 to 14, from the WENTWORTH Page Atlas of 1875. Note the interesting spelling of family names.

Mr. Haines allowed them the use of an enclosed porch for shelter or rest, and there they might be found at odd times, always friendly and mainly silent.

Not far from the Haines farm buildings was evidence of an early Neutral camp. A deep layer of ashes turned up with every ploughing, and, according to a handed-down story, an Indian burial ground was located near by, on a rise of land, across the road.

Only about six miles away, in a straight line, is the site of the Indian village of Tinawatawa (near Westover) of special historical significance. There, in 1669, La Salle and his party journeyed after landing at a spot believed to have been at, or near, the present La Salle Park at Aldershot. On the way, quite unplanned, and in a million to one chance, he met Joliet returning from explorations in the region of the Upper Great Lakes. Together, they visited the Indian village.

From there, two priests and seven other Frenchmen went on to winter at the present site of Port Dover, while La Salle and the remainder of his party continued to Niagara.

Settlers Arrive

It was unfortunate that our ancestors left no written record of their ocean trip or their experiences in establishing a home in thickly forested land. No doubt, the problems of providing food and shelter and fuel for winter left little time for anything that did not contribute to basic needs. Also, these people grew up in England in the time of child labour, with long hours, that left too little opportunity for education, so such a narrative may have been too great a task. And, the nearest place then, to buy paper and pencil, was Dundas.

The group of English friends who crossed the Atlantic together in 1835, included the families of Philip Johnson, John Revel (early spelling), Cornelius Hewins, Josiah Mount and Mrs. Mount's bachelor brother, Joseph Page. All were from Lincolnshire, except Josiah Mount, a native of Leicestershire.

They came by sailing vessel which, depending on the weather, would take from three to six weeks to reach Quebec. Their trip up the St. Lawrence, if it followed the usual custom of that period, would be by open barge, known as a Durham boat, which was propelled by pike poles, when not towed by oxen or horses. By day, passengers, if they wished, might stroll leisurely along the shore. By night, they slept on shore, hopefully under stars and not rain clouds. The trip across Lake Ontario might be either by sailing ship or steamer, with a stop over in Toronto to procure location certificates. Then, on to Dundas. The trip from Quebec to Dundas would take not less than three weeks.

They were still fifteen miles from their promised land, and faced the hazards of the Brock Road. This road, planned in 1827 to connect the budding town of Guelph with the commerce of Dundas, was still in a primitive state. In 1834, it was described thus: "It runs through a dense pine wood and extensive cedar swamps, with very few clearings. It is admirable travelling when frozen up in winter, but almost impassable in spring and autumn months, and but little improved in the midst of summer."

With the perils of the Brock Road overcome, the Lincoln group crossed their final two miles through trackless forest.

No one was ever accorded the honour of being the first settler. The English families from Lincoln were the nucleus of the later village of Mountsberg, but two Scottish families had settled earlier in the community. The Campbells of Lot 4, Concession 13 were there by 1832, perhaps earlier, and the Cameron brothers, Archibald and Duncan, arrived in adjoining Lot 3, in 1833. John Page, Lot 8, Concession 12 (older brother of Joseph) is thought to have been in the area, if not on that lot, before 1835.

Four of six Wingrove brothers, Charles, Thomas, George and James, may have arrived in East Flamborough at different times in the mid to late 1830's: Charles settled on Lot 10, southeast, Concession 12, and George, across the Mountsberg Road on Lot 10, northwest. Thomas chose Lot 10, southeast, Concession 13, and James took up Lot 9, alongside. They were from Northampton, England, and selected this area after a sojourn at Campden, near Vineland.

Abraham Purnell, Sr. from Gloucester, England, living on Lot 11, southeast, Concession 12, always was regarded as one of the very earliest settlers, perhaps before 1835. He joined the Lincoln group in founding the Mountsberg Methodist congregation.

Sometime around 1833, the related families of John Haines and William Barnes came from Wiltshire, England, and settled on Lot 2 of the 12th Concession, Mr. Haines on the northwest half and Mr. Barnes on the southeast half. At about the same time, George Lewis took up 50 acres at the southeast end of Lot 3. He seems to have been trapped in a problem resulting from the re-survey (as described later), and was forced to buy an extra 5 acres on which his cabin stood.

Also, there may have been squatters who vanished without a trace. One such abode is reputed to have been on a knoll in the otherwise flat land, northeast of the Community Park. With a good spring nearby, it would be a likely spot.

An Upper Canada Statute of 1838 gave instructions to assessors, and stated that persons unlawfully on the land must leave if a bona fide settler claimed the land. Otherwise, they must arrange to lease or purchase or leave. East Flamborough records began in 1841 with the first assessment; and that would mark the end of local squatters.

Other residents, not mentioned in the foregoing, whose names appeared in the 1841 assessment and census records were:

Concession 11—John Perry, Lot 6, southeast;

James Sullivan, Lot 7, southeast; James Smith, Lot 7, northwest; Andrew Smith, Lot 8, southeast; Joseph Beaty, Lot 8, northwest and William Savage, Lot 9, northwest. No deeds were recorded in the Perry or Beaty name.

Concession 12 -- Alexander Campbell, Lot 1, northwest; George Fearnley, Lot 9, southeast and Robert Kerr, Lot 11, northwest.

Concession 13-- Joseph Linn, Lot 1, southeast; Joseph Dixon, Lot 2, southeast; Thomas Revell, Lot 7, southeast and James Wheeler, Lot 8, southeast.

Concession 14-- Adam Darling, Lot 10 and Charles Buchan, Lots 11 and 12.

Early Surveys and Land Grants

Concessions 11 to 14

Settlement was slow in the northwest end of East Flamborough, as all the land, except Lot 7 in Concession 11, was tied up either as Clergy Reserves or Brock grants.

Back in 1792, Augustus Jones was appointed by Governor Simcoe to survey the townships around Lake Geneva (Hamilton Bay). One of his first tasks was to establish a Base Line, running from the east end of the bay, due northwest as far as Arthur in Wellington County. Part of that line became the townline between Wentworth and Halton.

In 1797-98, when John Stegman surveyed the lots of East Flamborough, he worked from this line, and numbered them from there. At that time, much of the first five concessions were occupied. As a result, the one-seventh for the clergy, provided for in the Constitutional Act of 1791, was crowded into Concessions 6 to 13. Thus, the Clergy controlled Lots 3, 6, 9 and 12 in the 11th and 13th Concessions, and Lots 2, 5, 10 and 13 in the 12th Concession. There was no 14th Concession then.

Nothing further happened until October 6, 1817, when all land that remained in Concessions 11 to 13, except Lot 7 in Concession 11, a total of 5000 acres, was granted to four brothers, heirs of General Sir Isaac Brock who was killed at Queenston in 1812. All four, Daniel De Lisle Brock, William Brock, John S. Brock and Irving Brock lived in Guernsey Island, England.

Many more years went by, leaving the land undisturbed except for roving hunters. Eventually, an effort was made to encourage settlement in this large tract of forest. In September, 1833, the Brocks transferred title to some of their land to William Henry Draper of York, in order to make sales easier for settlers. In the meantime, after 1827, a limited number of Clergy Reserves could be sold each year. Thus, in 1834 to 1838, Galt's Canada Company bought about 1000 acres in Concessions 11 to 14, all of which had been Clergy land, except Lot 2 in Concession 11.

John Galt (1779-1839), an author from Ayrshire, Scotland, came to Upper Canada, by appointment, in 1826, to promote settlement. His home and office was the first building in what became the City of Guelph. He was the chief founder of the Canada Land Company organized to open up the Clergy Reserves; clergy meaning the Church of England. The scattered lots were a deterrent to settlement and the cause of dissension among other religious denominations. Over much protest, the Canada Company succeeded in controlling two and a half million acres of former Clergy Reserves, gradually released for sale by the Crown.

Settlement began in the early to mid-1830's, and a re-survey of lots became necessary about 1835-36, before any deeds could be given. A shortage of land, due to early errors, resulted in considerable change, northwest of the 11th Concession Road.

Beginning with the 11th Concession, there were, henceforth, twelve lots in the width of the township, instead of thirteen, which explains why the Centre Road veers westerly at that point as lots became a little wider, northeast to southwest. No one was living on the 11th Concession, so those lots were reduced from 200 acres to 150 acres in order that people already on Concessions 12 and 13 might get their full 100 acres per half lot with the least possible inconvenience.

This meant that the 12th Concession road moved to the southeast, as did the 13th. Since roads at that time were mere forest trails that followed the line of least resistance, no road-building labour was sacrificed, but all settlers' cabins bore a changed relation to their public roads of the future. So that more than half the number of homes of that day were not left stranded midway between the new lines of the 12th and 13th Concessions, a new access road, narrower than the standard 66 feet, was incorporated into the new survey. In early times it was called the Cross Road; now Mountsberg Road.

The over-all change resulted in a surplus of land at the northwest end of the township; so the 14th Concession, with a road allowance and 45 acre lots, came into being. Clergy Reserves, which lost the vanished Lot 13 of Concession 12, as well as 200 acres in Concession 11, were given Lots 2, 5 and 10 in the new 14th Concession. The remaining lots of the 14th went to Brocks in lieu of the former Lot 13 in both the 11th and the 13th Concession.

There was one lot where the re-survey created a dilemma and changed the outlook of three founding families. The Lincoln group, after choosing their adjoining lots in Concession 12, built their log cabins as close as possible in the interests of communication; but, when new stakes were driven for wider, shorter lots, Cornelius Hewins of Lot 7, northwest and Philip Johnson of Lot 6, southeast, found themselves squatting on John Revel's Lot 6, northwest. John Revel seems to have been the chief victim of the survey error, but the three friends managed to work out their problem. Mr. Revel got a deed for his 100 acres in March 1837, and in January 1839, sold Cornelius Hewins 24 acres, alongside the 13th Concession, on which the Hewins buildings stood. By November 1847, a compromise was completed with Philip Johnson, which involved a trade of 34 acres, whereby Mr. Revel accepted a like acreage at the southeast end of Lot 6, southeast. But, since it was a less desirable, less accessible piece of property, 6 pounds went with the transaction. Egress from the seemingly landlocked 42 acres which John Revel kept for himself was effected by driving southwest to the lot line between lots 6 and 7, then southeast to the new given road.

In 1854, Clergy Reserves were abolished entirely. Before that date, as well as after, the Crown sold 1400 acres of Clergy Reserves to individuals. Most, but not all, of the buyers were resident settlers. Having in mind one other sale (Lot 6, Concession 11) there were but twelve families living in the four Concessions who received Crown deeds.

Still there were problems. Many people settled on Brock land not within the control of Mr. Draper, and they waited years to get a deed. A unique deed is the one obtained by Joseph Linn, when he paid 87 pounds, 10 shillings, for the 100 acres of Lot 1, southeast, Concession 13 (later the Harold Small farm). This deed, dated May 16, 1846, was signed in Guernsey, England, by Sophie Brock, sole heiress of Daniel De Lisle Brock who died in 1842. It was the only direct sale from the Brock family of Guernsey Island.

On January 19, 1849, all the Brock heirs and heiresses (by then involving children of the four brothers) known as Ferdinand B. Tupper, et al, put the remaining Brock land in trust to George Brock, a relative at Niagara, who had no claim to the Brock grant. On February 19, 1850, Mr. Draper turned over to George Brock the land he had not sold. In the few years of his duties, George Brock signed many deeds. On January 19, 1853, he was replaced by John De Haviland Uttermarck of Guernsey Island, England, who was appointed trustee of all unsold Brock land. One day later, the holdings were diminished by about 1,800 acres in an outright sale to John Hillyard Cameron, a Toronto judge (no relation to local Camerons).

This act of Judge Cameron was a favour to many settlers. Almost immediately many deed transfers were made to people who had been waiting about twenty years for title to their land.

Add to this the fact that Mr. Cameron bought some property that once had been in the name of William Henry Draper, and it is understandable that many lots had a bewildering history of land transfers before a settler had a chance to sign on the dotted line.

Topography, Land and Soil Classification

Looking northeast, Lot 6, Concession 13, into Concession 14.   A.R. Hewins.

'Rolling' is the description of the land. The hills and valleys are quite noticeable to anyone living here or driving along the roads. Across the community from No. 6 Highway to the Wentworth-Halton Townline along the Mountsberg and Campbellville Roads there are three hills.

The two hills northeast of Centre Road start near the 12th Concession road allowance. The hill close the Centre Road starts further down on the 11th Concession northeast of Centre Road. These hills widen and narrow and taper off at the lower land. They curve toward the west on the 13th Concession.

The overlay in these hills to the bed rock can be as deep as 25 or 30 metres. The soil is clay loam with a clay bottom, inclined to be a bit late in the spring and to get rather muddy in a wet fall where the surface drainage is poor. This clay loam can be rated high for its inherent productive capability.

The lower arable land is more level, inclined to be a sandy loam with a gravel bottom. Someplaces the bed rock rises to the surface, some of the land is a bit gravelly and there can be gravel knolls. This is earlier land. Its crop producing capability, one year with another, is about equal to the higher heavier land.

Most of the lowest land is not workable and has been left as wood-lots or pasture. A few of the lots in the area have very little working land. The McCrae Place on Lot 5, southeast, Concession 13 is an example. Most of the farms have some of this kind of land. It is by no means worthless as it has supplied pasture and forest products over the years. Features of this land are craggy bed rock, stones, swamp and some marsh.

There are two creeks, the Twelve-Mile Creek, of which the Mountsberg Dam forms a part, and the creek at the townline of what was East and West Flamborough, which is Bronte Creek. A hundred or more years ago, when there was more forest cover, there were more springs. There was a small year-round stream at the line fence between Lots 9 and 10 on the Mountsberg Road.

If the early pioneers didn't know before they came, they soon found out that this part of the country had stones, big and little. The hills and valleys were carved by a glacier that punched a hole in the Niagara Escarpment between Rattlesnake Point and Mount Nemo and scattered stones far and wide.

About 50 to 60 percent of the land is arable. This area cannot be classified as good farming country, but the soil is good.

Clearing the Forest

Southern Ontario was covered with forest before the early settlers came. The indigenous trees of this area were the same as the trees that still grow here. White pine was the dominant species on the higher land, mixed with hardwood, mostly sugar maple.

There was a lumbering industry in Ontario before 1800. It is unlikely, however, that any lumbering was done in this area before it was settled. White pine was the lumber most in demand. For many years, large quantities were shipped to England and Scotland in the form of "Waney" board. This was squared timber.

To form a mental picture of the forest at the time the land was settled is rather difficult. There were perhaps 75 trees to the acre. Some of the pine trees were magnificent specimens. They could be 4 feet or more at the stump and over 100 feet tall. Other trees would be much younger and smaller. It is quite likely a team of horses or oxen could be driven among the trees. There would be some fallen trees in different stages of decay. It was rather difficult to get through the cedar swamps.

Some people believe that the settlers, when clearing the land, cut the trees down, let them dry, and then burned them. This hardly seems reasonable. They built houses and barns at the same time they were claiming the land. The towns and villages were growing rapidly. Vast quantities of wood were used as fuel, for heating, burning lime, bricks, and charcoal, and firing steam engines. Logs were split into rails for fences. Lumber was used in manufacturing and exported to the United States.

It was near the end of the century before all the first growth was harvested.

Only good, sound, knot-free logs were saleable. The rest of the tree and trees for which there was no demand for lumber had to be burned unless they were used or sold for fuel. The smaller trees had to be cut down when clearing the land. Hardwood ashes were saved, leached, and boiled down to potash.

Lumbermen sometimes would buy the land that had not yet been logged, usually land not farmable, harvest the larger trees, and then sell the land back to the farmer from whom they had bought it. No farmer got rich cutting and selling forest products. They probably only made current wages.

Cutting a tree down is one thing, getting rid of the stump is something else. For many years the farmers had to work among the stumps. Each year they would clear some land until they had their farms all cleared. This took many years. The hardwood stumps rotted out in a few years. The larger pine stumps stayed in the ground until stumping machines came on the scene as early as 1850.

There are still a few stump fences left to attest to the size and durability of the white pine. The large stones also were a problem. They were removed by stoning machines and placed into fence-rows. There are still stone fences on the farms.

Farming in Mountsberg-1840 to 1900

By 1840 the settlers had taken possession of the farms pretty much as we know them today. There was a family on each farm. Good log houses and log barns were built. The foundation had been laid for the progress and prosperity of the next 60 years.

The Agricultural Censuses of 1851 and 1861 show the progress of farming in Mountsberg. They indicate that the farms were being cleared and operated quite similarly.

Here is the census information for 2 representative farmers.

Thomas Revell—Lot 7, Southeast, Concession 13

1851
Acres—100
Culivated—55
Crops—27
Pasture—27
Garden—1
Wild—45
Wheat—12 (200 bus.)
Peas—3 (60 bus.)
Oats—7 (230 bus.)
Buckwheat—0
Corn—1/2 (15 bus.)
Potatoes—1/2 (28 bus.)
Turnips—0
Hay—7 bundles
Wool—45 lbs.
Maple Sugar—120 lbs.
Fulled Cloth—17 yds.
Flannel—30 yds.
Bulls/Oxen/Steers—5
Cows—2
Calves—4
Horses—2
Sheep—13
Pigs—3
Butter—160 lbs.
Cheese—0
Beef—0
Pork—1000 lbs.

1861
Acres—100
Cultivated—51
Crops—43
Pasture—7
Garden—1
Wild—49
Value of farm—$3,500
Value of implements—$60
Fall Wheat—9 (250 bus.)
Spring Wheat—6 (120 bus.)
Peas—3 (50 bus.)
Oats—3 (150 bus.)
Barley—0
Potatoes—1 (150 bus.)
Turnips—0
Hay—7 bundles
Wool—54 lbs.
Maple Sugar—180 lbs.
Fulled Cloth—0
Flannel—36 yds.
Bulls/Oxen—3
Steers/Heifers—3
Cows—4
Horses—3
Value of Horses—$200
Colts—1
Sheep—16
Pigs—3
Value of Livestock—$549
Butter—0
Cheese—100 lbs.
Beef—0
Pork—5 barrels
Pleasure carriage—0
Value—0

John Hewins—Lot 7, Northwest and Part of Lot 6, Concession 12

1851
Acres—124
Cultivated—50
Crops—25
Pasture—24
Garden—1
Wild—74
Wheat—9 (150 bus.)
Peas—1/2 (10 bus.)
Oats—3 (150 bus.)
Buckwheat—0
Corn—2 (100 bus.)
Potatoes—1/4 (30 bus.)
Turnips—1)125 bus.)
Hay—13 bundles
Wool—35 lbs.
Maple Sugar—100 lbs.
Fulled Cloth—25 yds.
Flannel—125 yds.
Bulls/Oxen/Steers—0
Cows—3
Calves—8
Horses—4
Sheep—8
Pigs—5
Butter—320 lbs.
Cheese—0
Beef—400 lbs.
Pork—1200 lbs.

1861
Acres—124
Cultivated—64
Crops—45
Pasture—15
Garden—4
Wild—60
Value of farm—$3000
Value of implements—$150
Fall Wheat—15 (400 bus.)
Spring Wheat—6 (120 bus.)
Peas—4 (100 bus.)
Oats—4 (200 bus.)
Barley—0
Potatoes—1/2 (30 bus.)
Turnips—0
Hay—10 bundles
Wool—60 lbs.
Maple Sugar—0
Fulled Cloth—0
Flannel—0
Bulls/Oxen—2
Steers/Heifers—2
Cows—3
Horses—2
Value of horses—$125
Colts—1
Sheep—15
Pigs—3
Value of livestock—$400
Butter—240 lbs.
Cheese—0
Beef—0
Pork—700 lbs.
Pleasure Carriage—1
Value—$60

Fulled cloth is a textile term; actually, fulling means felting. The cloth is made dense with a smooth surface. Melton cloth is one example.

A bale of hay weighed 60 lbs.

Here is an extract from the 1860 Board of Agriculture Report for Nelson Township.

Exports for 1859

Fall Wheat (bus.)	125,192	Bbls. of flour manufactured out of above	12,353
Spring Wheat	27,190	Butter (kegs)	100
Oats	25,000	Lumber shipped (feet)	2,500,000
Barley	35,460	Lumber at Port Nelson and Wellington	
Peas	8,000	Square (Burlington)	1,000,000 bd. ft.

Cattle

From 1840 to 1870 most farmers kept a small herd of cattle; 3 or 4 cows, the young cattle and a yoke of oxen. Oxen were the main source of power for the first few years. These cattle were referred to in later years (1880's) as native cattle.

It is presumed they came from the United States with the United Empire Loyalists and later settlers. The steers grew into large oxen, up to 2,000 lbs. apiece, were very strong and quite useful in clearing the land. These cattle were horned, red, roan and white in colour and fairly large and rangy in conformation. As a guess, they may have been Teeswater cattle, an English breed from which the Shorthorns were developed. Maybe they were descendants of John and Priscilla Alden's white bull.

In England and Scotland, starting in the late 1700's, remarkable improvements were made in breeding livestock and developing purebred lines.

In the 1860's and 1870's these improved strains were being brought to Canada, mostly by business men whose trade took them to the old country. Thomas Mc-Crae of Guelph imported Galloways. This breed did not become popular. W.D. Flatt of Millgrove established a good herd of Scotch Shorthorn in the 1890's. The main breeds imported were Shorthorns, Herefords, Aberdeen-Angus and Ayrshires. The Shorthorns seemed to cross better with the native cattle. Until well into the 20th century most of the cattle in Ontario were grade Shorthorns or Durhams, as they were sometimes called.

Purebred beef cattle breeders in Ontario found a market in the Western U.S.A. after the Civil War, for breeding stock. The Texas Longhorns didn't last very long. The Herefords proved to be the best for ranching.

"Ringleader", Shorthorn bull. *A.R. Hewins.*

Swine

According to the 1851 census, every farmer kept pigs. In later years these pigs were called "native" pigs; also razor-backs, racers and alligator pigs. They had long legs, and snouts long enough to reach the second row of corn through a rail fence; not a particularly good strain for producing meat. Later, pure breeds were

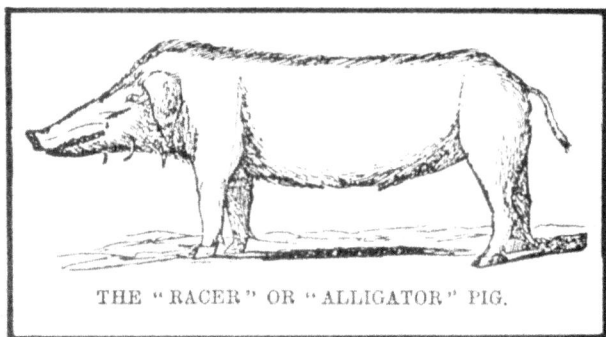

Native pig sketch. *G.A. Hewins.*

brought in from Britain—Suffolks, Berkshires, Essex, and Yorkshires. Poland China and Chester Whites came from the United States. These hogs went to the other extreme and were known as "lard hogs". The Berkshire was probably the most popular breed in this area at the turn of the century. Later, the Yorkshires took over as the Canadian Bacon Hog.

You will notice in the 1851 census that Thomas Revell produced 1,000 pounds of pork. It is doubtful that he sold much of it; more likely he cured it and ate it at home. Home-cured pork can be very good eating and

A large litter of piglets. *Mrs. A. Page.*

was a staple food. At that time, 70% of the people in Ontario were living on farms, and with little or no export, most of the food produced was consumed at home. Only one farmer in 3 or 4 kept a sow and supplied his neighbours with weaned pigs. They were kept until a year old before butchering and would dress out at 250 pounds. Later, as the population increased and some pork was exported, production increased. No farmer at that time got rich selling pork.

Horses

The farmers in this area soon began to keep horses. We don't know what breed they were, but they were road-horses, something like a big standard-bred horse of today, able to do farm-work as well. They were good horses but maybe inclined to be high spirited. Later, draft horses such as Clydesdales, Percherons, the Suffolk-Punch and Belgians were imported. Farmers made money breeding horses, with a good market in Ontario and the United States. As much as 25% of the land was used to grow feed for horses at the turn of the century.

Horse-drawn wire-wheeled buggy, Mrs. A. Bates driving. *Mrs. A. Page.*

John Gunby with horse-drawn plow. *Mrs. P. Pawlik.*

3 Horses drawing binder, Albert Hewins driving, 1925. *G.A. Hewins.*

Poultry

At a guess the first breed of chickens kept in Ontario were Dorkings, an old English breed brought into Britain during the Roman occupation. Later on, the Barred-Rocks and Rhode Island Reds were the favourite breed. A few geese were kept, maybe Toulouse, also Guinea fowl. A few farmers even had Peafowl.

Sheep

There were a few sheep on every farm. They were a long, coarse-woolled breed, referred to as "native". This long, coarse wool was preferred for home spinning. Towards the end of the century, considerably fewer farmers kept sheep.

Flock of sheep. *Wm. Wingrove.*

Dogs and Cats

Most farmers had a dog or two. They were known as English collies and many were excellent cattle-dogs. The cats were just plain "tabbies".

Barbara Revell, a friend, Alice Revell and their dog. *Wm. Revell.*

Fruit Growing

In the 1861 census, John Maddaugh's profit from his orchard is reported as $70. As it takes several years for an orchard to come into bearing, this indicates that apple trees were planted quite early. Every farm seemed to have an acre or more of apples. Bugs and diseases were not much bother. It seems that growing apples was fairly profitable, with an export market in Britain. Varieties were Spy, Baldwin, Greening, Russet, Snow and kinds we never hear of now. MacIntoshes were not planted then.

They also grew pears, plums, sweet and sour cherries, besides currants, gooseberries and can fruits. These were mostly for home use.

Farm Crops

Not much hay was grown in the early years. It was the natural grass that thickened up after the forest was cut. It was quite a few years before forage-seed became available.

Corn (i.e. maize) was the main crop for winter-feed for cattle. It was cut and stacked in the field in the Fall and later drawn in, to be put through a cutting box if the farmer had one.

Bill Revell on Case tractor, about 1943. *Wm. Revell*

Steam-engine power to fill silo at Lot 7, Concession 13
Tom Jordan

Both Spring and Fall wheat was the main cash crop grown. Before and during the American Civil War, the price was very high. It was wheat that built the substantial farm homes and made for prosperous times in Ontario. About 1870, the Spring wheat yield per acre became very low and farmers stopped growing it.

Peas were grown for both feed and sale. The pea-weevil got so bad that production was adversely affected.

Oats and barley were also grown. There was a market for malting barley, but it was never as profitable as wheat. Some of the good Methodists in this area would not sell malting barley. They were sworn enemies of John Barleycorn!

Other crops were mangels and turnips. With a good vegetable garden, fruit, dairy products, meat and cereals, a farm family could subsist very well with a balanced diet off the farm, only buying salt, tea, coffee and spices. Goitre was rather common due to a deficiency of iodine.

Prices of much of the farm produce were generally low, but as the farmers did not produce very much more than they consumed at home, it was not of much importance. Many of the farmers became prosperous selling wheat and raising horses. They were able to furnish their homes with fine furniture, buy organs and pianos, dress well and enjoy the good life. There was sufficient help available on the farm, so that people could visit friends and relatives. They would drive long distances with a horse and buggy or a team and democrat, putting up at a hotel for the night if the distance was over 50 miles. When the railroads came they were able to travel by train.

From 1835 to the end of the century the majority of the farms were cleared and fenced; good houses and barns built; all this in a short lifetime.

They bettered themselves by coming to Canada.

On way to farm meeting. Rear, Gerald Binkley, Hugh Wigood, George Campbell, Lyle Caswell, Michael Pasuta and Reginald Hewins. Front, Calvin Wigood, Gordon Hewins, Burdge Gunby, William Revell, Archibald Gunby and Ted Filtness. *Mrs. W.C. Cust.*

II

History of the Lots to the Present

Concession 11

Lots on the 11th Concession were reduced in size when resurveyed in the mid-1830's. Instead of 13 lots of 200 acres, they became 12 lots, said to be 150 acres, or half lots of 75 acres. Some seem to be just that. However, in recent surveys of farms, many are found to be much larger, making it difficult to state any acreage with accuracy.

In the early 1840's, an R.C. priest sponsored groups of Irish immigrants who left Ireland during one of its famines. They settled on the 11th Concession and, in time, had their own Separate School at the east corner of the intersection with Centre Road. The school was used until late in the past century.

In the allotment of school sections, the northwest half of Lots 1 to 10 was assigned to Mountsberg School, while Balaclava School at the 10th Concession, built in 1873, absorbed children from the southeast lots. For this reason, coverage of southeast lots on the 11th is less detailed, with emphasis on families and facts relating to Mountsberg. Because the 12th Concession Road is still unopened, except for two sections, not many people lived on the northwest lots of the 11th.

The area around Centre Road and the 11th Concession once was known as the "Stony Battery" or simply "The Battery". No one seems to know why.

Lot 1, southeast, Concession 11 **Brock Grant**

Zebina Fraser was given a deed for this 75 acres on August 11, 1857, the same day that John Haines, of Lot 2, Concession 12, received his for the northwest half. Each paid £93, 15s. In 1859, Mr. Fraser's tenant was a Mr. Thatcher. John C. McNiven and his brother, Daniel, bought the Fraser property in April 1867 and, two months later sold it to John Haggerty, but gave timber rights to 8 acres of cedar swamp to Samuel Newell. The estate of Samuel Newell passed the timber rights on to Robert Simpson. Eventually, they lapsed. Children of John Haggerty (born about 1812) and his wife, Johanna (born about 1823) were: Ellen, John, Michael, Robert, Thomas, Hannah and Margaret.

Subsequent land transfers were: June 1874—Johanna Haggerty, widow, to Henry Ashton; November 1891—Henrietta Ashton, widow, to Isaac Mitchell and his wife, Mary Ford; October 1916—to James Mitchell, brother of Isaac; April 1920—to Theophilus McCartney—Mr. Mitchell retained lifetime use of the stone house and January 1945—to Fred McCartney from the estate of his father, Theophilus. Between 1950 and 1971, Fred McCartney sold all the farm in a variety of acreages.

East Corner Group of Four Homes

A three-acre lot, its length facing the 11th Concession, was sold in 1950. Second owners, Arthur and Bridget Warford bought in 1958 and, in 1969, they sold half an acre at the corner to John W. Tenbrinke who built a house. Present owners, Reinhold and Gillian Roediger, bought the property in 1976. The remaining 2 1/2 acres, sold by Warfords in 1977, went to John and Lynne Walker who breed Siberian Huskies. They built their house that year.

Facing Town Line, northwest of Roedigers, is a lot of 3 3/4 acres first sold in 1970. Second owners, John and Dorothy Kent, bought in 1971 and had a new house built. They sold to Kenneth and Lynda Bonham in 1973. Boarding kennels were built later that year.

Next northwest, is a 2-acre lot bought in 1967 by Kenneth and Myrna Croall who built their house the following year.

Three Large Lots

A large part of the southeast end of the farm, amounting to 36 acres after deducting the corner lots, was sold in 1971, to Allen Lisson, a dentist and his wife, Loretta. Their property has some frontage on Town Line and also on the 11th Concession where their home was built the year they bought the lot.

Northwest of Lissons, a 10-acre piece of wooded land, across the full width of the farm was sold in 1967. Present owners, Norman and Ann Abbott, bought it in 1977 and the following year, built a house some distance from Town Line.

Vivian Muller, who raises golden retrievers, owns the northwest 20 acres, bought in two 10-acre parcels in 1965 and 1966. A new house was built in 1965, near the north corner of the former farm.

Lot 1, northwest, Concession 11

John Haines bought this 75 acres in 1857. It was meant for his eldest son, William, who worked it and, eventually, owned it. William and his wife lived there until November 1875, when they sold to Thomas Hopkinson and moved to Clifford, Ontario, and later to northern Michigan.

George Daley owned the farm from November 1889 to November 1906. His wife was a daughter of George Mitchell on Lot 2. Known members of the Daley family were: Jack, Jim, George, Bill, Mrs. Ford and Mrs. O. McCartney.

Following Daleys, the property passed through the non-resident ownership of Adolph Uberig, Amos McArthur and Sherwood Coulson. In November 1916, it was sold to the tenant, William Watson. "Billy" Watson was married twice. Two daughters of the first family were adopted after their mother died: Etta (later Mrs. Jim Roberts), by Mr. and Mrs. James Inglis and Bessie, by Mr. and Mrs. Truman Johnson. Both families were near neighbours of the Watsons in Nassagaweya. In the second family were: Leonard, Frank, George R., Eileen (McCartney), Winnifred, and Ruth (order unknown). All attended S.S. No. 1, Nassagaweya. The estate of William Watson, administered by Jennie Watson, sold the farm to William Cairns in April

1938. In November 1946, it went to John and Kathleen Chettle and, in March 1952, to Mrs. Beatrice Readman.

Gordon and Margaret McComb bought the place in 1957. Of their family of six, two daughters, Debra and Laura, attended Mountsberg school in 1963-64, before the family moved to Waterdown in the summer of 1964. The previous January, Gordon McComb kept 10 acres midway in the farm, including the original house, a lane's length from Town Line, and sold the land on either side to Richard Day of Timmins. Gordon's parents, Mr. and Mrs. Roy McComb, and their younger son, Richard, lived there until the 10 acres was sold, in 1969 to Stanley and Dianne Christensen. With their son and daughter, they made it their home until 1977 when they sold to the present owners, Frederick and Drusilla Collier.

Meanwhile, Richard Day quickly sold his two properties, separately, but neither buyer lived on the land. Since 1969, the 40.8 acres at the southeast end of the farm has belonged to Hermanus and Leona Vanderstar.

Frederick and Dorothy Smith have owned the 34.7 acres at the northwest end since 1965. Their new home, built in 1967, stands near the north corner of the former farm.

Lot 2, Concession 11   Canada Company

This Canada Company land was bought from the Crown in 1838, the company's only non-clergy land in the four concessions. It was sold, in 1862, to John White who had dealt in other local land. However, from January 1857, on, the entire lot had been rented in succession to three men, interested in lumbering. The last of these, John McDougall, bought the property in September 1862. He already owned a mill on Lot 5, near the Concession road and, since 1859, he had been operating a steam-powered sawmill on Lot 2, where he was assisted by his brother, Duncan, and three other employees, William Davis, Hiram Donelly and James Grant. Seventeen-year-old Anna Murray helped John's young wife, Sarah, care for an infant son and feed mill hands in their log house. Two other houses sprang up, occupied by worker families, Moggack and Sullivan. With the mill, the dwellings and the stables, it was a tiny community in itself. At one time, McDougalls had six others living in their home. Average wage for the mill hands was $11 per month, with room and board.

In March 1868, John McDougall sold the southeast half to his brother, Duncan, and the northwest half to James Gage. It is said that, in the late 1800's, a clapboard building, some distance back in the lot was used for Anglican church services.

The Southeast Half, later

Duncan McDougall (born about 1835) was married about 1865. While here, he and wife, Mary Ann had three children, Sarah Jane, John and James. In February 1874 they sold their land to George Mitchell, patriarch of the Mitchells of Lot 1 and 2. In 1919, the property went to George's son, Joseph Mitchell whose brother, James, was on Lot 1. Joseph remained on the place until February 1955 when he sold to William J. Bennett. Percy and Daphne Baker bought it in 1961 and remained until 1966. Between then and 1969, when it was bought by Bernard Zaionz, there had been three owners. The house is rented.

The Northwest Half, later

In November 1871, James Gage bought from Duncan McDougall a 40-foot lane off the southwest side of the MacDougall land to give access to the rear of the lot. He then divided his 75 acres for his two sons, giving the northwest part to James A. and the southeast part to George W. Each brother had a home, whether new or left over from the lumber era is not known. The Gage brothers sold their land to Edward Brown in January 1879.

In 1880 Mr. Brown sold his 75 acres to Patrick Gavin (See Lots 4 and 5), reserving timber rights to 10 acres. Three years later, Mr. Gavin redivided the lot as in the Gage ownership, giving the parts to his sons, Michael and Patrick. There followed many more in-family land transfers. Patrick died, and in 1957, his sons, Thomas, William and John, sold the property to Agro Brothers, Angelo and Frank. All deeds included the lane to the 11th Road.

Agros sold to Ursula Hunter in 1969. Three land sales later, it went to Charles Zaionz.

Lot 3, Concession 11   Canada Company

The Canada Company got the Crown deed for this Clergy Reserve lot in September 1838, calling it 200 acres. Early entries parallel Lot 2.

The Southeast Half

Thomas Allison, in September 1857, bought this property and in 1863, sold it to Andrew Foley, son of Michael Foley on Lot 5. When Mr. Foley sold it to Charles Stewart Jr. in January 1870, the acreage was given as 82. John Byrne owned the farm from April 1882 until January 1918, when ownership passed to Mary 1. Hearn. In September 1942, the title was transferred to Mrs. Hearn's daughter and son-in-law, Patricia and William Lacey.

In August 1957, correctly listed as 75 acres, it became part of the Agro Brothers large holding of land in the area. They sold it in 1969 and, after passing through four buyers, it was bought by Charles Zaionz in 1970.

The Northwest Half

Three years before James Gage bought the northwest part of Lot 2, he had purchased this northwest acreage from John McDougall, the owner of the sawmill on Lot 2. James Smith bought the land from James Gage in 1871 and, in 1878, sold it to his son, James Smith, Jr. The right-of-way through the southeast part of Lot 2, to the 11th Concession Road, went with all sales.

James Smith, Jr. sold the lot, in 1889, to George Mitchell who owned it until his death. In 1943, it went to his son, Joseph, and was sold with all his property, including the lane, to William J. Bennett, in February 1955. Two years later it was bought by Agro Brothers, who kept it until 1969, and since 1970 belongs to Charles Zaionz after the same multiple sales of the southeast lot.

Lot 4, southeast, Concession 11   Brock Grant

Dennis McCarthy, on this farm around 1842-43, was one of the first settlers on the 11th Concession, northeast of Centre Road. He was the ancestor of the many McCarthy families who, since then, have lived in various places around Mountsberg.

Family of Dennis McCarthy (1808-1887) of County Cork, Ireland, and his wife, Ellen Connor (1818-1902) of County Kerry, Ireland: *Ellen* (born about 1849); *Patrick* (1853-1896)—married Annie Hunter (1851-1922) —as a widow, Annie and her family rented Lot 6, northwest, Concession 12; *Dennis* (1854-1925)—married Margaret Burke (1856-1922); *Johanna* or *Joanna* (1857-1946) — married Thomas McKenna, parents of Dennis (See Lot 11, Concession 13) and Mary (Hearn); *Mary* (died Dec. 1938 at age 80)—married Alexander Hunter (brother of Annie), who died November 1923 at age 69.

Patrick McCarthy (1853-1896) and son, Jack.
Miss Christine Hanson.

The farm became Patrick's in July 1877. At that time, Patrick leased 5 acres to his brother, Dennis Jr. In 1908, Thomas McKenna and his wife, Joanna McCarthy, acquired the property. Ownership passed to their daughter, Mary Hearn, in 1920, and after her death it went to her daughter, Patricia, and son-in-law, William Lacey, in September 1952. Laceys sold, in 1957, to Agro Brothers who kept it until 1970 when it was sold to Tashan Construction. The house is rented at times.

Lot 4, northwest, Concession 11

Thomas Gavin's name (sometimes seen as Garvin) first appeared on the assessment roll for this lot in 1848, although his deed came much later. Thomas (born 1816) and his wife, Johanna (born 1811) had two sons, Michael, a sailor on the Great Lakes, and Patrick (18511944), both born in the storey-and-a-half log house, the first Gavin home.

In 1880, arrangements were made with the Township to make available the unopened Twelfth, beside Lots 4 to 7, as an access to Centre Road. It was used then, but most of it reverted to fenced-off farmland, early in the present century.

Patrick Gavin (1851-1944) and his wife, Mary Ann Foley (1857-1933), continued to live on the farm with their family: Lina (1887-1950), Tom (1889-1964), William (1891-1962), John (1893-1973), Florence, Margaret and Winnie (1898-1918). Lina, the only one to marry, became Mrs. James Hunter. They attended Mountsberg School.

In 1909, the family moved to Lot 5, southeast. At that time, Thomas gave to his daughter-in-law, Mary Ann, this 75 acres, as well as the northwest half of Lot 2, She passed it on to her husband, Patrick, in 1918.

In June 1938, Patrick Gavin, then a widower, sold 5 acres at the west corner of the farm, where the creek angles through. It was bought by Philip W. Hardie who built a small cottage for summer use.

Donald and Carol Wolverton bought from Thomas Gavin, son of Patrick, the Gavin farm also the 5 acres from the Hardie estate. That was in 1967 or late 1966 when a surge of nostalgia engulfed Canada in Centennial Year and left in its wake a keen awareness of our heritage. The Wolvertons planned a Pioneer Village as a business. That it became a trailer park may have been because the 12th right-of-way did not become an improved road from Lot 4 to Centre Road until 1978. That year, the Wolvertons sold their property to Donald and Marilyn Noseworthy.

Lot 5, southeast, Concession 11   Brock Grant

Michael Foley from Ireland (born about 1805), was assessed for this lot in 1843, but his deed was delayed until 1869. Mrs. Foley died in the early years of settlement and Michael continued to live in their one-storey log house with his family: Andrew, John, Thomas, Catherine and Mary Ann, the only one born in Canada. As years went on, John and Catherine remained with their father who lived to about age 85.

Also living on the farm as a tenant was Michael's brother, Thomas (a carpenter), and his wife, Bridget, and their children: Michael, Margaret, Honora, William, Mary Ann, Dennis and Henry. They had their own 1 1/12-storey stone house.

Edward Carrol held the property from 1893 until sold in 1909 to the Gavin brothers, Michael and Patrick; and the Gavin family moved there from Lot 4, northwest. Later, Patrick's family inherited the land. In more recent times, about 1960, a new Gavin house was built, beside the 11th Road. It was John's home until he died.

In February 1965, John kept his house and 2 1/2 acres and sold the remainder of the farm to Aage and Anna Jensen. It was bought in 1972, by Eugen and Maria Boehm who live in the old farm house, built in 1903. Maria Boehm bought John Gavin's new home and lot from his estate, in 1974, and sold it to Bruce and Carol Goodbrand in 1976.

The McDougall Mill Site

In 1859, John McDougall built a steam sawmill on 4 1/2 acres at the south corner of Lot 5 where the 12-Mile Creek divided his land into two triangles. Earlier, lumber interests had seen it as a choice spot for a mill, and three men, Pillars, Scarth and Stevenson, leased it from the Brock Estate. At the same time, they made a similar deal with the Canada Company for Lots 2 and 3. However, this lease or "interest" was registered and was sold and resold many times. John McDougall took it over, September 1859, from John Ferrier, and never held a deed to this mill site as he had done in Lot 2.

With two steam-powered saw mills in full operation, John McDougall was accorded the title of Lumber Merchant. He moved from Lot 2 into a new home he built on the north side of the Creek for his wife, Sarah, and children, Albert D., Jane, Sarah, John A., Hannah and James. He built a barn, too.

In 1874, with the lumber business past its peak, John McDougall sold his interest to Thomas and Philip Snell. Two years later, it was bought by William Emmons at the fabulous price of $2,700, when entire farm lots in the 11th were available for one-sixth that amount. When Mr. Emmons, in 1880, sold his interest to Michael Foley who owned the rest of the farm, the term "interest" became obsolete. Lot 5 was then all Mr. Foley's to do with as he pleased. He sold the 4 1/2 acres to his nephew, Henry, in 1884, after the mill had burned down.

Following the death of Michael Foley about 1890 and the settlement of his estate, the former mill property was owned by his son, John and Sarah E. Wilson, in 1893. Some time later, John Foley was killed when he fell from a wagon on Centre Road, not far from his home.

Morris Roberts, across the road on Concession 10, bought the mill site in 1909 and, for a time, it was occupied by his son, James, and wife, Etta. When it was sold to Thomas McKenna, in 1919, the price dropped to $665 from $2,800, indicating the time when the house and barn had burned.

The property was willed to Joanna McKenna, widow of Thomas, in 1932. In 1946 she, in turn, left it to her daughter, Mary Hearn, who transferred it to her nephew, Vincent McGuire, and his wife, Margaret, that same year.

Albert and Queen Hulme came from England with their children, Norman, Angela and Ursula, and bought the 4 1/2 acres and built a house, all in 1949.

Lot 5, northwest, Concession 11

Brothers, John and William Savage, on Lots 8 and 9, became interested in Lot 5, northwest, in the mid-1840's. They halved the 75 acres, and William was given a deed for the southeast 37 1/2 acres in 1861. Before then, John Savage worked all 75 acres until the early 1850's when John McKenna rented William's land and, before long, John's too. Mr. McKenna got a deed from William Savage in 1868. John Savage never owned his part, so the first deed from this Brock land went to John McKenna in 1876.

John McKenna and his wife, Mary, both born in the mid 1820's, came from Ireland about 1850 and lived in a log house on Lot 5. Tragedy struck the McKenna home in 1860, when a daughter, 11, a son 8, and another son 6, were victims of a scarlet fever epidemic. Honora, the eldest, Thomas, and Patrick, about a year old, survived. Younger members were Joanna (Mrs. John Byrne) and Mary.

John McKenna died about 1883 and the farm went to his son, Thomas (1851-1932) who married Joanna McCarthy (about 1857-1946), daughter of Dennis and Ellen McCarthy of Lot 4. Their children, attendants of

Thomas and Joanna McKenna, in front. *Mrs. R. Geraghty.*

Mountsberg School were: Mary-married twice-to John Sullivan, then Achilles Hearn; *John (Jack)*-always lived in the neighbourhood of the 11th; *Ellen (Nell)*-married Elmer McGuire-died when their only son, Vincent, was a young boy; Dennis-married Frances Player-lived on Lot 11, northwest, Concession 13; Jerry-married Florence Fletcher and lived in Hamilton; *Frances*-died when an adult.

For a few years, beginning in 1893, the lot was owned by Burdge Gunby (who may have been an older relative of Mountsberg's Burdge Gunby). Thomas McKenna bought it back in 1907 and, a year later, he and Joanna took over the McCarthy farm on Lot 4, but kept the Lot 5 homestead. Their daughter, Mary Hearn, inherited both properties; Lot 5, in 1952. It was turned over to Patricia and William Lacey that same year, and was bought by Patrick and Dorothy McCarthy in 1968.

The old McKenna house was burned in the 1970's and was not replaced. A small shack or shelter was put there for occasional daytime use.

Lot 6, southeast, Concession 11   Clergy Reserve

At the time of the first Township census, in 1841, John Perry was living on this lot with his wife, two sons, and three daughters. By 1843, he was cultivating 15 acres. When John Sanderson, a Scotsman, took over the land in 1850, 30 acres were cleared and in use. Nevertheless, the Crown deed went to Alexander Sinclair in August 1857, but the Sanderson family stayed on as tenants and, in 1860, James and Edward Sanderson, sons of John, bought the property. The boys were quite young, under 20. They lived in a frame house with their mother, Elizabeth, and younger members of the family, John, William, Elizabeth and Maria.

In October 1868, the Sanderson brothers sold the farm to John F. Wood who sold it the following year to Briton B. Osler. John McDougall, of the sawmill on Lot 5, owned it from 1870 until 1875 when it was bought by Richard Watson, and for 70 years it was "the Watson place". Edward Watson, son of Richard, became owner in January 1907. He sold the acreage, less one lot, to William C. Campbell, in August 1946. The next month it went to Charles and Mary McCarthy.

In 1949, McCarthys sold all their land on the southeast lot to Charles and Jessie Prudham, but, in 1951, Edwin Manto owned 56.6 acres, all the southeast lot, except for three properties along the Concession road. Mr. Manto's trustee, Cornelius W. D. Kort, sold his land to George H. Stone in 1969. The tenant is Mr. J. Hutchison.

The East Corner

Edward Watson made the first land separation from the farm in September 1936. It was for 2 acres at the east corner, sold to George C. and Eva A. Elder who built a house the following year. With additional land purchases in 1939, 1943 and 1947, the lot was increased to about 6 1/2 acres, including some of the creek. Lorne and Joan Henwood owned the property from 1951 to 1975. For a year it belonged to the Roman Catholic Episcopal Corporation and was used during the summer of 1975 by Bishop Paul Reding. It was sold in 1976 to Miss Edith Murray and Mrs. Elaine Sharp.

In 1946, William C. and Maria Campbell bought from Edward Watson, 10 acres near the east corner. This right-angled piece of land borders on the rear and southwest side of the corner lot. The Campbell estate sold the property, in 1973, to the Scholey family. Mrs. Harold Scholey was formerly Leila Gray, daughter of Percy and Cora Gray who lived on Lot 8, southeast, many years. The cottage that had been there, burned in 1975. The present Scholey home was moved from Burlington and remodelled.

The South Corner

Charles and Mary McCarthy built a house at the south corner, in the mid-1940's, and, in October 1947, sold it and 3 acres to Florence Williams. She sold to Victor and Evelyn Dunk, in March 1958. The property went to Waine and Wendy Bertsch in 1966-67, and to David Whidden in 1975. Since 1976, it has been owned by Ann and John Kane who enlarged the house.

Lot 6, northwest, Concession 11

The Canada Company became less active after John Galt resigned his appointment in 1838, and returned to Scotland. But, until 1854, Clergy Reserves were being released for sale and Guelph men were encouraged to rent or buy Clergy lots still lying idle. Lot 6, northwest was one of these. At an unknown time it was leased by A. McElroy who assigned his claim to John and Bridget McKenna, assumed to be the parents of John McKenna on Lot 5. The elder McKenna died and Bridget released her interest to Thomas Collier, but it was William Macdonell who was given the Crown deed in May 1856.

James Watson bought the lot in July 1859, only to sell it in September 1860 to brothers, Timothy and James O'Donnell who, since the mid-1840's, had been living on the place with their parents. Their father, Dennis O'Donnell (born 1807) and his wife, Margaret (born 1813), from Ireland, had in their family: Timothy (1837), Hannah (1839) and James (1841), born in Ireland; also Mary (1847) and Dennis (1851), born in Canada. As they were said to be Anglicans, they would attend the log school at Mountsberg.

Dennis O'Donnell and his sons operated a water-power sawmill near a bend in the creek, but little is known about the length of time the mill was used, or the extent of its work.

In December 1880, the brothers divided their lot. James had the northwest part and Timothy, the southeast, giving each about 38 acres. At the time of division, a 20-foot right-of-way was designated along the southwest side of James' land and continuing northeasterly along the dividing line, thus giving Timothy access to that part of the 12th Concession road, then in use.

James, no doubt, lived in the early log home, its location discernible for many years as a grassy hollow beside a flowering shrub and close to the road allowance. James sold his part of the lot to Edmund Freed in 1926. William and Mildred Revell bought it in April

1945, to use as pasture. They sold it to Johan Rikkerdink in 1979.

Timothy lived on the east side of the creek, in a house built by his father, Dennis. In 1892, he sold his land, with use of the right-of-way, to Arthur Smith of Lot 8. Two years later, Mr. Smith gave his wife, Margaret, formerly Mrs. Hunter, title to the property. In 1933, the stepchildren of Arthur Smith sold the land to John D. Wheelihan, and in 1945, it was bought by Charles and Mary McCarthy. From 1949 to 1957, it was owned by Silverine Didero who sold to Agro Brothers.

Lot 7, Concession 11

This lot is unique. It is the only one in the four Concessions, 11 to 14, that had had no involvement with Clergy Reserves, Brock Grants, or the Canada Land Company.

The Southeast Half (Sullivans)

In the resurvey of 1836, the newly-aligned Centre Road veered westerly and separated an 11-acre triangle at the south corner from the rest of the farm. James Sullivan settled on the lot about 1840, and began the task of turning virgin forest into a farm. Ten years later, he had 30 acres cleared, but the only property registered in the Sullivan name was an acre in the triangle, at the west corner of the road intersection. It was deeded to James in 1868 with the log house already used many years and, for the next hundred years, it remained Sullivan's acre.

In 1882, the lot went from James to his son, Bartholomew (born about 1819) and his wife, Margaret, about 12 years younger. Their children were Patrick, James, Michael, and Hannah. It was home for Bartholomew's family until after the death of Michael when it was sold, in 1931, to Patrick, then over 70, and his wife, parents of Bartholomew, William, and Margaret (Mrs. Neil Hunter).

William (Bill), a bachelor, was the last Sullivan in the home which he shared with Jack McKenna for several years. Bill died in December 1968, at age 72 and, the following year, the acre was sold by Margaret (Sullivan) Hunter, who never had lived there.

Back around 1850, James Sullivan waived his claim to the southeast lot. It was taken up by John Steele who received a deed from the Crown, in 1859. John Steele (Ontario-born about 1833) and his Irish wife, Margaret, while there, had children, Timothy, James and Hannah, and lived in a 2-storey, frame house at the south corner of the main part of the farm.

Innes Sutherland owned the farm from 1869 until 1875 when he sold it to Alexander Ross. Eight years later, it was bought by Patrick and Annie (Hunter) McCarthy. After Patrick's death in 1896, his brother, Dennis, worked the land until his death in 1925 and, in July 1926, the farm was registered in the name of Dennis' wife, Margaret. She died in 1927, and the place was rented many years before her estate was settled. At this period the Dennis McCarthy family lived in the Sullivan house. Finally in January 1953, the farm was sold to George and Daisy Bowman, already living there. All the many deeds carried the phrase "less one acre" (Sullivans).

Beginning in 1967, the Bowmans sold their property in lots of varying sizes. Moving from the west corner of the farm, along the angle of Centre Road towards the 11th Concession, properties on the left are:

10 acres—Sold in 1967 to Thomas and Stella Gillespie who built a house in 1968. They moved to Campbellville Road (Lot 5, Concession 12) in 1978, after selling to Dennis and Lesley Happy.

10 acres—Bought by George and Mary Gramme in 1968; house was built that year.

10 acres—Bought in 1968 by James and Margaret Runciman who built their house in 1969.

10 acres—Bought in 1968 by Errol and Sylvia Domenico. They built their house that year.

12 1/2 acres—First sold in 1968. Third owners, Mimmo and Julianne Lostrocco bought in 1969 and built their house in 1970.

1 acre—Bought in 1979 by Cecil and Elizabeth Buttenham who are building a house. They are third owners of this piece of land sold from a 15.8 acre parcel in 1968, owned by Walter and Mary Cuculich.

Building Lot—vacant. Elfriede Juraschka, third owner, bought the lot in 1975. It had been sold, in 1974, by Sydney and Margaret Stringfellow, then owners of the larger acreage.

The corner property with the farmhouse, less the two building lots, was sold by the Stringfellows in 1974 as 13.9 acres. Four sales later, in 1979, it went to Lola Stone, wife of George Stone, and is rented to G. Jones.

The Triangle after 1969

Edwin and Georgina Bridle bought the Sullivan acre in 1969. It was owned later by Neil and Joan Boyle before being sold to Arthur and Susan Schwab, in 1975.

Bowmans sold the rest of the triangle, 10 acres, to Hamilton and Helen Cooke, who have a house facing Centre Road.

In 1972, Cookes sold a lot on the 11th Concession, next to the corner lot, and a house was built that year. Third owners, Francis and Susan Cuvaj, bought it in 1975.

Kaj and Freida Rasmussen bought slightly more than an acre in 1974. The lot included all the remaining frontage on the 11th. They built a house close to the south corner that year and in 1979, split the lot and sold the section with the house to Wendy and Wayne Elliott, then built themselves a new home, northeast of the one they sold.

The Northwest Half

James Smith was given a Crown deed in June 1861, when he was in his mid 50's. However, he had been on the land since 1840 and, by the time of the first assessment, in 1841, he had 10 acres cleared and in use. James and his wife, Bridget, lived in a frame house. Both were born in Ireland, but their children, Arthur, James, Ellen, and Thomas, were born in Canada. As Roman Catholics, they would attend the R.C. school at the corner of the 11th.

Arthur (Attie), born in the early 1840's, inherited the farm. Well past his youth, he married a widow, Margaret Hunter, who had four children: Cecilia, Mrs. Dunn of Detroit; Frances, Mrs. Ed Organ of the 6th Concession, East Flamborough; William, of Toronto, and Lottie, Mrs. J. McKenna. A son, Daniel, died at age 22 in 1894. They attended Mountsberg School.

Arthur Smith put his property in Margaret's name in 1894, but lived for some time after that. Later, however, the farm went through a long period of renting. Not all tenants are known. Percy and Cora Gray, married in 1914, lived there before they bought their own place on Lot 8, in 1919. Bill Sullivan had it a few years before 1920. Mr. and Mrs. Dennis Hunter went there for a year or two. Their daughters, Stella and Rose attended Mountsberg School. Later, the Cramer Zimmerman family were tenants, but their children continued at Balaclava School. James Hunter followed (see Lot 8).

In December 1933, Frances and Lottie, executors of their mother's estate, sold the property to John D. Wheelihan. He sold it to Charles and Mary McCarthy in 1945. The next year, McCarthys sold 18 1/2 acres to Albert and Lillian Borthwick. This acreage at the south corner of the farm was bought, in 1948, by J.K. Hall Parry and his wife, Barbara, whose daugther, Susan, is Mrs. David Cook of Hamilton, and son, Robert, married Betty Taylor, in Lynden.

Parrys live in the stone house, built by Smiths at an indeterminate time, thought to be early 1870's or before. They have done much to preserve the lovely old home in its original state. Its symmetry and unassuming dignity earned a bid for designation as an historic dwelling by the Architectural Conservancy of Ontario. There were no other buildings when Parrys went there in 1948, just the crumbling remains of the stone foundation of a large barn.

Parry house, 1950. *J.K.H. Parry.*

In 1972, Parrys kept the house and 1 1/2 acres, and sold the remaining 17 acres to Ira and Violet Gilmore who built a house, east of the stone house and some distance from Centre Road. McCarthys sold the rest of the farm to Silverine Didero in 1949. Agro Brothers bought it in 1957.

Lot 8, southeast, Concession 11   **Brock Grant**

Andrew Smith (born about 1801), older brother of James on Lot 7, northwest, settled here in 1840. Apparently, the brothers and their wives left Ireland together. All children in both families were born in Ontario. Andrew and his wife, Elizabeth, had Catherine, James, Margaret, Elizabeth and Andrew.

Andrew, Sr. obtained his deed in March 1876, probably some time after the family had moved from their log cabin into the handsome stone house that receives admiring glances from passersby on Centre Road. At that time, a lime kiln was situated some distance back of the farm buildings. In October 1887, Andrew turned the farm over to his son, James (then in his 40's) and his wife, Margaret, the same day that Andrew Jr. was given the northwest half of Lot 8.

James Smith sold the farm in April 1919. It became the home of Percy A. Gray and his wife, Cora Coulter of Lowville, and remained theirs until they retired and moved to Carlisle late in 1965, one year after celebrating their golden wedding in December 1964.

Family of Percy Gray (1894-1979) and Cora: *Carl*—married Connie Coulson, lives in Freelton; *Gordon*—married Laura Buttenham, lives in Freelton; *Lorna*—Mrs. David Smith of Hamilton; *Leila*—Mrs. Harold Scholey of Lot 6, Concession 11; and *Morley*—married Ruth Gunther, lives in Waterdown.

At the time they retired, Grays began selling large lots off their farm.

Lots Facing the 11th Concession (moving southwesterly from the east corner of the farm)

9 acres—John and Theresa Boka bought the lot in 1967 and built their house that year.

About 1 acre—At the south corner of the Boka property; sold by J. Boka in 1972; fourth owner, Lynda Dunham, bought the lot with a house from David and Bonnie Doxey in 1979.

10 acres—Sold in 1967, third owner is Arthur Pudwill who bought in 1974 and rents the house to Allan Brown.

10 acres—Bought in 1966 by Werner and Luzie Gruenberg who built their house forthwith.

4.7" acres—Part of a 10-acre parcel, sold by Grays in 1966 and bought, in 1969, by L., L.M., and A.Z. Zsadanyi who divided their property in 1971. Third owners of this section are Harry and Margaret MacKay who bought it, with a house, from Jack and Winnifred Surerus in 1975.

5.3 acres—The remainder of the 10 acres; at the south corner of the farm; now owned by Joseph and Suzanne Restivo who bought the lot in 1978, with a house, from Frederick and Eleanor Lapp.

Northwest Part of Gray Farm (homes facing the Centre Road)

At the northwest border, 14.4 acres were sold to Roger and Miriam Challinor, in 1966. They built a house near the east corner of their property. In 1969, Challinors sold to their son, Roger, and his wife, Lynne, a half-acre lot at the north corner. They built a house in 1973, and sold, in 1976, to Michael and Sally Hole who sold to Faith and Thomas Schofield in 1979.

Beside this lot is the home of John and Terri-Ann Gushie, built in 1974. This lot was purchased in 1972 from Terri-Ann's parents, Mr. and Mrs. Challinor.

Ernest and Marjorie Warren bought 29 acres, including the stone house, in 1966. A lot, at the north corner of his property, was sold in 1971 to Fritz Cohrs who built a house. Three sales later, it went to Arthur and Cheryl Hebert in 1979, from Donald and Lynda Wigood.

Lot 8, northwest, Concession 11

The earliest settler on this land was Joseph Beaty (Beatty) who arrived in 1840 and stayed three years. The first two assessments were in the name of "Batie". That's what happens when an Irishman gives his name to a phonetic speller.

William Savage, who had been living on adjoining Lot 9, took over the work on Lot 8 for his son, John, a child at the time. However, in 1849, the occupant was listed as John Savage, Jr. Twenty years later, in April 1869, John procured a deed, only to sell his property to John Page, in January 1871.

It remained in the Page name until February 1880, when it was brought by Andrew Smith of the southeast lot. He gave it to his son, Andrew Jr. in October 1887. Andrew died about 1918 and his brother, James, took over the farm from the widow, Ellen, and sold it to John Gray in April 1920. Gray's son, Hanley, attended Mountsberg School; later married Helen Leslie.

There followed a period of rental. From about 1924 to 1932, the tenant was James Hunter whose wife was Lina (Pauline) Gavin, daughter of Patrick, on Lot 4. Their small children went to Mountsberg School as soon as they were old enough: *Florence*—Mrs. St. Pierre of Stoney Creek; *Walter*—married Mary Walsh, in Freelton; *Frank*—married Maxine Gartley, in Freelton, and was a member of the School Board, 1963-69, and a Councilor, 1969-1980; *Eileen*—Mrs. Richard Kelly of Hamilton; and *Theresa*—Mrs. Frank Jamieson of Freelton.

Frank and Annie Svab bought the farm from the Gray estate in May 1932, beginning 20 years of farm turnover; to Elsie Mae Simons in November 1934; to Marguerite Sharp in September 1943; To Thomas and Minnie Prowse in 1944. A joint tenant of the Prowses, O.G. Empey, sold his share back to them in 1952.

In 1958, Minnie Prowse began making separations from the farm. That year she sold 7 acres at the north corner to Arnold and Eileen Waller who built a home about 1968. In 1971, they sold .6 acres in the corner to Frederick and Dorothy Bolingbroke who have two daughters, Esther and Eileen. In 1975, the remaining 6.4 acres were sold to Kenneth and Eileen Grant who have three children, David, Ian, and Kathy Ann. They breed Labrador retrievers with the kennel name "Oaklea".

Southeast of Grants is a 4 1/2 acre parcel first sold in 1960. Sixth owners since then are Margaret and John Hughes who bought it in 1975. They have a son, Richard.

Karl and Rosemarie Hellenbroich bought 50 acres, in 1950, this being the northwest part of the lot, less the three smaller properties. Hellenbroichs sold 40 acres to Sharon Elms in 1973. In 1977, it was sold again to Nikola and Margit Dulic.

In the meantime, Minnie Prowse had sold 2 1/2 acres on which stood the red brick, Smith farm house, to Claude Thompson in 1963. John and Isabel Simms bought it the same year and lived there until they sold in 1967, to Brian and Jacqueline Thornborrow who owned it two years before selling to Edward and Elizabeth Cook. The next year, 1970, Cooks bought 10 acres from Rosemarie Hellenbroich giving them a property of 12 1/2 acres, which they sold to Louis and Beverly Schnepf in 1974. Their children, Jennifer and Paul, are in their teens.

Back in 1959, Mrs. Prowse sold to Andre and Dora Kirk, 19 acres at the southeast border of the farm. Kirks are still there, but, in 1971, they sold a half acre at the north corner of their property to Betty Jean Gyrpstra. The same year, it was purchased with a house by Karl and Donna Gonnsen. Donald and Cheryl Peters bought the house and lot in 1976. Cheryl is the daughter of Eileen and John Bellingham of Lot 12, Concession 12, near Beechgrove. The Peters have a son, Donald, and a daughter, Kerri.

Hunters on the Eleventh

No Hunter family owned land in our four concessions, but the name appears repeatedly. Their numbers are infinite. Those who left their mark on the 11th Concession are descendants of Dennis and James, two brothers of a large family which came to Canada from County Antrim, Ireland, in 1844. In the second generation, the name of their cousin, Daniel Hunter, entered the local story.

Dennis Hunter married Helen McKenzie from Scotland and lived at the northwest end of West Flamborough. The Hunter name first appears, locally, when two of their children married children of Dennis and Ellen McCarthy of Lot 4: *Annie*—married Patrick McCarthy and, from 1883 to 1926, owned Lot 7, southeast,—about 1910, Annie, then a widow, and her family rented Lot 6, Concession 12, and stayed 10 years; *Alexander*—married Mary McCarthy and, at one time, lived in Nelson Township; *Frank*—died leaving five children—his widow, Margaret, married Arthur Smith of Lot 7; *Dennis*—married Catherine McLaughlin—around 1920, they rented the Arthur Smith place; *Neil*—had a son, Neil, who married Margaret Sullivan, granddaughter of Bartholomew.

James Hunter married Jane McMullins and lived in Nassagaweya. Their son, Dennis, married Margaret Hunter, daughter of Daniel Hunter and his wife, Anne

Stuart. James, son of Dennis and Margaret, married Lina (Pauline) Gavin, daughter of Patrick and Mary Ann (Foley).

About 1922, the James Hunters rented the Arthur Smith farm and, two or three years later, also rented Lot 8, northwest, across Centre Road. For a year or more they worked both places before they moved over to Lot 8 where their family is shown. They left in 1932. *Hunter family information courtesy of Theresa Jamieson.*

Lot 9, Concession 11   **Canada Company**

The Canada Company bought this Clergy Reserve lot in two sales, the northwest half in November 1832 and the southeast half in September 1838. It did not sell readily. The southeast half was almost forgotten when James Smith on Lot 8, got a lease from the remnants of the Canada Co. in 1884, with the option of buying. It was finally released to him in February 1904. Wm. D. Flatt bought the property from James Smith in 1927, and sold it five months later, February 27, 1928, to Henry Slater, reserving all cedar and tamarack with a three year right-of-way for getting the trees out. The next day, Henry Slater sold it with its restrictions, to Darius Springer. It is now owned by Muriel M. Stevens and Elmer S. Springer.

The Northwest Half

The first time the Savage name appeared in records was in 1841 when William Savage, his wife, Catherine and two young sons, John and William, put up a log house and began clearing this land. In one year they were cultivating 10 acres and, by 1843, had 30 acres tilled and were ready to assume work on the northwest part of Lot 8 which eventually was deeded to his son, John Jr., in April 1869.

The "Junior" distinguishes him from William's younger brother, John, whose wife, Honora, and children, James, Honora and Johanna were in the community for a while (see Lot 5, northwest). Another brother, Thomas, with his wife, Margaret, and eight children, at one time, owned two properties on Concession 10 facing the 11th Concession, one at the east corner of the intersection, .the other opposite the Mc-Dougall mill.

William obtained a deed for his Lot 9 land in December 1859 and died two years later. Catherine carried on a few years but eventually lost the property. The next 50 years turned out a sheaf of documents: a few sales and transfers by Canada Company shareholders and their heirs; deeds; quit claims and just about everything that can happen to a piece of land. Finally, in 1896, it was consolidated into the name of one man, Christian Kloepfer, a carriage maker of Guelph.

There was little to recommend it. The 12th Concession, which William Savage had used with a team and wagon was choked with trees and brush, leaving Lot 9 landlocked. And so it lay until 1919, when bought by Mark Leslie of Lot 10, southeast, Concession 12. It was easily reached from the east corner of his farm, across the 12th Road allowance into the west corner of Lot 9. It has remained annexed to the Concession 12 farm, going to Samuel and Sidney Shanks in 1943 and to Dr. J.R. Kearns in 1972.

Lot 10, southeast, Concession 11   **Brock Grant**

Bernard and Jane Murray came to this lot in the mid-1840's. In time, they owned the farm and passed it on to their son, Duncan. It was owned by William and Mary Johnstone from about 1886 to 1908 when bought by Patrick and Michael Sullivan. In 1943, Dennis McCarthy (son of Dennis and Margaret, Lot 7) and his wife, Annie Higgins bought a small piece of land at the south corner of the farm from the Patrick Sullivan estate, and built two houses.

The one in the corner is now the home of the fourth Dennis McCarthy, in direct succession. The other one owned by a brother, Charles, was sold in 1961 to Joseph and Mabel Mitchell; owned by Alvin and Verlie Finkbeiner from 1968 to 1973; now the property of Hugh Smith and rented.

The farm with its house was bought from the Sullivan estate by Thomas and Mary Bojeski. Northeast of the Bojeski home is a house, on a lot bought from the Sullivan estate by Roy D. Pearson, and sold in 1966. Third owners since are Robert and Elsie Carr who came in 1969.

The Northwest Half

This was one of the lots, overlooked by John D. Uttermark in the matter of taxes, as in Lots 1-4 on Concession 14. Consequently, E. Cartwright Thomas, the sheriff, sold 18 acres off the southeast end in March 1856, to George B. Rousseaux who resold to Edward Brown in 1861. The same two men had a parallel deal in Lot 3, Concession 14, in 1861. A month after buying the 18 acres, Edward Brown sold it to John Evans who held it several years.

No early use was made of this lot. James Wheeler, Jr. settled on Lot 11, before 1850, and soon assumed work on the northwest 57 acres of Lot 10. His son, Joshua, kept up the use of this property, but it was never owned by Wheelers.

A Drummond family bought the 57 acres in October 1889; first owned by Hugh and William, later by William, only. In February 1920, Cecil Drummond bought the 18 acres and, two months later, sold the entire 75 acres to William Waygood (Wigood), then living on Lot 11.

Lot 11, southeast, Concession 11   **Brock Grant**

Philip and Patrick Smith worked on this lot in 1849-50, but, by 1851, John and Mary Hood were there and, in 1859, were given their deed. About 1894 the lot was divided lengthwise. David Brown had a claim to the northeast part which was passed on to John Brown in 1894 and released to a younger John Hood in 1908.

More recently, it was owned by Edwin and Nellie Manto who sold it to Vera Cumming in 1969. Dorothy Tuinstra bought it in 1970 and divided it further into two long, narrow lots. She sold the northeast 20 acres beside Lot 10, in 1973, to John and Patricia Traas who built a large home. In 1978, Leslie Maszaros, who lives there, was appointed their trustee. Alexander and Joanne Seggie bought the other 20 acres in 1977. They built two houses; one is rented.

The 37 1/2 acres on the southwest side was owned first by John R. Johnstone. After 1895 it was in the name of three other members of the family until sold, in 1912, to Edward Gartley; on to Wesley McCuen in 1929; to Roy A. Harris in 1961 and in 1967 to E. Manto, who sold it to Pieter and Hendrika Hollander who have a home there. In 1971, Hollanders sold .7 acres at their south corner for a Hydro station.

Lot 11, northwest, Concession 11

James Wheeler, Jr., son of James Wheeler on Lot 8, Concession 13, settled on this land in the 1840's. In less than ten years he also was working part of Lot 10 beside him and, in 1864, he received his deed for the property on Lot 11.

James Wheeler Jr. (born 1819) was married three times:
1. Christiana (Purnell) (1815-1853) was the mother of the children: Joshua (born 1844); Martha (1846-1919), Mrs. Roger Maynard; Ada (born 1849), Mrs. Thomas Monkhouse; Benjamin (born 1852).
2. Esther Ann Figsbee (1817-1867). The first two wives were buried in the Methodist Cemetery.
3. Rose Ann (born 1827).

In 1873, the farm went to the two sons, Joshua and Benjamin, and six years later, Benjamin sold his share to Joshua. In the Methodist Cemetery is a stone to "The children of Joshua and Sarah Wheeler", giving no names or dates. In 1885, Joshua sold the farm to Charles E. Galloway and, in 1905, he sold it to Samuel Zimmerman.

In 1915, William Waygood (Wigood) (1860-1951), son of Robert of Lot 4, northwest, Concession 12, bought the property with his wife, Margaret Weir (1869-1953), sister of William Weir on Lot 12. They bought adjoining Lot 10, in 1920, giving them a total of 150 acres. In 1954 the farm went to their son, William T. (1899-1961) who was married to Alma Laking, daughter of Fred and Mary Jane on Lot 9, northwest, Concession 13. Alma's brother, Harvey, married Eileen, sister of William T. Alma is living in Morriston. She has two sons; Murray, who married Diane Miller and lives on Concession 10, West Flamborough, and Glen, married to Joan McKenna, daughter of Dennis of Lot 11, northwest, Concession 13. Glen and Joan and their children, Beverly, Donna and Mark, live on the family farm.

Lot 12, southeast, Concession 11   Clergy Reserve

The first person on this Clergy Reserve lot, close to Freelton, was Joseph Smith who held a Crown deed, dated May 8, 1856. In 1875, the land was still in the name of his heirs, but later was bought by William Weir, son of Thomas, on the northwest end of Lot 9, Concession 10.

The Weir family has a tie with Mountsberg through William's aunt, Isabella, sister of Thomas, who came from County Sligo, Ireland, with others of their family. Isabella married Robert Kerr of Lot 11, Concession 13. The mother, also Isabella (1786-1864), wife of Thomas Weir, Sr. is buried in the Mountsberg Methodist Cemetery.

Lot 12 is still a Weir farm, owned by William R. Weir, who followed Raymon V. Weir.

Lot 12, northwest, Concession 11

Abraham Purnell, born about 1823, was given a Crown deed for this lot on August 23, 1848. He was a nephew of Abraham Purnell on Lot 11, Concession 12. Parents of the younger Abraham, Thomas Purnell (1792-1876), and his wife, Mary (1797-1879), came from Gloucestershire with him. They are buried in the Mountsberg Methodist Cemetery.

Young Abraham and his wife, Elizabeth Mary College, lived in a 1 1/2-storey log house south-west of the creek. Their children, with approximate birth dates, were: John (1853); Mary (1855); Ann (Annie), (1857), married Tudor Eaton; William (1859); Charles (1860), went to the U.S.A.; and Alfred.

Alfred Purnell (1863-1950), and his wife, Sophia Schultz (1860-1934), lived at the north corner of the intersection of Brock Road, now Highway 6, and the 13th Concession Road, now Regional Road 18; the spot long-known as Purnell's Corner. They were the parents of Selena, Mrs. Gordon Wingrove, and Charles, who married Marion Pickett.

Abraham died January 2, 1914, and is buried in Carlisle Cemetery with his second wife, Mary Shaw, who died in 1904.

Later owners of the farm were Mr. and Mrs. George Shead who bought in 1874 and were there many years. William L. Beaton owned the farm from 19301942. The present owner is Llewelyn Cooke who bought it from Grace Hopkins in 1970. Since the Freelton bypass took a strip off the southwest side of the entire lot, several years ago, this northwest half now has 67 acres and the southeast half is a 66-acre farm.

Concession 12

Farms in the southeast half lie between the Mountsberg Road and the 12th Concession, which is unopen except for two short sections. As a result, all farms face Mountsberg Road. When surveyed in 1836, the road allowance was there and was used to a limited degree. It remained a dirt road with no improvements and fell into disuse. Parts were fenced off and used by adjacent farmers. A section from Highway 6 always gave access to Lots 11 and 12, and in 1978, the Region reopened the 12th from Centre Road through Lots 7 to 4. Lots 11 and 12 lie outside the boundary of the former No. 6 School Section of East Flamborough.

In the northwest half of Concession 12, which lies between Mountsberg Road and Concession 13, the farms also face Mountsberg Road, except Lots 1 and 6, using Concession 13 and Lot 8 on the Centre Road. In early times, Mountsberg Road was known as the Given Road. Villagers called it the Cross Road. Few of the lots on Concession 12 and 13 listed as 100 acres are exactly that; many are several acres over that total.

Lot 1, southeast   Brock Grant

After John Haines was well settled on Lot 2, northwest, he branched out to acquire this 100 acres of Lot 1. His deed dated August 11, 1857, indicates the delay in getting a sale of Brock land finalized. James Campbell of the northwest half got his deed the same day.

Earlier, about 1850 when McLean and Clark had a sawmill on Lot 5, Concession 13, they obtained timber rights on this lot. The privilege was passed on to Thomas McCrae when he took over the mill, and lasted until all the excellent tall pines were gone. Some became ship masts. The stumps were used for fences, traces of which still may be seen.

No one lived here. The land passed from John Haines to Thomas Haines to Marshall Haines who sold to Matthew Harris in 1920. Later, it belonged to Morley Harris who sold to Milford and Alice Watson in 1955. It still has much woodland, well bestrewn with pine. Since 1966 it has belonged to Grace and Edward Chester, but the Chester home was built on a 34-acre parcel of Lot 2, bought at the same time.

Lot 1, northwest

Alexander Campbell, who was working on this land in the late 1830s, posed a puzzle for the present generation. In 1841, he was there, apparently alone, and had cleared 10 acres. Study indicates that he was the father of Archibald (Lot 4, Concession 13) also Peter and James. Later mention of a widow, Jane, born about 1791 and living on Lot 4 with her son, Archibald, supports the conclusion that she had been the wife of Alexander who never reached old age; that they settled on Lot 4, Concession 13, later known as Archibald's farm, and that the work on Lot 1 was for the benefit of the younger sons. James, first mentioned in 1845, had title to the land in 1857. Peter, older than James, lived there also, before marrying and having a home in Nassagaweya.

James Campbell, born about 1819, married Isabella, daughter of Archibald Cameron, Sr. of Lot 3, Concession 13. They had no children but provided a home for nieces and nephews. About 1845, a Campbell family of half-grown brothers and sisters arrived from Scotland. Among them was Janet, 10 at the time, who later married Duncan Cameron. Catherine, who married Donald Cameron, seems to have been a sister. Colin Campbell, born about 1833, and in the neighbourhood about 30 years, was apparently a brother. John Campbell's position in the family tree is hard to find. Believed to be a younger brother of James, he could have been the eldest of the Campbell family who came to live with him. Around 1870, John, born about 1824, and his wife, Ann, were living not far away, on Mountsberg Road, working on a farm where a house was provided. As the children arrived, they were given family names. With approximate dates of birth, they were: *James* (1853), *Catherine* (1854), *Margaret* (1856), *Donald* (1858), *Ann* (1860), *Colin* (1867), and *Jessie* (1870). In the 1880s, when the John Campbells were living in Nassagaweya, near Townline, above the railway tracks, John was killed when thrown from a cutter.

About 1860, Alexander (Sandy) McKenzie, a young nephew of Mrs. Campbell's, was welcomed into the home and remained to inherit the farm.

The first Campbell home was a log cabin with a new orchard growing up around it. The second home, a two-storey frame, still stands on the hilltop on the southwest side of the lane. This became the McKenzie home in 1876 when James and Isabella had Peter Davidson build the stone house across the lane, for their own use. It, too, in time became the McKenzie home.

A hurricane in 1879 destroyed the barn of that period. It was replaced the following year by the barn still in use.

A feature of the farm is the double row of large maples lining the lane and extending a short distance along the roadside. Appropriately, the farm was named *Maple Hill*.

The stone McKenzie house, Maple Hill Farm. *Mrs. A. Elliott.*

Alexander McKenzie (1854-1938) and his wife, Isabella Cameron (1855-1942) of Lucknow, had a family of three: *Christina (Tina)*—lived all her life on the farm and died there in 1963; *Isabella (Bell)*—married John Pinkney, lived on a farm in Morriston, later in Guelph; *Kenneth*—died in Guelph in 1965, a year and a half after selling the farm.

In 1963, Kenneth had sold the frame house and an acre of land to Douglas and Menedora (Millie) Dredge about the time they married. They had five boys, Douglas, Cameron, Mark, Jeffrey and Barry. The family moved to Campbellville in 1977 when they sold the property to Richard and Marie Manger who made extensive renovations to the house.

After the farm was bought by Allan and Isabel Elliott (Lot 6, Concession 12) in 1964, the stone house had three short term tenants. It burned in the early morning of March 31, 1969 when occupied by James and Jane Bell. Following the fire, John DeVries bought about 14 acres at the corner of the Town Line, containing the stone ruin. He rebuilt the house and sold the property in 1973 to John and Claire Tigchelaar. In 1976, Tigchelaars sold about an acre on the hillside, facing the 13th Road, to Claire's parents, David and Sylvia VanderSchaaf. They built a house and, two years later, sold to Kenneth and Theresa Fox who moved from Burlington with their children, Jennifer and Stacie.

In 1979, Tigchelaars sold their property and moved to Lot 9, Concession 14. New owners are Frederick and Constance Hall who came from the U.S.A. in 1972. Both are in the teaching profession. They have a son, David. Their land is mainly reforested with 1,200 spruce trees and with apple trees on the hillside near the lane.

In 1969, Elliotts sold 10 acres at the east corner of the farm in the angle of the Nassagaweya Town Line and Mountsberg Road to David and Marion Wood. A house was built in 1971 well back from the corner. Woods sold, in 1973, to Mary Szollosy, and built a new house on Lot 3, Concession 13.

Donald Stevens and his wife, Brenda Elliott bought about four acres at the south corner of the farm and built a house in 1974. They have a son, Mark.

Lot 2, southeast (see also Lot 3)   Clergy Reserve

The Barnes family who first lived on this lot included William (born about 1805) and his wife, Jane Murray from Ireland; also the father, John Barnes (1775-1855) and his wife, who were parents of Ann (Mrs. John Haines) who had been on the northwest 100 acres of the lot for a year or two. Both the Barnes and the Haines were from Wiltshire, England.

The first Barnes home was a storey-and-a-half log cabin, and the first death recorded in the area was that of Emmanuel, son of William and Jane Barnes, who died January 1839, at age two months. They had another son, James, born about 1845.

In the very early years, William Barnes took over 45 acres of adjoining Lot 3 that faced Mountsberg Road. For a considerable period, including the 1860s, a Scottish couple, James and Ellen Baxter, lived on the Lot 2 Barnes farm, their known children being John, Margaret, James, George, Andrew, Thomas and Ellen. They were renting and left Mountsberg for Hamilton.

In 1875, William Barnes leased his 145 acres to Robert Marshall of the 14th Concession reserving about two acres in Lot 3 where a new frame house stood. In 1904, all were sold to Thomas Haines by James Barnes, sole heir of Jane (Murray) Barnes.

Marshall Haines, son of Thomas, who later owned the land sold the 100 acres of Lot 2 to Matthew Harris in 1920. It passed to a son, Morley Harris, who sold about two-thirds of the lot to Hugh Wigood in 1939, retaining a triangle of 34 acres at the north corner. Wigoods since 1916, had owned all of Lot 3. The later story of all Wigood property in both lots is told with Lot 3.

Along with Lot 1, Milford and Alice Watson bought the 34 acre triangle from Morley Harris in 1955. In 1966, Alice (Watson) Hurren sold both parcels to Edward and Grace Chester who built a home the following year on the Lot 2 property. In the Chester family *are: John,* married Cheryl Sellar, in Islington; *Edward,* of Vancouver; *Saranne (Lawson),* Mrs. Ian Luke of Aurora; and *Caroline,* married David Stupple of Calgary.

Lot 2, northwest, Concession 12   Clergy Reserve

For more than 80 years this was the Haines place, although in early times the family name appeared as Haynes. Soon after John Haines and Ann Barnes were married in Wiltshire, England, about 1833, they left for Canada. They came by sailing vessel to Quebec. Ann was one of the fortunate few of the working class who had some education, so during their six weeks at sea, she taught John to read. They reached their location in East. Flamborough by way of Dundas and put up a dwelling of cedar logs, adding an enclosed porch, not common at the time. That was where Indians were welcome to rest when roaming the surrounding forest. The cabin was on high ground northwest of the present farmhouse, and it was there that their six sons were born.

Family of John Haines (1808-1890) and Ann Barnes (1807-1845): *William*—see Lot 1, northwest, Concession 11; *James*—married Elizabeth (Betsy) West, lived near Mildmay, Ont.; *John* (born about 1839)—married Elizabeth Heath, daughter of his father's third wife, moved to Listowel; *Edward* (born about 1840)—in 1863, married Margaret Inglis of Nassagaweya, later lived near Wingham, both died about 1920; *Thomas* (1842-1927)—married Margaret Ann Marshall (1842-1899), daughter of Robert, on Concession 14, remained on the farm; *George* (about 1843-1937)—married Jane Dimond, lived near Mildmay, later near Teeswater.

In 1845, Ann and a newborn only daughter died (story of funeral is told with Methodist Church). A year or more later, John married Jane Inglis of Nassagaweya. She is said to have been a kind mother to the six small boys. After her death in 1876, John Haines married a widow, Mrs. Heath of Morriston and lived out his years on the farm he founded.

The fifth son, Thomas, and Margaret Marshall, were married in January 1865. About that time a new stone house was built, a short distance in front of the log house. It was a stately home of 10 rooms, two fireplaces and a handsome door with side lights and a fan light, all further enhanced with hedges and flowers around the house and maples along the lane, a lane that, in those days, was southwest of the present lane. It entered through stone gateposts, among tall trees near a spring, then led to the new house in a graceful curve. It may have been at this point that the name *Clover Lea Farm* was chosen.

This Clergy Reserve was not released for sale until 1852. In 1869, Thomas took it over from his father, John, along with Lot 1, southeast, Concession 12.

Family of Thomas and Margaret Haines: *John* (1866)—tried homesteading in South Dakota for about three years, there he married Sybil Lougheed, returned to Bruce County about 1890; *Marshall* (1867-1946)—spent a year with John in South Dakota, tried farming in Bruce County, owned Lots 11 and 12 on Concession 14 from 1894 to 1899, married Lucinda Kitchen in 1895, returned to home farm; *Margaret Jane* (1869-1952)— married Job Revell, see Lot 7, southeast, Concession 13; *Anne (Annie) (1870-1971)*—married James S. Inglis of Nassagaweya, farmed in Saltcoats, Saskatchewan, as a widow, she lived with her sister, Lillie McIntyre, in Guelph, for a time, returned to Saskatchewan, died at Yorkton; *George* (1873-1947)—his career was horses, first in New York, then as trainer at Hancock Farm in Lexington, Kentucky, worked with the famous *Man 0' War,* married Dora Peel in 1917; *Ida (1875-1970*—a nurse, married August Anderson, a Lutheran minister of New York, who died about a year later, retired in Guelph for some years, married James S. Ford, travelled extensively before settling in St. Petersburg, Florida; *Mabel* (1877-1949)—married Benjamin Wyse, lived in Beverly Township, daughter, Olive, married Charles Stewart of Lot 11, southeast, Concession 13; *Lillie* (1879-1970)—a nurse, married Joseph McIntyre who died in 1950, lived in Guelph and vicinity, died at son Don's in Montreal; *Evelyn (1881-1968)*—a nurse, married Clayton Brown, M.D. of Buffalo, New York; *Ethel* (1885-1946)—married Alex McPhee, lived in Guelph and Hamilton.

The Haines family had all the usual farm animals, and grew tree fruit, small fruit and vegetables. They went to Hamilton market every second week to sell the products not needed at home. As was common then, they kept sheep. Every spring the sheep were washed and clipped, and the wool was taken to Rockwood Mills to trade for blankets, yarn and cloth. Home spinning and weaving was abandoned in the 1880s. They made maple syrup every spring. They kept bees, too. Thomas made his own hives and some years had 1,000 pounds of honey.

This was a musical family where members played accordion and violin and where all the girls took organ lessons on one of the first reed organs in the community. In those days, the music teacher called at the home to teach all but advanced students.

About the time Marshall and Lucinda Kitchen were married, in January 1895, the house was divided and a stone addition was built on the northeast side to provide a second kitchen and woodhouse. The first barn was struck by lightning and burned in 1896. It was rebuilt by Jim McLean of Morriston and his crew. Later that year, Thomas transferred ownership of this farm and Lot 1, southeast, to Marshall.

Mrs. Thomas Haines died in November 1899 at age 58, the result of a horse and buggy accident in their own lane. Thomas continued to live on the farm and made a home for his unmarried daughters. Ethel was with him until her marriage. Thomas spent his last few years with his daughters, Margaret, Ida and Lillie in their homes, all in or near Guelph.

Family of Marshall and Lucinda Haines: *Thomas* —farmed in Nicol Township north of Guelph, when his wife, Della Philpott of Puslinch died, he retired in Guelph; *Agnes* (1900-1971)—Mrs. Charles Borthwick of Puslinch Township; *Alfred*—he and his wife, Martha, lived in Buffalo, New York, retired in Tennessee; Jeffrey—unmarried, living in Tavistock; *Bruce* (1906-1907); *Margaret*—Mrs. John Coburn of Aberfoyle.

Marshall Haines was a township councillor from 1904 to 1907. Lucinda died March 1913, in her 42nd year. In 1915, Marshall married Janette (Nettie) Bryce of Teeswater. Their son, Clayton, was born soon after they moved to Aberfoyle, after selling the home farm to Roy Harris in 1917.

Roy Harris, unmarried at the time, had his family living with him in the former Haines house. Parents were Matthew Harris (1865-1926) and Ada (1875-1939), a sister of Burdge Gunby and Mrs. Albert Campbell (Harriet). The family included: *Roy* (1896-1977)- owned the farm until 1948, married Elaine Collins, lived in Fort Erie, later on a farm on York Road, near Waterdown; *Ivan*—married Ethel Simpson, lives in Acton; *Morley* (1902-1969)—married Mabel Colling, lived in the farmhouse while under Harris ownership, later in Freelton, their daughters Marie, Phyllis and Shirley attended Mountsberg School; *Mona*—married John Lyons, in Dundas; *Idella*—married Roy Laking of the Freelton Mill.

The Harris family seemed beset with adversity, although one unfortunate event ended happily. That was when Morley, as a young man, miraculously recovered from a siege of tetanus. The barn burned about 1923 and was replaced. In 1926, Matthew Harris was killed when kicked by a horse, and, a year after losing their mother, Ada, the house burned in the early months of 1940. It was rebuilt on the same site.

New owners, in 1948, were Harvey and Jessie Prudham who stayed little more than a year. Charles and Mary McCarthy then had the farm for two years before selling, in June 1951, to Fred and Margaret Beeforth.

In January 1954, Milford and Alice Watson bought the 100 acres and moved there with daughters, Linda and Lois. A son, Harold, and his wife, formerly Verna Klodt of Waterdown, also lived in the farmhouse. A year later the Watsons also bought a triangle of 34 acres across the road (see Lot 2 southeast). Milford died in December 1962. Some time later, Alice married Robert Hurren of Campbellville and under the name Hurren sold the farm in parts.

Thirty acres with the farm buildings were bought, in 1965, by Robert and Elizabeth Corman, who had two girls and a boy. Cormans sold an acre of the south corner in 1970. Third owners of this lot, Errol and Roslyn Alexander, who bought in 1972, meant it for a home and built their house in 1973. They came from South Africa in 1968 and had lived in Burlington in the meantime, where the older two of their family, Roger, Neil, Kevin and Wendy, were born.

In 1972, Anna Spencer of the Mohawk Inn bought the remaining 29 Corman acres and lived there with her two boys, Tom and Ben, until 1979. Present owners are Brian and Dianne Houston, farmers from the Ingersoll area who have two children, Christine and Vincent, attending High School.

An acre at the north corner of the lot facing the 13th Concession was sold in 1973 to Lois Mitchell, a Watson daughter. The property changed hands two more times that year, but it was William and Elizabeth Finlay, who bought in 1974, who had a house built and lived there until 1978. It now belongs to Christopher and Margaret (Margie) Maby and children Mark, Hannah and Robin.

The remaining large acreage beside the 13th Concession was bought in 1973 by Comin Brothers Farms.

Lot 3, southeast, Concession 12 (see also Lot 2)
Brock Grant

When George Lewis settled on Lot 3, he probably intended to buy the 100 acres. No doubt the resurvey of 1836 upset his plans. He had built his log cabin a reasonable distance from what he expected to be the 12th Concession, but was left a long way from the newly aligned 12th, used but little and never more than a dirt trail in the Lewis era, and even now improved only in limited sections.

As this lot was in the first group of Brock Lands to be sold, George Lewis had a deed for the southeasterly 50 acres by 1839, but it was not until 1856 that he held a deed for an extra five acres that included his home. Earlier, in 1852, William Barnes of Lot 2 had obtained a deed for the northwesterly 45 acres which he had been using for several years. The second Barnes home, a frame house, was built on Lot 3 very close to the Lot 2 line and had, as well, the usual cluster of farm buildings. A short extension of his farm lane gave George Lewis access to Mountsberg Road.

Little is known of the Lewis family. John Lewis, living on Lot 8, Concession 14 in the 1860s, almost certainly was a son and there may have been a daughter, Mary. The 55 acres were sold in December 1864 to Oliver and Elizabeth Ferrier who had been living on the place a few years, while also renting Lot 2. The Ferrier children included James, Edward, William, Amelia and Mary. Many short-term owners followed: William Wingrove, October 1866 to October 1871; Elizabeth Cooper, 1871 to December 1885; Alexander Milne, 1885 to January 1887; Charles and David Wilkerson, 1887 to 1890; and for a few years it became the property of James Barnes, son of William.

The old Lewis cabin had several tenants. For some time at the turn of the century, Henry McLaren, a tea merchant, lived there. Mr. McLaren obtained tea from imports, blended it himself, according to the taste of certain customers, and sold it in decorative tin caddies of 5 pounds, 10 pounds, or the large size, a 9-inch tin cube that could be counted on to last until his next horse-and-buggy visit, when caddies could be refilled.

McLarens were followed, about 1903, by the Simons family who stayed a few years. Their only son, Clifford, later of Detroit, attended Mountsberg School and the Methodist Sunday School.

Owing to age or poor health, the William Barnes farm (45 acres in Lot 3 and 100 acres in Lot 2) was rented after about 1860, reserving 2 acres and the house. In 1875, William Barnes, still around, leased his land to the Marshalls of Concession 14, for an extended period.

As William's widow, Jane remained in the home. Her son, James, and his wife, Sarah Ann Allison of Carlisle, also used the home until James, as sole heir of his mother, Jane (Murray) Barnes, in 1904, sold all the Barnes property, then including all of lots 2 and 3, to Thomas Haines.

Marshall Haines, son of Thomas and later owner, used the Barnes house as a home for his hired help. It burned about 1915-16 while occupied by the Freestone family with sons, Harry, Richard and Britton. Marshall Haines put up a small, frame house on the hillside of Lot 2, close to the road, for the Freestones, and sold Lot 3 to Robert Wigood in 1916.

Robert Wigood and his son, Hugh, in 1923, built a large, red brick house on Lot 3, in the general vicinity of the one that had burned. In 1920, Hugh had married Annie Scott, daughter of Jonathan and Jennie of Centre Road, and had been living in the homestead house on Lot 4 where their oldest son, Lyle, was born. As soon as the new house was finished, the three generations moved in.

When Hugh bought two-thirds of Lot 2 from Morley Harris in December 1939, the link between Lots 2 and 3 was rejoined. Hugh moved the Freestone cottage close to the farm buildings to become a chicken house.

Family of Hugh Wigood (1893-1964) and Annie Scott (1899-1972): *Lyle* (1921-1959)—remained on the farm, married Mary Free, had two sons, Allan and Larry. Several years after Lyle died, Mary married Donald Small, son of Harold on Lot 1, Concession 13; *Lorene*—married Al Watson, lived in Guelph; *Calvin*—see Lot 4, northwest, Concession 12.

The Survey—all of Lot 3, southeast
and two-thirds of adjoining Lot 2

Hugh Wigood died in December 1964 and the following June, Annie sold all the land to Harry S. Pett who had it surveyed into lots averaging slightly over 10 acres. All the lots were sold in 1966. Between then and 1971, when John DeVries built all the new houses, ex-

Looking north on Glenron Road from the Cormack's.   D. Cormack

cept on Lots 5 and 6, most of the properties changed ownership several times.

Lots are numbered from the west corner of the Lot 3 farm, moving northeasterly. Lots 1, 2 and 3 face Mountsberg Road, then enter the blind Glenron Road into the survey where numbering is counter-clockwise, with a turn-about between lots 9 and 10, bringing one back to Mountsberg Road.

Lot 1. Owned by Ronald G. Purdy; no house.

Lot 2. Anthony and Marjorie (Cooper) Davies bought the property in 1968 and in 1976, a large house was built some distance from the road. They have a son, Richard, and a daughter, Leslie. Davies also own, in part, the house and Lot 13.

Lot 3. Owned by Donald Plouffe; no house.

Lot 4. The house was built in 1971, the barn in 1973 by Dieter and Katherine Brandes whose children, Dieter and Kathy, are in elementary school.

Lot 5. George and Norma Sonnenburg, with two daughters, Marie and Holly, bought the property in 1975. They had the house built that year and the barn a year later.

Lot 6. Wayne and Gayle Hutt bought the lot and built the house in 1972. In 1979, they sold to Donald and Judith Cooke who moved from Carlisle with children, Timothy, Todd and Christine.

Lot 7. Francis and Tomasina Field, known as Bud and Ina, bought the house and land in 1971 and moved from Hamilton. A son, Bill, and his wife, Tina, live in Hamilton.

Lot 8. When Donald Cormack married Marilyn Henderson, they combined their children from previous marriages into a family of eight, all born between 1955 and 1964, and have lived there since 1971. The Henderson family includes Michael, Kurt, Lyndsay, Caroline and Peter. In the Cormack family are: Wendy, Susan and Steven. Since 1976, a shed and greenhouse have been built, and a sundeck and fireplace added to the house.

Lot 9. George and Jean Monas bought this new home in 1971 and moved from Ancaster. George served in W.W. II almost 6 years.

Lot 10. Around the bend is the home of Norman and Beverly Matthews who moved from Ancaster in 1971 with two sons, Jon and Adam. A third son, Brock, was born since then. In 1972-73, the Matthews built a two-storey barn. In 1974, a log cabin behind the barn was another family project and in 1977 they added a room to the house.

Lot 11. Peter and Gerda Burger left Holland in 1953 with three children and lived in Vancouver and Toronto before coming to Mountsberg in 1971. The next year they built a barn for their horses. They had five in their family: John, who lives at home; Cornelia

(Elsa), (1949-1971); Matthew, married Kathleen Hyndman and lives in Calgary; Paul, married Carla Bruurs and lives in Campbellville; Rosemarie, Mrs. Michael Hawkrigg lives in Hamilton.

Lot 12. John and Brenda Cottrell bought the property in 1971 and had the house built that year. They have two children, Darren and Mandy.

Lot 13. Anthony and Marjorie Davies bought this house and lot in 1976, in order to have a place to live while building their home on Lot 2. Since 1978, it has been rented to Jerome and Teresa Lassaline whose family includes Ronald, Susan, Denise, Laurie-Ann, Jeffery and Sandra.

Lot 14. Owners in 1971 when the house was built, were Stanley and Carolyn Lytle. They sold to Giacoma and Liberata Marinucci of Toronto in 1976. Their children are Adrianna, Enio and Anna.

Between the Marinucci home and Mountsberg Road, is a 27-acre property containing the former Wigood farm buildings. The house, built in 1923, has been made a duplex. It was bought in 1966 and is owner-occupied by Murray and Jessie Smith who have a family of three: Stephen, married to Julie Skelly; Brenda, and her husband, Geoffrey Aston live in the house with their two sons, Brett and Stephen; Mary married William Fearns who died in 1974.

Lot 3, northwest

Perhaps a relative of Catherine Griffin (Mrs. Thomas Wingrove), Joseph Griffin seems to have begun the task of clearing this 100 acres, a year or two before the arrival of John Millman, about 1848. Mr. Millman set about buying the property for which he received a deed in August 1857.

The Millman family left the neighbourhood early in 1873 and now little trace of them remains. A gravestone in the Methodist Cemetery tells a sad story. In February 1849, just four days apart, John Millman lost first his two-year-old daughter, Margaret Ann, then his 25-year-old wife, Sarah Ann.

The census of 1861 shows that John Millman had remarried, his second wife also named Sarah. At that time their children were James, Mary Jane, Isabel and John, and they were living in a 1 1/2-storey log house. That house stood behind the present-day barns, and eventually burned. The well, in use then, was a considerable distance to the northeast.

William Dougherty (1834-1905) bought the farm in January 1873 and sold his 35 acres at the northwest end of Lot 9, northwest, Concession 13. His first wife and the mother of his children was Mary Anne Revell (1842-1882), eldest of the Thomas Revell family. In their family were: *Sarah (about 1863-1928)*—Mrs. Henry Wise of St. Catherines; *Nathan (about 1865-1939)*—he and his wife, Louisa, lived in Buffalo, New York; *George (Feb. 1868-Feb. 1928)*—remained on the farm.

William's second wife, Elizabeth Smith, is buried in the Roman Catholic Cemetery at Freelton. He was a

William and Mary Anne Dougherty. *Mrs. Wm. Payne.*

George and Harriet Dougherty. *Mrs. Wm. Payne.*

township councillor for two or more years, including 1881-82. Later, his son, George, held the same office for four years, 1908-11, and again in 1913.

George succeeded to the farm. His first wife, Harriet Clark (1873-1903) had five boys: *Leland (1894-1917)*—killed in W.W. I, in 173rd Highland Battalion; *Earl (1896)*—remained on farm; *George (1898-1971)* — married Rilla House of Bartonville, lived in Hamilton; *Nathan (1900-1917)*—also a casualty of W.W. I, in 129th Battalion; *Elvin (1902-1963)*—known as "Kelly", lived in the village with his grandmother, Mrs. Clark Foster after his mother's death, married Marie McGuire and lived in Detroit, but Marie was killed in an auto accident May, 1938.

George's second wife was Margaret Zimmerman. They left the farm to Earl and moved to Waterdown when the four children of the second family were quite small: *William*—now of Guelph; *Mary*—a United Church minister who had been a missionary in China for five years, now retired in Hamilton; *Orville*—of Hamilton, died in 1971; *Ellis*—of Hamilton.

Earl married Flossie Hood of Freelton. Their family: *Grace*—Mrs. John Bell of Beechgrove; *Lyle*—married Florence Reed of Appleby, in Mississauga; *Doreen*—Mrs. Lloyd McGeachy of Galt; *Betty*—Mrs. William Payne of Flamborough Centre.

In the summer of 1956, Earl retired and he and Flossie moved into their home on Mountsberg Road (Lot 11, southeast). The farm was sold to Brock Howard, whose wife was formerly Irene Campbell, daughter of Albert. They had lived in Halton County And had three daughters: *Freda,* Mrs. McFadden of Milton; *Marie,* married Doug Ford, a veterinarian of King City, and *Sharon,* who went with her parents to Concession 7 near Harper's Corner, when they sold to Alfred and Annie Stoeckner in 1961. The Stoeckners and their children, Hannelore, Marie and Fred, stayed less than three years then moved to Highway 5 near Oakville, where Mr. Stoeckner died a year later in 1965.

In April 1964, the present owners, Lloyd and Faye (Bryant) Coverdale moved from Cedar Springs.

The age of the farmhouse is unknown, but with square-cut nails, wide pine board floors and nine-foot ceilings, it has seen more than a century and, probably was built about the time William Dougherty bought the farm. The barn complex is three separate buildings: a small very old barn, a large second barn and the latest small one, built about 1913 to use for the beef ring which George Dougherty took over from the Linns.

After the separation of five lots, the Coverdale property consists of about 80 acres. At the north corner of the farm, facing the 13th Concession, a half-acre building lot was sold in 1973 to Marilyn Coverdale, a daughter, and her husband, Glen Buttenham, who built their house that year. They have a son, Jeremy.

Beside them on the southwest, is the home of Ross Laking and his wife, Camilla McCrory of Montreal, and their children, Barbara and Murray. They bought the lot in 1969 and began building that year.

Farther southwest, is the 10-acre property of Steve and Mary Smutylo, bought in 1968 and where they built a large house in 1975.

Facing Mountsberg Road at the east corner of the farm, a 10-acre lot was sold to Alfred and Dorothy Houston in 1967. They built a house and, in 1976, sold to George and Arlene Best.

Between them and the Cloverdale farmhouse, Thomas Coverdale, a son, and his wife, Susan Mann, built a home in 1975.

A younger son, David Coverdale, married Laurie Stutt and lives in Dundas.

Lot 4, southeast, Concession 12   **Brock Grant**

Joseph Page, already settled on Lot 5, southeast, early decided to include Lot 4, southeast, to make up a 200-acre farm. Mrs. R. Kerr (daughter of Dr. John H. Page) has two deeds for the sale of this Brock land to Joseph Page. The first deed was dated March 1, 1850; the price—£125. The second deed, same lot, same price, was made out on August 11, 1857. The first one, dated 10 days after a change in Brock agency, was never registered. Perhaps a legal requirement had been overlooked and not rectified until a later trustee, John D. Uttermark, had been in charge for four years.

Following Joseph Page, sales of Lot 4 were included with Lot 5 through the ownership of Jeremiah Hunt, Marshall Hunt and Dr. John H. Page to Charles and Mary McCarthy in 1916. In April 1954, McCarthys sold 16 acres beside Mountsberg Road, northeast of the Creek, to A. Riley Armstrong, M.D. of Chedoke Hospital. The Armstrong home was built that year with additions in 1962 and 1968. It is now unseen from the road, screened by a new evergreen forest. Dr. and Elizabeth Armstrong have a grown family.

In January 1960, the remainder of the Lot 4 farm passed briefly through the hands of Bernard and Lorraine McCarthy to Eugene Zaborowski of Oakville and his wife, Dr. Janine Zaborowski of Joseph Brant Hospital. The Zaborowskis built a summer home on their land. They sold to Gilbert L. and Joan Cooper in 1969.

Lot 4, northwest

This Brock lot was late in settlement. In 1849, it was assessed to Thomas Wingrove of Lot 10, Concession 13; but that seems to have been a brief venture. The following year, the 100 acres was divided into two farms of equal size.

The Southeasterly 50 Acres (Beside Mountsberg Road)

George Hopkinson of a Nassagaweya family worked on this property during the 1850s. He did not buy, but remained in the vicinity as an auctioneer. In 1860, the 50 acres became the Wigood farm and is still partly owned and occupied by Wigood descendants.

Change in the spelling of family names was common, but perhaps no local surname saw greater variation that that of Wigood. The first deed of land, under the date August 18, 1864, was to Robert Weygood. Later, it became Waygood and, still later, Waggood and Wagwood. The present form, Wigood, has been in general use, locally, since around 1900.

Robert Weygood, or Wigood, was born in 1822, if one checks the family Bible, or in 1824, if his tombstone is correct. He died in December 1869. He came from Somerset, England, met Martha Ross (1828-1909) from Monaghan, Ireland, and they were married February 17, 1858 in Kilbride. They lived on Dundas Street (Highway 5) before coming to Mountsberg in 1860. Their family: *Annie* (1858-1930)—Mrs. Robert Clugston of the Freelton area; *William* (1860-1951)—born at Mountsberg, married Margaret Weir (1869-1953), see Lot 11, Concession 11; *James* (1862-1922)—married Rhoda Hambleton, see Lot 7, Concession 14; *Robert* (1864-1954)—married Emily A. Smith (1869-1896), remained on farm; *Martha* (1866-1922)—married James H. Smith, older brother of Emily; *Jacob* (1869-1939)—married Fanny Sutton (18661936), lived in Freelton.

Apparently, George Hopkinson had not lived on the lot. It was Robert Wigood Sr. who put up a large log cabin near the road on a knoll rising from the 12-Mile Creek; the site perhaps chosen with an eye to beauty as well as convenient water supply. That home still stands, its logs unseen behind modern siding.

Wigood homestead, circa 1915. William Jr. and Hugh standing, Robert and Robert Weir sitting, Martha Smith, Eileen Wigood and William, Sr. *Mrs. C. Wigood.*

Robert Jr.'s wife, Emily, died in 1896 when their only child, Hugh, was three years old. Robert's sister, Martha, a widow with a small daughter, Edith (Mrs. Percy Haskell), joined the farm household where the grandmother, Martha, still lived.

When Robert bought the Barnes place and moved there in 1923, with Hugh's family (see Lots 2 and 3, southeast) they kept the homestead, which was rented from time to time. The Shanks family lived there 1924-26, and Mrs. George Eaton and her three boys occupied it for a short period before 1940 but it had been vacant for some time before Hugh's son, Calvin, was married in 1947. When Calvin, born and raised in the new house, married Marjorie McLean of Badenoch, the early dwelling, once again became home to a Wigood family. Calvin and Marjorie have two sons, great, great grandsons of Robert Sr.; Peter, living at home, and

Four generations of Wigood, in 1949. Robert, Jr., Calvin, Hugh and baby Peter. *Mrs. C. Wigood.*

Paul, who married Marnie Robinson of Puslinch, and lives in Puslinch Township.

In April 1967, Calvin sold 45 acres to Dunbar Heddle, a retired lawyer, and his wife, Flora, who built a new home on the hill, some distance from Mountsberg Road. Family members *are:* Dr. John Heddle of York University; Frances, Mrs. C.H. van Mil of Lowbanks, and Margaret, at home.

As the original barn is on Heddle property, Calvin built a small barn on his remaining 5 acres.

Heddles, in 1970, sold 3 acres to Gary Kempenaar who built a home on the hillside before he married. Now, he and his wife, Allie (Sybersma) have three daughters: Rosalee, Valerie and Suzanne.

The Northwesterly 50 Acres (Beside the 13th Concession)

In 1859, Solomon Dawson, newly arrived from England, worked on this farm which Jacob Wright was in the process of buying. The Dawsons lived across the road (site of Jack Watson's home) on 50 acres which Jacob Wright also owned during a non-Campbell interlude of 20 years. Dawsons remained there until buying the Johnson farm (Allan Elliott's) in 1856.

Jacob Wright sold the timber off the acreage in Concession 12 and is said to have operated a lime kiln there. In 1873 he sold all his property to Archibald Campbell Jr. The 50 acres on Concession 12 passed on to Archibald's son, Alex L., and was sold by his estate to Jack and Florence Watson in 1953.

Watsons, in 1969, divided the lot into two 25-acre parcels which were bought by two Toronto couples that year. John and Helga Novak built a home in 1970 on the southwest part. Their sons, John and Rick, live in Toronto. Kurt and Irmgard Tennigkeit built their home in 1974 on the northeast half, hidden among trees near the east corner of their property.

Lot 5, southeast, Concession 12   Canada Company

Joseph Page settled on this lot while still a bachelor but had family nearby; his brother, John, on Lot 8, and his sister, Mary (Mrs. Josiah Mount) across the road. Ann Revel, whom he would marry, was a five-minute walk away on Lot 6; all in the central part of the 12th Concession. Around 1840, Joseph and Ann were married and lived in a storey-and-half log house on the northeast side of the farm lane.

Joseph Page's deed, dated June 29, 1846, states the price of £75. When, in August 1857, he got a deed for adjoining Lot 4 from the Brock estate, the price was £125. Inflation seems to be an old story.

Family of Joseph Page (1808-Jan. 1, 1892) and Ann (1820-1903): *Charles W. (1843-1929)*—he and wife, Arsinoe (1845-1934), later lived in Jerseyville; *Elizabeth (1845-1859); Mary Ann (1848-1928)*—married twice: first to James Clark, two daughters, Annie (born 1870) (Mrs. James Hurren) and Harriet (1873-1903) (Mrs. George Dougherty), and son, Charles A. (died June 16, 1877), then married William Foster, one son, Elvin; *John Albert (1854-1922)*—married Mary Ann Gunston (1856-1910), later owned the entire farm; *Daughter (born 1860)*—died at 18 days.

In his early years on the farm, Joseph's father, Matthew, came to live with him. His mother had died, and England was urging the elderly who had children in Canada or any colony, to go to them. Matthew's life in Canada was brief, and he was buried on the farm. Joseph's two married sisters, Ann and Maria, may have come at or about the same times as their father. Maria (Mrs. Cottrell) lived in Carlisle, but Joseph built a storey-and-a-half frame house beside the lane near the road for Ann, close to him in age. Ann and her husband, William Walker, had four young children, born in England: *Maria*—(Mrs. David Vivian), perhaps the eldest; *Rebecca (born about 1839)*—married William John Beatty; *Jane (1840-1875)*—became Mrs. James McCormack, lived at the village corner; *Moses*—two or three years younger than Jane.

In the early 1860's, Joseph Page set about building a grand new home made of buff brick, hauled from Streetsville. The house had three storeys and was reputed to be the largest in the area. The old house across the lane, later was enlarged, renovated and sided with red brick, making a good home for sons of the family, first Charles, then Albert.

A year after Joseph died, Ann assigned the farms to the two sons, retaining for herself, lifetime use of her home and stipulating that each son pay his sister, Mary Ann, $1,000 within two years. In 1905, Charles sold his share to Albert.

Family of Albert Page and Mary Ann Gunston: *Talbert (1877-1893); Finton (born in 1879)*—"Fin", married Ruby Carey, a barber in Hamilton; *Burnice (1880-1958)*—"Bun" married Hannah Emmons (18801969), lived in Mountsberg vicinity; *Russell (born 1883)*—died at less than one year old; *Amasa (1886-1949)*—"Am" married Ruth Hood, lived on northwest half of Concession 9, East Flamborough; *Flossie (1891-Feb. 1976)*—married James Gray of Centre Road, Concession 10.

In 1905 the big house, then occupied by Albert and his family burned in a spectacular, early-afternoon fire. The following year, Albert (John A. Page on documents) sold all 200 acres, as well as the 6 acres of former parsonage property on Lot 6, to Jeremiah Hunt. The once magnificent home was rebuilt on a more modest scale to become the residence of Mr. and Mrs. Jeremiah Hunt. Their son, Marshall, and his family lived in the red brick house. In 1911, the entire property became Marshall's. At that time the Marshall Hunts had six children: *Walter*—later in Rockwood; *Stanley*—minister in Oregon; *Florence*—later Mrs. Walter Harris; also *Hazel, Victor* and *Grace*.

Dr. John H. Page bought the entire acreage from Marshall Hunt in March 1914, but held it only two years. This John Page, son of Peter, was a great nephew of Joseph and had an interesting career in teaching and medicine. Trained at the Hamilton Model School, he taught three years in Binbrook Township where he met his future wife, Alice Beattie. They were not married until 1896 when he graduated with an M.D. degree from University of Detroit and began to practice in Fostoria, Michigan

It was during a respite from medicine, while helping his father on the farm (now Allan Elliott's) that a year-old daughter, Ruth, died in November 1900 and was buried in the Methodist Cemetery. There followed an 8-year medical practice in South Dayton, N.Y. and a further stint of teaching at Sinclairville, Ontario. He left a practice in Kennedy, N.Y. when he bought the Mountsberg farm to restore his health in country living. In 1916, he returned to medicine in Falconer, New York and there he and his wife remained the rest of their lives.

John H. Page (Dec. 1868-April 1935) and Alice Beattie (died in 1959) had the following family with them at Mountsberg: *Bessie*—attended Hamilton Normal School during the Mountsberg interlude, married Earl Mitchell, then of Binbrook, who died in 1960, now Mrs. R. Kerr; *Arnold*—a M.D. specialist in dermatology in Erie, Pennsylvania, married, died in 1934 aged 32; *Gladys*—a nurse, Mrs. Marvin Nelson of Falconer, New York; *Hadley (1907-1942)*—married, killed in a truck accident.

In November 1913, when a McCarthy family was living on Lot 6 (present Elliott farm), the second son,

Family of Mary Ann and Albert Page; Burnice, Anton, Amasa and Flossie. *Mrs. K. Zimmerman.*

Family of Charles and Mary McCarthy; rear, Bernard, Mary, Dorothy, Anne, Loretta and Patrick. Middle, Charles, Father, Paul, Mother and John. Front, Edward, Sarah and Margaret. *Mrs. Vince O'Connor.*

Charles, married Mary Mooney of Freelton. Early in 1916, they bought Lots 4 and 5 from Dr. John Page and, for more than half a century it remained a McCarthy home. Family of Charles McCarthy (1881-1959) and Mary Mooney (1890-1975): Charles—second wife, Olga Mailer, in Hamilton; *Mary*—Mrs. Vince O'Connor of Hamilton; *John*—married Winnifred Leslie, died in 1974; *Anne*—of Flint, Michigan; *Loretta*—married Verne Hall, lived in old Methodist parsonage, now in Hamilton; *Dorothy*—in Toronto; *Patrick*—married Dorothy Fritz, in Burlington; *Bernard*—married Lorraine Close, later owners of the farm; *Sarah*—Mrs. William Ward of Dundas; *Paul*—married Rose Sterner, see Lot 9, Concession 12; *Margaret*—Mrs. Merlin Misner, lives on 5th Concession, East Flamborough; *Edward*—married Joyce Parkinson, in Hagersville.

About 1927 or 1928, the barn was struck by lightning and fired. That it was saved with relatively little damage makes it a rare event, especially at a time when the only fire protection one had was good neighbours.

Charles McCarthy was a township councillor from 1940 through 1951.

Bernard and Lorraine owned the farm from 1960 until they sold to Vratislav Kraus in 1968. With children, Mark, Charles, June and Barbara, they moved to Millgrove. Mr. Kraus has a nursery business on Centre Road, near Carlisle, and grows trees and shrubs on this farm.

From time to time there have been tenants in the red brick house. In the 1920's the Dan McGuire family was there, following his death. The children were: Cecil, Jack, Marie, who married Elvin Dougherty, Jim and Basil. Young married members of the McCarthy family used it at times. In the 1960's, McDougalls lived there with daughters, Heather and Debbie. There were others. Since owned by Mr. Kraus, David and Shirley Jones with daughters, Janet and Pamela, have been tenants.

Gilbert and Joan Cooper of Lot 4, bought from McCarthys about 2 acres at the north corner of Lot 5, in 1968. They sold half of it to their daughter, Sheila in 1973. She sold her part in 1975 to Barry and Patricia Vegh. William Moskalyk bought it in 1978, built a house and lived in it briefly before selling, in 1979, to Tony and Judith Bayer who have two children, Mark and Rebecca. Coopers still own an acre at the north corner.

Lot 5, northwest, Concession 12   Canada Company

This lot was bought by the Canada Company in September 1832. Three years later the northwest 100 became the home of pioneer Josiah Mount, patriarch of the Mounts of Mountsberg. Mr. Mount obtained his deed July 12, 1840. The price was £75.

Although the village name honoured the Mount family, it was here at the homestead that the name persisted longest. Two of Josiah's grandchildren spent their entire lives on the farm, Matt who died in 1957 and Jennie in 1959. With their passing there were no Mounts left in Mountsberg.

Josiah Mount (1794-1873) of Leicestershire and his wife, Mary Page (1797-1875) of Lincolnshire were married in England, where six of their eight children were born. In their family were: *John (1817-1867)*—see Lot 7, southeast, Concession 12; *Richard (1821-1901)*—moved to Iowa; *Matthew (1824-1904)*—see village; *Jane (1827-1912)*—Mrs. Bernard Griffin; *Page (1830-1865)*—see Lot 6 adjoining; *Charles (1832-1890)* —see Charles Mount's House, Lot 7, southeast; *Alpheus (1836-1918)*—remained on farm; *Mary Ann (1838-1882)*—Mrs. John Taylor.

About 1860, the Mount family built a house in the village for their parents. They occupied it briefly before returning to the farm. The change in their plans was due to the early death of their son, Page.

Alpheus Mount married Hulda Wingrove (1842-1921), daughter of Thomas Wingrove, Sr. Their children were: *Gilbert (1865-1890); Mary Catherine (1867-1947); Tom (1869-1947); Charles (1872-1953)*—see Lot 10, Concession 14; *Janet (Jennie) (1875-1959); Matthew (Matt) (1878-1957); Laura (1882-1959)*—Mrs. Joshua Allison, Moffat.

Alpheus and Hulda Mount with 2 of their children.
The late Miss Jennie Wingrove.

In 1889, Mary Catherine and Tom took over from Ralph Hewins a farm east of Guelph Line on the Middle Road (Queen Elizabeth Way). There they remained as long as they were able to keep up the farm work. In their late years, they returned to the home farm where Jennie and Matt were living. Matt was interested in Indian history and as a hobby, collected Indian artifacts found on his land, the most rewarding site being the flats beside the 12-Mile Creek.

Of all the Alpheus Mount family, only Laura married. In June 1962, Harold Allison, only surviving grandchild of Alpheus, sold the farm to Douglas and Opal Dent of Waterdown.

With the passing of the Mount family, misfortune fell upon the homestead. On Thanksgiving Day, October 12, 1964, the barn burned. Tenants at the time were Mr. and Mrs. George Ballantine. They, with their eldest son, Brian, were not at home. Others of the family, Bruce, Tommy, Donna, Joey and a baby of one year had a narrow escape.

Only a few months later in January 1965, the two-storey frame house, the century-old Mount home, was badly damaged by fire. It was repaired and later occupied by two families. The house had been built about 1870, beside the early log home which became the kitchen of the later dwelling.

Fritz and Ursula Kopp, both from Germany, bought a building lot in 1972, located near the east corner of the farm and, two years later, built a home for themselves and their two small daughters, Lillian and Karin.

In 1977, about 28 acres was sold and a house built near Mountsberg Road. In 1979 it was sold by John DeVries to Gordon and Margaret Boyd McNeil who have three children, Christine and Stephen Boyd and Victor McNeil.

Flamborough Centre Properties, who had bought most of the farm in 1977, sold the northwest 67 acres to Thomas and Stella Gillespie in 1978. The Gillespies moved a cabin to their property for temporary use and began building a house facing the 13th Concession on this attractive acreage with the 12-Mile Creek coursing through it. Along the creek is the spot once known as the "swimmin' hole", a small section of the stream three or four feet deep, the same spot used by the Baptists until early in the century for their baptismal ceremonies.

In spite of the ideal location, the Gillespie building program was fraught with more than the usual unforeseen delays. In the 1960's there had been a chemical waste disposal site near the 13th Concession road southwest of the creek. Although it operated only a short time before being closed by the Board of Health, it left a hidden predicament with underground concrete storage tanks and the problem of locating a safe water supply.

The Gillespies raise beef cattle. Their family includes Randy, Rhonda, Darlene (Mrs. Marcel Poirier) and Jeffrey.

The remainder of the farm, including the Mount house, is still owned by Dents. Paul, son of Douglas and

Opal, with his wife, Merejean, and children, Vicki, Douglas, James and Duane have lived there since 1967.

Lot 6, Concession 12   **Brock Grant**

In looking at an 1859 map of East Flamborough, one might wonder why the northwest half of Lot 6 was divided into three parts. Early Surveys and Land Grants, tells how the re-survey a year after settlement, placed the new log homes of Philip Johnson and Cornelius Hewins on John Revel's Lot 6, northwest. Mr. Revel paid for the lot in 1837 and, two years later, sold 24 acres at the northwest end to Cornelius Hewins to add to his 100 acres of Lot 7. In 1847, John Revel and Philip Johnson completed a trade whereby Mr. Johnson received 34 acres on the northwest side of Mountsberg Road, where his buildings were located and Mr. Revel accepted 34 acres at the southeast end of Lot 6. That left Mr. Revel with about 42 acres and his home, midway in the northwest hundred, and a lane to Mountsberg Road that he had reserved at the southwest border of the lot.

Charles Revell (the spelling was changing) inherited his father's land and, in 1870, sold the 34 acres at the southeast end of Lot 6, beside the 12th Concession road allowance, to Thompson and Laking of the Shingle Mill. Four years later, it was William Laking's only, when he became sole owner of the business. In order to reach the property, the mill used a trail through the main farm, southwest of the church. In 1880, the 34 acres was sold back to the farm, then owned by Peter Page.

No farm home ever existed on the southeast hundred, but a small barn stands beside Mountsberg Road on the hilltop. The Methodist Cemetery is on this land and the Methodist Church stood there from 1854 to 1969 (not far from the west corner) and the old Methodist parsonage remains at the north corner, astride the line between Lots 5 and 6.

The Former Parsonage

The initial use of this house with six acres is told with the Methodist Church, that era lasting from 1861 to 1889. During the following eight years, the home was owned by Margaret Dawson (not of the Solomon Dawson family). As a widow, she moved from Morriston with her family of eight, to become caretaker of the church. In 1897 she sold out to Peter Page, then owner of much of Lot 6.

Whether by error or design, the house site squarely on the line between Lots 5 and 6. Early deeds are confusing. Three were signed in 1861. In the first Solomon Dawson, then of Lot 6, sold 6 acres at the north corner of the southeast half to Charles Revell for $480. Very soon it went to Joseph Page of Lot 5 for $1,375. That apparently included the house. Then Joseph Page sold it to the trustees of the church for $700. Obviously there were conditions, for when the church sold to Margaret Dawson, she received only a fraction of an acre and most of the 6-acre parcel reverted to Joseph Page.

Mr. and Mrs. Peter Page retired in the old parsonage in 1905. The following year, J. Albert Page, son of Joseph (deceased) sold to his cousin, Peter, a strip of land 200 by 4 1/2 feet, to add to one side of his lot. Later, in 1914, when Peter's son, Dr. John H. Page, owned all the former Joseph Page land, including Lots 4 and 5, southeast, and the almost 6 acres in Lot 6, he sold the 6 acres back to his father.

Samuel Shanks bought the property from Peter Page in April 1926, and the Shanks family lived there until 1943 when they bought a farm, (see Lot 10, southeast, Concession 12). They sold the house and 6 acres to Charles McCarthy, then owner of the lands founded by Joseph Page. So, once again the roving 6 acres became an adjunct of Lot 5. For seven years the boundary remained fixed. It was during this hiatus that Charles McCarthy's brother, John (Jack), lived there after the death of his wife, and there he died in 1949.

In 1950, the one-time parsonage took on new metes and bounds when McCarthys sold to their daughter, Loretta and her husband, Vernon Hall, through the Veteran's Land Act, the house and three acres of land, part in Lot 5 and part in Lot 6. The remainder of the 6-acre parcel is still with Lot 5.

Following is the family of Loretta and Vernon Hall: *Gail*—Mrs. Paul Kachiuk of Millgrove; *Ronald*—married Lois Watson, in Hamilton; *Larry*—died in 1952 at 16 months; *Edward*—married Angela Morrison, in Hamilton; *Raymond*—married Gwen Mosher. Also *Dennis, Laura, Marilyn* and *Leonard.*

After the Halls moved to Hamilton where Vernon is a druggist, Francis and Lena McGroty owned the house and lot from 1965 to 1972. McGroty's built a new home on Lot 3, Concession 13. Now Gordon and Mary Harris own the former parsonage and live there with their family, Nancy, Sandra, James and Wayne.

With the re-survey problems resolved, Philip Johnson owned a 100-acre farm, two-thirds of it in the southeast half of Lot 6. His buildings remained on the 34 acres in the northwest half, beside Mountsberg Road.

When Philip Johnson and his wife, Ann, arrived from Lincolnshire in 1835, they had a family ranging in age from mid-teens down. Known members were: *William (1819-1886)*—see Lot 7, northwest, Concession 13; *Elizabeth (1821)*—married John Wingrove, son of Charles, see Lot 10, southeast, Concession 12; *Benjamin (1823-1896)*—married Ann Hewins, lived in Nassagaweya and Mountsberg village; *John*—uncertain, believed to have married and lived in Burford area.

Little is known of Philip Johnson, personally. He was a Methodist. He gave a piece of land for a cemetery about 10 years before the frame church was built in 1854. His wife, Ann (1792-1852) is buried there, but there is no record of Philip who was still living in 1861. At least two early graves are known to have been on the Johnson farm in the southeast part. Presumably, the deaths occurred before there was a cemetery. According to a township record, in 1841 there were six males on the Johnson farm, one under 16, and two not otherwise accounted for.

In January 1856, Philip Johnson sold his land to Solomon Dawson who moved there from Lot 4, Concession 13 (present Jack Watson place) where he had been a tenant. Solomon Dawson (1826-1911) and Sarah Laking (1827-1901) were married a year or two before leaving England. Sarah was the older sister of John, Joseph and William Laking. Following is the Dawson family, information incomplete: *Charlotte (1849-1912)*— Mrs. James Inglis, Sr. of Nassagaweya; *Elizabeth (born 1851)*—Mrs. Shortreed, lived on farm north of Guelph; *John (1853-1929); Harry (1854-1937)*— lived on farm northeast of Guelph, which is now city; *Walter (born 1856); Robert (1858-1939)*— farmed north of Guelph; *Effelinda (born 1860); Solomon (1861-1862)*— buried in Methodist Cemetery; *Caroline (Kate) (about 1863-1927)*—Mrs. Ben Freure of Guelph; *Christopher (1865-1927)*—lived in Guelph, latterly in Hamilton; *William (born 1868)*. Although he lived in the neighbourhood only 22 years, Solomon Dawson's name is remembered as one who was involved and interested in local happenings of, his day. He moved to Guelph after selling the farm, less the 6-acre parsonage property, to Peter Page in February 1872.

Despite the fact that Peter Page's tombstone gives his years as 1835 to 1931, he is believed to have been born in 1836 with the honour of being Mountsberg's first baby, the son of John and Catherine Page of Lot 8, Concession 12.

Peter Page and Susannah Hurren had been married almost 12 years when they moved to this farm. When first married they lived in a small log house, on Lot 8, Concession 14, owned by Susannah's uncle, William Hurren. From 1863 to 1867, Peter had title to 50 acres on Lot 8, Concession 13, and they may have lived there. However, at one stage of their early years together, Peter and Susannah spent a period at Erin, Ontario; but Mountsberg lured them home again.

Family of Peter and Susannah Page: *Elizabeth (1861)*—Mrs. John Carlson, Carlisle; *William E. (1863-1902)*—died of pneumonia while working away from home, buried in the Methodist Cemetery; *James A. (1864-1896)*— died as the result of an accident, buried in Methodist Cemetery; *Philip (1867-1935)*—unmarried, taught school, obtained a Ph. D. degree, then spent much of his life operating a chicken farm new New Westminster, British Columbia; *John H. (1868-1935)*—married Alice Beattie, see Lot 5, southeast, Concession 12; *Jane (1871-1956)*—Mrs. Sam Cairns of Nassaga-weya; *Nettie (1878-1958)*—married Tom Wingrove, see Lot 10, southeast, Concession 13.

Little is known of early farm buildings. As of 1861, Solomon Dawson was living in a storey-and-a-half stone house, probably the second house on the farm. A barn built by Peter Page in 1874 still stands.

In January 1880, Peter Page bought back from William Laking the 34 acres at the southeast end of Lot 6 and, in 1885, added the central section of the northwest half, giving him a farm of about 170 acres, all of which he sold to John Harris in March 1905. He then moved into the former parsonage which he had owned since 1897.

Susannah Page was noted for her many crafts. She made quilts and mats, as did all the neighbouring ladies, but with imagination and creativity, her fingers fashioned rarer arts. Her flowers of dyed feathers were airy bits of beauty. Her worn-out pots and pans were not thrown away. In time, they, along with cans of all shapes and sizes, reappeared as vases, bowls, and jardinieres, covered with plaster of Paris, inlaid with colourful fragments of broken china.

I once stayed overnight at the Pages in the old parsonage, and slept under a new "Star of Bethleham" quilt, even then recognized as an exceptional piece of handiwork. Now, people gladly lay down $200 and more for less meticulously sewn-by-hand quilts.

Mr. and Mrs. Harris stayed only a year, a tragic year for them. Their only child, Winnifred, died from scalds in a home accident on December 17, 1905. She was 4 years and 8 months old.

Dr. Arthur Jones of Kilbride owned the farm from 1906 to 1921, but did not live there. First tenants were Arthur Peer and his family who were there about three years. Of their family, Lawrence, Nellie and Violet attended Mountsberg School.

Annie (Hunter) McCarthy, widow of Patrick McCarthy, came next with her grown family. Her eldest daughter, Annie, had married Augustine (Gus) Carroll

Peter and Susannah Page. *Mrs. H. Rennick*

of Carlisle and died in August 1911 at age 28. The others were: *John (Jack)*—married Eliza Foley of Kilbride, as a widower, lived in the former parsonage, died in 1949; *Charles (1881-1959)*—married Mary Mooney, after 1916, on Lots 4 and 5, Concession 12; *Patrick (1886-1963)*—married Gretta Mooney (1897-1958), lived at Kilbride and Freelton; *Hunter (1888-1973)*—married Eva Smith (1888-1961), lived in Freelton; *Ella (died September 1910)*—shortly after coming to Mountsberg, she died; *Christina (Tina)*—the only one to attend Mountsberg School, married John Hanson and lived in Guelph, died about 1977.

Two McGuire brothers, Bill and Elmer (Al), a widower with a young son, Vincent (Mickey), and their mother, were on the farm a few years before Dr. Jones sold all the property to Charles Elliott of Morriston, in March 1921.

Following is the family of Charles W. and Isabella (Campbell) Elliott: *Mervin*—married Helen Bowman, lived a short while in the home built by John Hewins on Lot 6, later moved to London where Mervin died in 1970; *Allan*—married Isabel, daughter of David and Jane Stewart, remained on the farm; *Wanda*—Mrs. Walter Amos of Stratford; *William*—married Anne Fox, in Dundas; *Freda*—Mrs. Glen Mohr of Stratford.

In 1958, Allan took over the farm. He specializes in dairy farming with his herd of Elleetta Holsteins. The parents retired in Morriston where Mrs. Elliott died in September 1959, and Charles in April 1961.

Family of Allan and Isabel Elliott: *Murray*—not married, on the farm; *Shirley*—married Alexander(Sandy) Cleghorn of Guelph, a great-great-grandson of the first Thomas McCrae, now lives on a farm near Elora; *Marlene*—in Guelph; *Barbara*—married Joseph Scanlon and lived in Fergus, Barbara died July 26, 1973 at 25 years old, leaving a one-year-old son, Justin. Joe remarried and went to Spain; *Brenda*—Mrs. Donald Stevens of Lot 1, northwest, Concession 12.

Centre Part of Lot 6, northwest

When John Revel came to East Flamborough, he expected to own the 100 acres of Lot 6, northwest with his friends beside him, Josiah Mount on Lot 5, Cornelius Hewins on Lot 7 and Philip Johnson on the southeast half of Lot 6. But it didn't work out that way. The settlement of the land dilemma, completed in 1847, shows Mr. Revel to have been an agreeable and obliging man. He was left with 42 acres in mid-lot with access to Mountsberg Road by way of a 30-foot lane at the boundary line with Lot 7.

John Revel (1780-1851) had been married twice in England. He and his second wife, Mary (1793-1855) had two children, Ann (1820-1903) who married Joseph Page, and Charles (1827-1895) who later lived on Lot 10, Concession 12, also in the village. Perhaps a brother of John lived with him. A stone in the Methodist Cemetery is to the memory of Thomas Revell, son of Charles and Jean Revell of England, who died in 1853 at age 78. From this lone fact, the relationship is merely an obvious assumption. John's son, Thomas, of his first family, came to Canada five years after his father and settled on Lot 7, southeast, Concession 13.

John's son, Charles, sold the 42 acres to Page Mount, son of Josiah. Although the deed is dated April 1865, the Page Mounts had been living there about five years. Page Mount died November 1865 at age 35. His wife, Elizabeth Dougherty died December 1881 at age 43. In their family were: *William Leonard (Len)* (18601923) who was the neighbourhood thresher for many years. He had a daughter, Ethel (Mrs. William Anderson) and a stepdaughter, Minetta Coleman. Len had two sisters, *Isabella (Bella)* and *Caroline (Carrie)*, and a brother, *Richard*, who died March 1865 at 8 months.

Peter Page bought the property from Len Mount in September 1885 increasing the main farm to about 170 acres. The old Revel cabin, unoccupied, remained standing for another quarter century.

Northwest 24 Acres of Lot 6

Cornelius and Ann Hewins left England with their children, Ann and John, along with their Lincolnshire friends and their families. They left a homeland where labour and housing conditions were poor, and where their working children had little chance of education or advancement. It was a gamble and the stakes were high, but they were inured to hardship, so the struggle and toil of turning a lonely forest into a farm did not faze them. And "Corney"' was a tough, tenacious man. He proved his mettle on the outward journey.

Cornelius Hewins, original settler. *Mrs. W.C. Cust.*

Their crossing of the Atlantic by sailing vessel was long and arduous. Wholly dependent on the elements, they encountered cold and stormy weather. At one time the superstructure of the ship became coated with ice. Navigation was impossible when the weather vane, atop the mast, became fixed in one position. The captain found that not one of his crew could scale the slippery spar. He appealed to the passengers, and offered a 40-ounce bottle of whiskey to anyone who could free the frozen vane. Cornelius Hewins was the hero and received his reward.

Believing they were well settled on Lot 7, Cornelius and Ann faced the unforeseen problem of having to buy this 24 acres from John Revel in order to keep their year-old buildings. That, accomplished in 1839, gave them a 124-acre farm. By the time of the 1841 township assessment, Cornelius, with the help of his son, John, then 17, had cleared and was cultivating all 24 acres, as well as 17 acres on Lot 7, and he owned 2 oxen, 3 cows and 3 young cattle.

A story that clings to Ann's name is a clue to her nature. She was busy baking bread when the opportunity came to visit a neighbour. Did she decline? Not Ann. She wrapped up the rising loaves warmly, took them along, and baked them in her friend's oven.

Family of Cornelius Hewins (Sept. 6, 1793-Feb. 8, 1864) and Ann Drewry (1791-Sept. 11, 1854): *Mary* (April 10, 1817-1820); *Elisabeth* (born Jan. 1, 1819); *John* (Apr. 27, 1824-Apr. 9, 1893)—October 4, 1845, John married Margaret Sutton (1822-1911), daughter of Samuel and Elizabeth (Slater) Sutton who lived beside present Highway 6 on Concession 10 of East Flamborough; *Ann/Anne* (both spellings used) (Nov. 25, 1833-Sept. 9, 1893)—married Benjamin Johnson, son of Philip.

The first Hewins home was the standard, small log building, designed to provide quick and comfortable shelter that would tide them over the lean years. It stood 100 feet or more from the road, midway between the later house and barn. Its site was close to the east corner of the stone workshop which John built at a later date. John's hobby was woodworking. He produced articles for either barn or house use. Today, a restored pine cupboard, carefully crafted by John, graces the home of his great grandson, Reg Hewins, on the farm across the road.

In its aged and crumbling era, the workshop was demoted to a hen house and pig sty. But the end came slowly. The roofless ruins remained part of the scene for many years.

In 1856, Cornelius deeded the 24 acres to John who, in 1860, built the brick house still in use. John and his friend, Thomas Revell, shared a house plan. Although basically the same, modifications gave a varied appearance to the houses. The Hewins place had a veranda facing the road and continuing along the southwest end to a roomy open space that gave access to a one-storey kitchen and to a woodshed, all of brick. No doubt, the veranda originally encircled the house to meet at the kitchen, as was the style of the day.

John and Margaret had two sons, Ralph (1846-

John and Margaret Hewins. *G.A. Hewins.*

1915) and Aaron (1847-1905) who later lived across the road on Concession 13. A niece, Mary, grew up with the family.

Ralph married Janet Wingrove in 1871. Some time later, a three-room addition was built at the north corner of the house. It was entered by a door at the end of the veranda and had direct access to the main house. Ralph and his family lived there until 1885 when they went to a farm on the Middle Road (Queen Elizabeth Way) in Nelson Township. Later that year, John sold Lot 7 to William Laking. Ralph returned to Mountsberg four years later (see Lot 8, southeast, Concession 12).

In the meantime, Ralph's son, Richard, remained with the grandparents and continued to spend most of his time there until several years after John died in 1893.

Margaret had a knack with herbs, which gave her a certain status in the neighbourhood. With no doctor within reach, people had to treat their ailments as best they could. Margaret's lore was a legacy from her grandparents, John and Ann Sutton, who brought their family to the Hamilton area from Pennsylvania in 1795. In those primitive days home remedies were a matter of life and death and were only slightly less so in the northerly reaches of East Flamborough in the mid 1800s.

When a member of the family or a neighbour became ill, Margaret went off to the woods with a basket, and returned with an assortment of plants that might include Indian turnip (Jack in the Pulpit), catnip, witch hazel, wild mustard, foxglove, belladonna, balsam, pine and maybe just a bit of balm of Gilead to add a touch of perfume to a poultice. Then, according to the need, she brewed up a potion to be swallowed or an ointment to be rubbed on. Some plants, such as hops or flax, were grown near the home. For winter use, medicinal herbs were dried and stored. Most families tried to keep on hand two standby remedies: sulphur, that was taken for just about any ailment and turpentine for external use.

The vacated north wing of the house had occasional tenants. Around 1890, Harry Elvin and his wife, Sarah Laking (daughter of Joseph) lived there for a few years. They were newly-arrived from England with their family, Mary, Charles, George and William. The last occupants where Richard Hewins and his bride, Mary Ann (Dolly) Roberts, who were there in the winter of 1905-06.

Margaret Hewins left her farm home and moved to the village in the late 1890s. The house and property on Lot 6 was rented to Emanuel Mount's family until about 1904. Joseph McIntyre of Morriston was a tenant for a season before the 24 acres was sold to Emerson Carton in September 1905.

The following January, Mr. Carton bought from Charles Hewins 48 acres at the southeast end of adjacent Lot 7, northwest, thus renewing, in part, the link between Lots 6 and 7. During his ownership, he demolished the north wing of the house, took down the front veranda and built a porch over the front door; jacked up the barn, turned it 90 degrees and had stables built within the new foundation.

Emerson and Ellen (Nellie) Carton stayed on the place seven years before moving to Rockwood. In the early part of the Mountsberg period, their daughter, Elsie, died at age 5. Younger children were Bertha, Ross and Laura.

In April 1912, the farm (24 acres on Lot 6 and 48 acres on Lot 7) was sold to Matthew Patton of Freelton and his wife, Amy Nicholson, daughter of Mr. and Mrs. George Nicholson of Lot 11, Concession 13. Mr. and Mrs. Patton had a daughter, Muriel, who married Morris Scott of Flamborough and a son, Bruce.

In the mid-1920s, Matthew Patton purchased from Charles Elliott a 30-foot lane beside Lot 7, extending from the 24 acres through to Mountsberg Road. This included the section of lane that, in early times, had been John Revel's.

Bruce, who never married, took over the farm in 1938 and was alone for many years. In 1954, he made an agreement of sale with Henry and Georgette McDermid, whereby he continued to live in part of the house with the McDermids and their children, Robert, Marlene and Ricky. Bruce died the following year, and his interest passed to his sister, Muriel Scott.

On January 1, 1959, the barn burned and was not replaced. In November of that year, the McDermids and Muriel Scott sold all of their property on Lots 6 and 7 to Remi Desender of Lot 3, Concession 13. Several tenants followed. The Sheppard family with children Morris, William, Thomas, Bruce, Harold, Susan and Allan, came in 1959 and stayed about a year. They were followed by Walkers and their children Larry, Bob, Carol, Irene, Fred and a baby girl. Mr. and Mrs. William Hysert, who had shared the Desender house on Lot 3 Concession 13, also came in 1960 and for a few months shared the house with the Walkers until they left. Mrs. Hysert died in 1963 and soon after, Mr. Hysert and his children Merle, Fred, Sheila, Glen (now of Burlington) and James moved away. Before leaving the neighbourhood, Desenders lived in the house, briefly.

In the meantime, ownership had changed and the property passed through the hands of Eleanor London to Fenrock Ltd. in November 1962. In 1966, the Fenrock Company made an agreement of sale with Edward and Patricia Edmar who were already living on the place. Edmars made changes to the house and its surroundings. The front porch was removed and a large dormer on the southeast, or rear, changed the roofline. In the Edmar family were: Dianne, Raymond, Belinda, Stephen, Calvin and twin boys.

In 1977 Edmars sold their equity and moved to Milton. New owners were William and Eileen McDonell who made extensive renovations and improvements to the house, as it neared the age of 120 years.

Lot 7, southeast, Concession 12   Brock Grant
John Mount's Farm and Mountsberg Village

The village that sprang up at the intersection of Centre Road and the Cross Road (or Given Road, now known as Mountsberg Road) owes its beginning to four sons of Josiah and Mary Mount's family of eight children. John, the eldest, was 18 when the family came from England in 1835 and settlefd on Lot 5, northwest, Concession 12. About 10 years later, John and his brother Richard began clearing Lot 7. John bought the southeast hundred, but did not hold a deed until 1866. His log cabin and farm buildings were close to Centre Road, midway on the lot.

About 1850, Matthew, the third son, took over an acre at the corner and built a blacksmith and carriage shop. He was married but had no family. Richard worked along with Matthew a few years before leaving the community. Charles, the fifth son, worked in the carriage department. One of the first employees was Harness Kelk (1828-1891), not long from Lincolnshire, who spent the rest of his life working for Matthew and succeeding blacksmiths.

Showing horses was only a small part of the blacksmith business. Matthew made just about every small implement used on a farm, from square-cut nails to ploughshares, including shovels, hoes, axes, chains, hammers, crowbars and mat hooks for every household.

The Mounts built three village houses, and all three still stand. Their first, in the early fifties, was for Charles and his family. It was on a lot adjoining Matthew's and faced the Cross Road. On Matthew's lot, between his shop and Charles' new house, they built a retirement home for their parents. About 1860, Mr. and

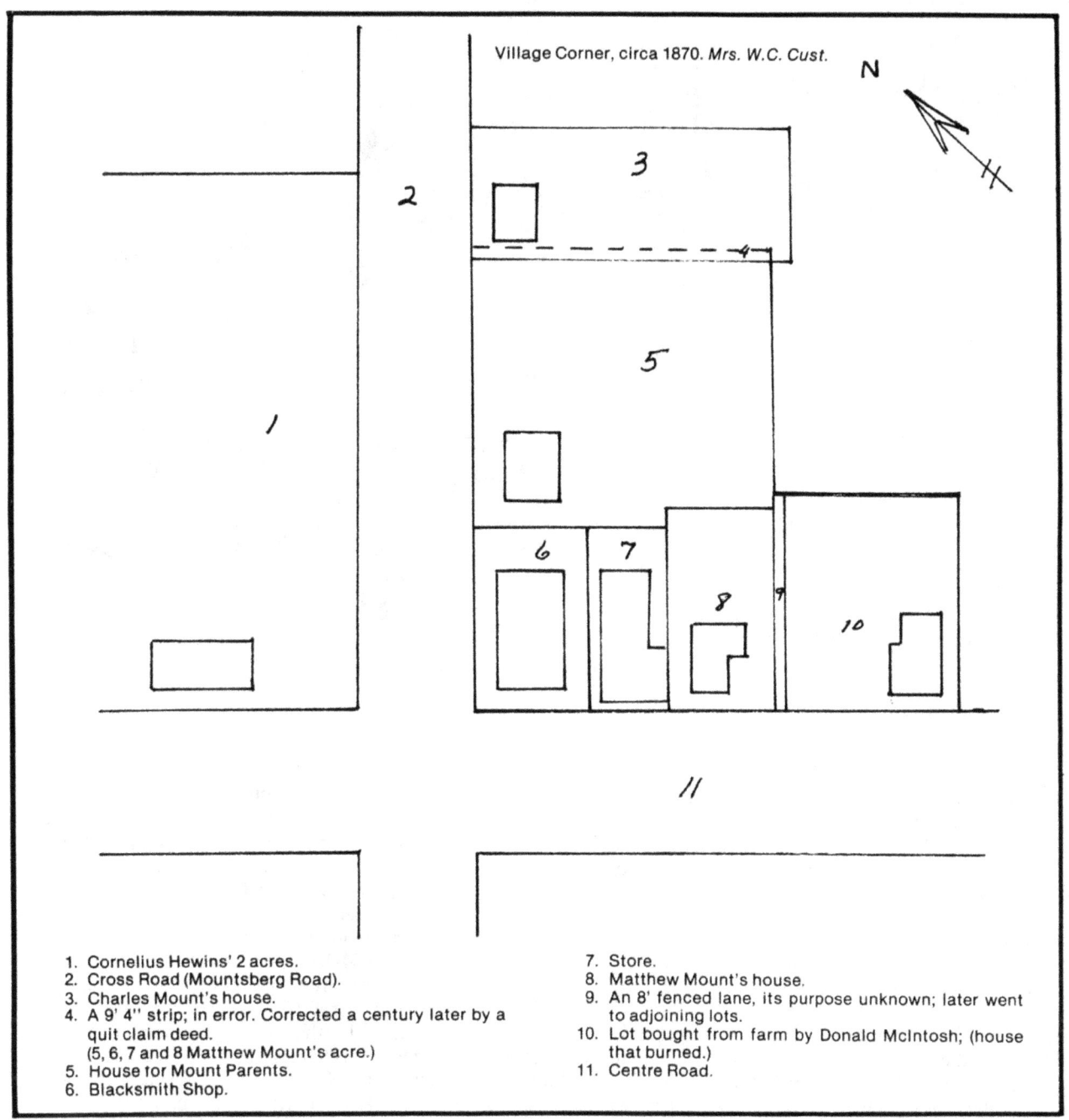

Village Corner, circa 1870. *Mrs. W.C. Cust.*

1. Cornelius Hewins' 2 acres.
2. Cross Road (Mountsberg Road).
3. Charles Mount's house.
4. A 9' 4" strip; in error. Corrected a century later by a quit claim deed.
   (5, 6, 7 and 8 Matthew Mount's acre.)
5. House for Mount Parents.
6. Blacksmith Shop.
7. Store.
8. Matthew Mount's house.
9. An 8' fenced lane, its purpose unknown; later went to adjoining lots.
10. Lot bought from farm by Donald McIntosh; (house that burned.)
11. Centre Road.

Mrs. Josiah Mount moved in but, in 1865, returned to their farm on Lot 5. Their son, Page, had died and the youngest son, Alpheus, needed their help.

Matthew built a house on his acre, facing Centre Road (Bryant home) and moved his family from their quarters above the blacksmith shop. In the early 1860s, James Paine built a frame store on Matthew's lot, behind the shop and facing Centre Road.

The Farm

John Mount married Mary Ann Wheeler of Burlington. Their eight children were born in the log house on Centre Road, the youngest, William, after the death of his father. John Mount gave Charles a deed for his quarter-acre on May 23, 1866, a mere five weeks after receiving his own deed. Matthew's deed from John for the acre at the corner is dated June 10, 1867. John died July 19, 1867. This flurry of documents indicates that John's health was such that a settlement of his affairs was imperative. John was 50.

Emanuel (Manny), the eldest child, 17 when his father died, assumed charge of the farm, assisted by

Emanuel Mount. *Miss Fanny Mount.*

Jane Mount. *Miss Fanny Mount.*

Jacob (Jake) six years younger. When Emanuel married Jane Ford, they lived in the Mount log home where seven of their 10 children were born. Needing more room, they rented the John Hewins house and property on Lot 6 from 1896 to 1904. The farm house was left for Jake who had married Annie McPherson. During the 1860s part of the farm was rented to Thomas and Mary Connor, a young Irish couple with children, Pachein, Joanna, Mary and Thomas. They had their own log house.

When the John Mount estate, finally, was settled in 1903, Jacob had the southeast 50 and continued to live in the homestead. Emanuel had the northwest 50, less five village properties. To go with it, he bought back the house built for his grandparents and moved into it in 1904.

The Farm Families

John Mount (1817-1867), eldest son of Josiah, and Mary Ann Wheeler (1828-1902) of Burlington (not related to James Wheeler of Concession 13): *Emanuel* (1850-1926)—family listed separately; *Emily* (1852-1947)—married George Trask who worked at the Laking mill; *Minerva* (1854-1948)—married James McNiven of Nassagaweya; *Jacob* (1858-1935)—family listed separately; *Ann* (1860-1940)—unmarried, lived in Dundas; *John* (1862-1935)—married, in Milton, later in Hamilton; *Irene* (1864-1924)—Mrs. Cummins of Dundas; *William* (1868-1935)—unmarried, owned and operated a dry goods store in Dundas.

Family of Emanuel Mount (1850-1926) and Jane Ford (1856-1947): *Herbert* (1877-1957)—went to Saskatchewan, married twice, had no family; *Eleanor* (1880-1970)—Mrs. Theodore Marcy, in Detroit; *Edna* (1882-1956)—worked in Hamilton, retired with her mother; *William* (1884-1960)—married Annie Sault, lived in Beverly; *Mary* (1886-1943)—private secretary and purchasing agent for P.B. Yeates, Hamilton; *John* (1888-1971)—married Bertha Dent of Lowville, lived at Beechgrove; *Hannah* (1891-1974)—;operated her own lunch bar business in Hamilton until retiring; *Elmer (1897-1971)—in* banking in Hamilton, married Muriel Coverdale, went to Montreal, attended Sir George Williams University with his second daughter, Mary, graduating in 1956; Frank—banker, married Rita Nichols, in Toronto and Victoria, **B.C.,** after retiring in 1963, wrote and published a Handbook of Bank Rules; *Janet Viola (Fanny)—remained* with parents, in Beechgrove, then Hamilton.

Family of Jacob Mount (1858-1935) and Annie McPherson: *Jean—died* when a young adult; *Roy* (1895-1917)—died in W.W. I; *Lorne* (1897-1936)—died of war disability; *Joe* (1900-1963).

Jacob and his family moved to Waterdown in November 1908. They sold their 50 acres to Walter and

Elizabeth Emmons who were the last to occupy John Mount's old log cabin. The Emmons children were: *Clifford* (1901-1973)—lived in Hamilton; *Hazel*—Mrs. Guy Wetherall, Dundas; *Nellie*—Mrs. Norman Bowman, Hamilton; *Russell*—of Hannon, killed in an auto accident in 1963; *May*—Mrs. Edward Case, Millgrove.

Walter Emmons sold the farm to Burdge Gunby in 1914 and moved his family to the 10th Concession. He joined the army and was killed overseas in 1917.

In 1928, two years after the death of Emanuel Mount, John and Vera Gunby bought his house and land. The following year, John built a barn down the hill from the village, beside Mountsberg Road, and farmed both his and his father's fifty, 96 acres in all. In 1957, Burdge's land was transferred to John and his wife, Vera, thus restoring Lot 7, southeast to the original unit, less the village lots. The following year, John and Vera kept their house and sold the farm to their daughter, Marion and son-in-law, Peter Pawlik.

Charles Mount's House

Charles Mount (1832-1890) was the carpenter of the family. He built his house on a small lot off his brother John's farm sometime in the early to mid-1850s. He and his wife, Rachel, had the following family: George, 1855; Henry, 1857; Josiah, 1858; Franklin, 1860, who became a professor of music in Bay City, Michigan, and also a daughter.

About 1867, the family left Mountsberg and moved to Michigan where Charles continued in the carpentry and wagon-making business.

James McCormack (1839-1890) and his wife, Jane Walker (1840-1875) moved into the house and in 1872, completed buying it. Mr. McCormack was known, mainly, as a shoemaker, but he also made sashes, doors and window blinds. The McCormack children were: William, Annie, Sarah, Moses and Margaret (1873-1950). As a widower, James McCormack married Margaret McCrae and had a second family of six children, some of whom, including Delila (1881) were born before the family left Mountsberg in 1884 and moved across the line into Puslinch Township.

John Albert Page, son of Joseph, owned the house from 1884 to 1907 but did not live there. During this time it was rented. In the mid part of this period, Mr. and Mrs. Peter Redpath lived there with their family of nine: Mary, Rachel (who married Charles Laking, son of John), Nellie, Jack, Roberta, Bella, Margaret, Mina and Clark. The Redpaths moved to Dundas.

Walter Emmons bought the house from J. Albert Page in April 1907 and, in June 1908, sold it to his parents, Mr. and Mrs. William Emmons, when they retired from their farm on Lot 10, Concession 12. Later that year, Mr. Emmons bought an acre across the road and slightly north, where he built a small barn and grew vegetables. He died in 1918.

When Mrs. Emmons' health failed, her son, Albert, unmarried, who had worked in Brantford and Hamilton, came home and cared for her. From the time of her death in 1929, until his own death in 1950, Albert lived there alone. During that time, he was caretaker of the Methodist Cemetery and worked at times for people in the neighbourhood.

In August 1951, Albert (Bert) Page and his wife, Evelyn Wingrove, bought both properties from the Albert Emmons estate. Bert is a nephew of Albert Emmons and a grandson of J. Albert Page. They made changes and improvements to the century old home, inside, and replaced the kitchen at the south corner with a garage. Here, their family grew up: Mervyn, now in his own house not far away on Centre Road; Donna, in Brampton; and Ronald, married to Donna Crowdy, in Acton.

Pages sold, in 1968, to Robert and Marilyn Stevens with two daughters, Heather and Brenda. The house only, on its small lot, was owned by Jane Tennant and Jeffrey Daw from 1975 to 1978 and, since then, by Glenn and Linda Stewart, living there with their two daughters, Karen and Valerie.

House Built for the Mount Parents

After living in their new home five years or less, Mr. and Mrs. Josiah Mount returned to the farm (Lot 5, Concession 12) and the house was rented. A known tenant was Joseph H. Smith, teacher, who became the first public school inspector of Wentworth County. He was there in 1866-67. The next teacher, James McLean, who stayed two or more years, probably, also lived in the Mount house.

In the fall of 1874, Charles Revell (1827-1895), son of John, sold his farm on Lot 10, Concession 12, and bought both the store and this house. He kept the store until 1889, but lived in his home until his death. About 1880 Mr. Revell built an extension on the southwest end of the house and finished it in time for the marriage of his daughter, Mary, to John Connell. When Mrs. Revell, the former Delilah Sutton, died in 1901, the house went to Mary Connell. For a year or two it was rented to Mr. and Mrs. Samuel Thurston, who came from Badenoch with their family of two boys and six girls.

Emanuel Mount bought the place in 1903 to be close to his farmland and, the following year, the Mount family moved in from the John Hewins property on Lot 6, which they had been renting. There was an excellent well near the house and farther back, a good bank barn; the barn, so long gone that few people remember its existence.

In 1928, two years after the death of Emanuel Mount, his widow, Jane, sold the Mountsberg property to John Gunby and spent the rest of her life at the home of her son, John, at Beechgrove. John Gunby and his wife, Vera Binkley, had two daughters, Marion Pawlik, living in the village, and Lois, Mrs. Calbert Mitchell of Burlington. Soon after John's death in 1971, Vera sold the house and lot to Stanley and Louise Carpenter who have a daughter, Lizabeth Mia.

The Blacksmith Corner

About 1850, Matthew Mount built his blacksmith and carriage shop close to the intersection, its length parallel to Mountsberg Road where the entrance was located. A decade later, he permitted James Paine to build a store behind his shop, facing Centre Road. About the same time that Charles left Mountsberg, Matthew also pulled up stakes and moved to Victoria Harbour, where he continued as a blacksmith and maker of carriages and wagons. Before leaving, he obtained a deed and divided his acre into three parcels: his own house; the parents' house which remained in his name, and the combined store and blacksmith shop site, which he sold to the Paines.

It is uncertain how long the blacksmith shop remained in use, operated by people who rented the premises. According to records, John McLaren followed Matthew Mount. Francis Dawson was there in a period including 1871, and John Connell 1880-1888. Others, if any, are unknown. Finally, the shop, unoccupied for several years, remained standing until about the end of the century.

The House That Dick Built

In 1906, a year after Richard (Dick) Hewins and Dolly Roberts were married, they bought the store. At first they lived in the quarters behind the store where their eldest child, Byron, was born. Later children were Elmer and Vera, both of whom died in their teens.

In 1907, Dick built a large house of concrete blocks, abutting the northwest side of the store, with direct access. It stands on the site of the blacksmith shop.

George Hinton and his wife, Catherine (Kate) Roberts, former storekeepers, returned in 1910, rebought the store, and lived in the three-year-old house, new to them. Their children were Olive, John and Harold, the only one to return to Mountsberg School.

George and Annie Bogle bought the house and business from Mr. Hinton in 1916, and moved from the Carlisle area with their young son, Wilfred. Another son, Calvin, was born at Mountsberg. They left about 1928 and for two years, Charles and Myrna Bryant rented both the house and the store. The store was razed in 1931.

For a few years the house and land was held by an Anderson estate, during which time it was rented; to Arthur Peer and his wife, formerly Sarah Sutton, in the 1930s, and to the Alfred Smith family, including Alfred, Louise, Reginald and Dalton, who came in 1939. Asahel Bates of the 10th Concession owned the property three months in 1945 before he sold to Oscar and Louise Pegg. They moved from Cedar Springs and stayed. They also own two acres at the north corner of the road intersection, across Mountsberg Road from the house. The two units have been connected since 1911. The Pegg family includes: *Donna Tweedle*—a niece and part of the family from infancy, now Mrs. Frank Laking, of Lot 10, Concession 14; *Norma*—Mrs. Walter Sardella of Dundas; *Jean*—Mrs. Palmer of Strabane; *James*—married Jacqueline Roberts, now a widower in Millgrove; *Charles*—married Avaline Bohm, in Calgary; *Joanne*—Mrs. George Raymond of Hamilton.

The Mountsberg Store

By some private agreement, James Paine, in the early 1860s built his store beside Matthew Mount's blacksmith shop. Later, the Paines bought the property with the two buildings, the deed being made out to one Nathaniel Paine. J.C. Crooker seems to have had a close association with the store, between 1866 and 1871.

Following the Paine family, the store had many owners:

Dec. 1872-Dec. 1873—William Emmons.

Dec. 1873-Oct. 1874—William Laking & Oron Thompson; operated by Mr. Thompson.

Oct. 1874-March 1889—Charles Revell (son of John).

March 1889-Dec. 1889—Levi Revell (son of Charles).

Dec. 1889-April 1896—Benjamin Johnson (son of Philip).

April 1896-Jan. 1906—Charity Linn (daughter of Benjamin Johnson; during this period, the store was rented; at one time to Jake Maddaugh, later to George Hinton, who obtained a deed in time to sell to Richard Hewins (Mrs. Hinton and Mrs. Hewins were Roberts sisters).

Feb. 1906-Feb. 1910—Richard Hewins; during the latter part of this period, George Hinton returned and

Dick and Dolly Hewins. *Mrs. W.C. Cust.*

rented for a short time before buying back the store. The first time George Hinton ran the store, he lived in quarters at the back. Richard Hewins also lived there a year before building a house in 1907 (the Pegg home), abutting the store, with direct access.

Feb. 1910-May 1916—George Hinton; during some of this time he was assisted by his brother-in-law, Jim Roberts.

May *1916-1931—George* Bogle; rented to Charles Bryant 1928-1930.

1930-1933—Charles and Myrna operated a store in their home next door; the store was torn down in 1931.

(A description of the store is on page 29 of *Waterdown and East Flamborough* 1867-1967).

The Post Office

For several years, Mountsberg pioneers had to get their mail in Dundas, so it meant going weeks, or even months, without a letter.

Waterdown had a Post Office in 1841, which may have been more convenient for some people. However, when Carlisle got theirs in 1848, that became the mailing address for most of the Mountsberg residents. By the mid-fifties, there were Post Offices in Freelton, Puslinch and Campbellville, and some families in those directions found them more convenient.

Mountsberg got its own Post Office in 1864, and it was then that the name became official. In those early times, mail came via Carlisle. Later, it arrived in Freelton, by stagecoach from Hamilton. Someone was appointed to pick it up there. A few old timers can remember when Emanuel Mount or his son, John, performed this duty every week-day afternoon.

The Post Office was usually, but not always, located in the store. Post Masters were:

1864-68—M.M. Crooker—in store, presumably. It would seem that Mr. Crooker worked from the Carlisle Post Office.

1868-82—James Paine—in store.

1882-92—Charles Revell—in store; Mr. Revell sold the store in 1889, and the Post Office may have been in his home, next door on the Mountsberg Road, in the period 1889-92.

1892-95—William Foster—in his home (Bryant house). It was during this period that Mountsberg got daily mail rather than three times a week.

1895-1903—Jacob Mount—in farmhouse, on Centre Road.

1903-06—George Hinton—in store.

1906-09—Richard Hewins—in store.

1909-16—George Hinton—in store.

1916-28—George Bogle—in store.

Rural mail came, about 1913, from Campbellville, and reached people living on the 13th Concession and on the Mountsberg Road. The Post Office closed in 1928.

Matthew Mount's House

Until Matthew Mount built a house at the southeast side of his acre, around 1860, his family had been living in quarters above his blacksmith shop. Matthew and his wife, Rachel Chambers, had several children. Names remembered are: Mary, Josiah, Bethany and Dan. After a few years in the new house, the family moved to Victoria Harbour on Georgian Bay, where Matthew continued as a carriage maker.

Mary Ann Mount, widow of his brother, John, moved into the Mountsberg house, and, later, bought it in 1873. After eight more years, Mary Ann moved to Milton with the youngest members of her family. Her daughter, Emily, and son-in-law, George Trask, who worked at the Laking Mill, had been living in Mountsberg and bought the house. The Trask family included John, George, Amelia, Joseph, Irene, Victor and Jacob. An isolated item of 1869 lists "Trask and Paine, Butchers."

A year after buying the house, the Trasks sold it to Mary Ann and William Foster, and moved to Orillia. William Foster (1831-1910) was a wagon maker and had his own shop beside the house, which building remained standing until about 1840. Three Foster children died when quite small: Balinda, in 1881, at 8 months; Gertrude Bell, in 1886, at 10 months, and Clarence Wilfred, in 1891, at 21 months. The youngest son, Elvin, a carpenter, worked along with his father. Later, he went to Guelph where he married Fanny Taylor.

Mrs. Foster had been married before and had two Clark daughters: Annie, later Mrs. James Hurren, Jr., of Michigan who died in 1961 in her 93rd year; and Harriet, who married George Dougherty. When Harriet died in 1903 at 30 years, Mrs. Foster took Elvin, the youngest of five Dougherty boys, and cared for him several years. Already, Mrs. Foster was giving lifelong care to handicapped girl, Addie, a relative who lived to middle age.

In March 1908, the Fosters went to Guelph and sold the property to Margaret and John Wingrove who moved in from their farm on Lot 10, Concession 12. For a time, John worked by the day when farmers needed light help, but before his death in 1922, he was, for many years, a bedfast invalid. Mrs. Wingrove sold her home to Charles and Myrna Bryant in October 1930, and went to Toronto to live with her son, Osborne and his wife, Etta.

The Bryants, originally from Lowville, came to the Mountsberg store in 1928 from the store at Guelph Junction which they had operated for three years following their marriage. From 1930 to 1933, their store was in the front room of the house, a house which since has seen many structural changes. Were the spirit of Matthew Mount to return, it would find few familiar places to haunt. Inside, Bryants removed and realigned partitions to create an entirely new floor plan. The stoop, along the southwest and southeast sides, was taken away in the Wingrove era, and the front fence disappeared a little later. Time was when every house in the village had a picket fence and a gate; a taken-for-granted necessity when cattle pastured along the roadside.

Family of Charles Bryant (1902-1978) and his wife, Myrna Coulson: *Raymond* (1926-1979)—married Elizabeth Peace, lived in Burlington, then Vancouver; *Faye—Mrs.* Lloyd Coverdale of Lot 3, Concession 12;

Everley—married Joyce Beckett of Hagersville, in Kitchener; *Anne—Mrs.* Lawrence French of Hamilton.

The House That Burned

Sixty years have just about erased all memory of a village house that once stood on the site of the present Pawlik home. It was in 1870 that Donald McIntosh, a tailor, obtained a deed for a lot, 93 feet by 117 feet, southeast of Matthew Mount's property on Centre Road, and granted by the John Mount estate. Mr. McIntosh paid $40 for this piece of land where already he had been established for three or four years. That he put up a building for his trade, is indicated by the price of $175 which he received for the property in 1873.

James Gordon was the owner for five years and following his death, James Ford for two years; but it is not know what use these two men made of the place.

In June 1880, John Connell, the new tenant of the blacksmith shop, married Mary Revell (daughter of Charles) and together they bought the property from Mr. Ford. Without delay, they built a storey-and-a-half house of board and batten construction, using the small building, already on the lot, for a roomy kitchen and woodshed. Across was a veranda about 10 feet from the picket fence and, outside the fence, beneath a maple tree was a "stand" with steps to make it the right height for getting into or out of a buggy or democrat.

The house had an outstanding feature, a magnificent dumb waiter. It was built-in and placed, conveniently, in the passage between kitchen and dining room, and had the appearance of a fine, floor-to-ceiling cabinet. The china section at the top had glass doors, while the doors of the large base were panelled and, if opened between meals, one looked into a vast, empty space. A crank at the side was used to lower the shelves of the base into the cool cellar. The kitchen had a sink with a pump, and waste water was carried away in buried tile. These innovations were the mark of an ultra modern, country home 100 years ago. Praiseworthy they were, but the outhouse was still out.

Not all the Connell children were born at Mountsberg. The eldest was Alena (1882-1968) who married William Tufgar of Millgrove. Others were Jessie, Charles, Bertsel and Harold.

The Connell family moved to Millgrove in 1888. Thomas Revell bought the house but did not live in it. Indications are that this was the home of the Rev. Alexander Gay, his wife and children, Jack, Arthur, Ruby and Pearl, while Mr. Gay was pastor of the Baptist Church in 1890-92.

In October 1896, Mrs. Thomas Revell, then a widow, sold the house to Ralph and Aaron Hewins. It was for their mother, Margaret, who had been a widow since 1893. She left her farm home and lived in the village house until her death in September 1911. Margaret outlived her son, Aaron, so Ralph bought the half-share from Aaron's estate, and when Ralph died in 1915, the property went to his son, Albert.

From 1911 on, there were tenants, perhaps not all recalled. Before 1915, Jim and Etta Roberts were there a year or two while Jim worked in the store. Their two eldest children, Charles and Mary were of school age. Roberts were followed by Percy and Edith Haskell who lived there in 1915-16, while Percy worked for Albert Hewins. Mrs. Patrick McCarthy, Sr. was the tenant on that eventful Sunday of July 13, 1919, when the house melted from the Mountsberg scene in fierce and vicious flames that threatened the entire village.*

Later, Albert Hewins moved a shed, spared by the fire, across the road to his farm, where it became a garage. In May 1928, the lot returned to the farm from whence it came, then owned by John Gunby; and for 30 years, a quiet corner of a farm field gave no hint of its history.

Then, 40 years from the devastating fire, phoenix-like, from the long-cold long-buried ashes, sprang the modern, brick home of Marion and Peter Pawlik and their children, Karen, Kerry and John David.

In 1972, Pawliks, who had owned the farm since 1958, sold a building lot beside the Centre Road, to Flamborough Centre Properties. A house was built for Foppe DeVries and his wife, Glenda Clugston, who have two children, Christopher and Amanda. The new home is located a few yards northwest of the spot where John Mount's log cabin and barn were a hallmark of Mountsberg's pioneer portrait.

Lot 7, northwest, Concession 12

From the time of settlement, this 100 acres was regarded as the property of Cornelius Hewins. But because Lot 7 was not included in the first group of Brock lots to be sold, it took a long time to "draw up the writin's". It finally was accomplished in 1853, through Judge John H. Cameron of Toronto, and was registered in the name of John Hewins, son of Cornelius. By that time, John and Margaret Sutton had been married eight years and had two sons, Ralph and Aaron. Cornelius and Ann then were living in their new frame house on two acres at the south corner of the farm, later to be known as the Village Corner.

Although the Hewins farm buildings were on Lot 6, there were many early structures in the northwesterly part of Lot 7. In the late 1830s, the log schoolhouse is believed to have stood on the northeast side of Centre Road, not far from the 13th Concession, and was used until 1866. About 1860, George Green established a shingle mill a short distance southeast of the present park, beside a tiny stream. The mill is remembered as the Laking mill, as it was bought by William Laking and Oron Thompson in 1866 and, seven or eight years later, was owned solely by William Laking.

Between the mill and the log school were, at least, two houses; one of logs was about opposite the brick school. Before its final degeneration, it was downgraded to a horse stable for Fred Fearnley's team. Southeast of it was a frame house large enough for two families. It was here that William Laking lived after he married Martha Revell, daughter of Thomas, and here their three children were born: *Elizabeth* (born 1872)—later

* An account of the fire is on page 28 of *Waterdown and East Flamborough* 1867-1967. (M.C.)

Mrs. Albert Woodhall of Hamilton; *Mary Jane (Minnie)* (1874-1939)—unmarried; *John* (1877-1917)—drowned in Haliburton.

During the Laking-Thompson partnership, the house was shared with Mr. and Mrs. Oron Thompson and their children, see Lot 10, southeast.

Farther back from Centre Road, on a knoll, two hollows mark the site of early log buildings, believed to have been used by squatters about the time the settlers arrived. According to an olden tale, the first religious meeting in the new community was held there.

For all the many signs of activity on John Hewins' property, there were no land transactions until December 1885 when William Laking bought the 98 acres. The mill business was just about finished at that time and the land was mainly for the use of William's brother Joseph and his family, recently arrived from England. All lived in a new, two-family house which William had built across the Centre Road on Lot 8, on 50 acres bought in 1880.

After a 17-year lapse of Hewins ownership, Lot 7, northwest, went back to John's grandson when William Laking sold it, in 1902, to Charles Hewins of Lot 6, southeast, Concession 13. Four years later, Charles sold the southeast 48 acres to J. Emerson Carton who, in 1905, had bought the 24 acres on Lot 6 from the John Hewins estate.

In January 1907, Mr. Carton sold to his father-in-law, William Dutton, 4 1/2 acres beside Centre Road and lying northwest of the 2 acres, still in the Hewins name with Cornelius' old house still standing. In August 1908, Emerson Carton sold William Emmons an acre, northeast of the Hewins 2 acres and facing Mountsberg Road.

Mr. Carton was left with less than 43 acres on Lot 7 which, along with the 24 acres on Lot 6, were sold to Matthew Patton in 1912; to Bruce Patton in 1938; from Muriel (Patton) Scott and Mr. and Mrs. H. McDermid to R. Desender in 1959 and, through Eleanor London to Fenrock Ltd. in 1962. The Fenrock Company divided the land, not otherwise owned, into four lots of slightly more than 10 acres and one smaller lot. According to their survey, the original quarter lot, regarded as 50 acres, is larger by about 3 acres.

The lots are not numbered officially. But, for ease in identifying the new homes, they are, herewith, numbered from the east corner and follow Mountsberg Road to the village corner, then along Centre Road to the west corner.

1. This lot, the largest, has 11 acres and includes a section of the 30-foot lane in Lot 6. It was bought in September 1961 by Edwin Harris. In 1967, he sold the land to Mrs. Ruby Maher who built a house that year and stayed six years. Her daughter, Mrs. Burbridge, and two Burbridge grandsons, Rick and Larry lived with her. From 1973-1974 the lot was owned by Stanley and Dorothy Dziepak before being sold to Robert and Lynne Petch who made changes to the house. They have a son, Jefferson.
2. In 1964, Fenrock Ltd. sold this 10-acre lot to Anthony and Yoskyl Webb who built a house in 1967. They sold in 1971 to Barry and Eimar Hall who made several additions to the house. Two Hall daughters, Debbie and Kerry, attended the Roman Catholic school in Waterdown. Owners since 1977 are Peter and Anne Martin with children, Kenneth, Theresa and Jeffrey.
3. Ronald and Bertha Harris bought this 10 acres of woodland from Fenrock Ltd. in 1964. During the next 15 years, it passed through the hands of six more speculators until sold in 1979 by Lyn Crawford Lewis to Brian and Leslee Taylor. That same year, the Taylors built an attractive home among the trees.
4. This lot, a bit larger than an acre, was separated from the farm in 1908 by Emerson Carton, and soldto William Emmons, then retired and living across Mountsberg Road. Mr. Emmons put up a small barn with a hayloft, in order to keep a cow and a horse and buggy. The land was used for grazing and for a vegetable garden. The two properties remained together through three changes in ownership until a construction company bought the acre, only, in 1976, from Robert and Marilyn Stevens. A house was built, slightly west of where the barn had stood. Later, that same year, it was sold to Gary and Susan Warren who moved in with their young sons, David and Peter.
5. *The Cornelius Hewins Corner:* Thus far, it would seem that every property at the village corner, originally carried the Mount label. Not so. Around 1850,and perhaps as early as 1845-46, Cornelius Hewins built a frame house at the south corner of the family farm; this, at a time when the village was not even the concept of a fertile mind. The small house faced Centre Road with a door in the exact middle of its length. Northwest of the house was a small barn. Both buildings were close to the road.

Records show that Cornelius was living there alone in 1861, his wife, Ann Drewry, having died in 1854. Cornelius died in 1864, but meanwhile had remarried. His second wife, Margaret Coverdale, - returned to her family in Lowville. Much younger than Cornelius, she lived many more years, but never married again.

At a later time, the house was occupied by Cornelius' daughter, Ann, and her husband, Benjamin Johnson. This was before their daughter, Charity, married William Linn, or their son, Trueman, married Emma Heath. Benjamin owned and operated the general store from 1889 to 1896 and presumably they lived in the store's living quarters during that time. Ann died in 1893; Benjamin in 1896, seven months after leaving the store.

Two short term tenants are recalled; Thomas and Mary Ann Hillyard lived there for a time when Mr. Hillyard worked for Archibald Campbell on Lot 9, along Mountsberg Road. Fred Chandler also lived there, probably about 1890.

It was not until John Hewins sold the farm (Lot

Ann Johnson. *Mrs. W.C. Cust.*

Benjamin Johnson. *Mrs. W.C. Cust.*

7 only) in 1885, that the house was allocated a two-acre lot, and reserved in the Hewins name.

At an uncertain time, around 1890 to about 1904-05, the place was leased to George Cartwright (not to be confused with a distant relative of the same name on Lot 11, Concession 13). Mr. Cartwright turned the small barn into a blacksmith shop and, with sons to help, had a good business. Son William followed his father's trade and became a legend in Freelton as one of the last of his kind. Children of George and Minnie Cartwright (order uncertain) were: *Minnie* (1886-1896); *William* (1888-1966) of Freelton; *Oscar* (1890-1910); *George* (1892-) of Dundas; *Isabel* (1895-1896); *Spencer,* went to Toronto; and *Harry,* to Port Credit.

Cartwrights were the last to live in the old house. Richard Hewins used it for storage while he ran the store, and, eventually, he bought the property from the John Hewins estate. He sold the two acres to George Hinton in 1912, two years after selling him the store. Since then, the two corner properties have been linked in ownership, although the store was demolished in 1931. Early in this union, the Hewins house was moved to the northeast side of the lot and later vanished. Since 1945, Peggs have owned the land. In 1946, they moved one of the two sheds from the Methodist Church to the corner, across Mountsberg Road from their house.

6. William Dutton bought 4 1/2 acres, beside Centre Road and abutting the 2-acre corner lot, from his son-in-law, Emerson Carton in 1907. He used the virgin land as a vegetable garden. Mr. and Mrs. Dutton owned and lived in the red brick house, later to be the Baptist parsonage. When they moved to Rockwood in 1912, they sold both properties to Mr. and Mrs. Archibald Campbell. Mr. Campbell died in 1928; his wife, Isabella, in 1929. Martha (Campbell) Gunby, who inherited the lot from her parents, sold to Willy Korb in 1961. A house was built about that time and several farm buildings went up later. Korb children Evelyn, Heinz and Karen, also a stepson, Peter Jordt, attended Mountsberg School.

In 1965, Karl and Wiltrant Korb bought the 4 1/2 acres from Mr. and Mrs. Willy Korb and, at the same time, bought the 10 acres at the rear from Fenrock Ltd., giving them a total of almost 15 acres. This land, later in the name of Harry S. Pett, was rented in 1970 to Ronald and Ruth Mundy with children, Ronald, Robert, Paul and Kim. Since 1978, Bryan and Susan Sharp and daughter, Sarah, have been there, also as tenants.

7. Fenrock Ltd. sold these lots as one parcel of 4.7 acres to Ronald and Bertha Harris in September
8. 1964. A house was built in 1965 and sold to Edgar and Phyllis Smith in 1966. Smith children are Roy, Sharon, Elaine (Mrs. Robert Pasuta of Lot 4, Concession 13) and Edmond.

In 1975, the lot was divided, giving the northwest 2 acres to Roy Smith, who sold to Stanley and Anne Rudge, and a house was built, all in 1975. Roger Burge bought house and lot in 1976 and the next year, sold to James and Ruth McMurdo, an English couple whose children, Allison and Duncan, were born in Canada.

Meanwhile, the Smith family continued in their home until selling the property of about 2 1/2 acres, in 1978, to James and Barbara Senier who made improvements to the house and landscaping.

Changes took place in the northwest 50 acres after Charles Hewins sold the southeast 50. In 1920, a 3-acre parcel beside Centre Road was sold for a Community Park, dedicated to the memory of four Mountsberg men who died in World War I.

After Charles' death in 1941, his eldest son, Roy, owned the land until he sold to his brother, Reg, and sister-in-law, Violet, in 1960. In 1972, a builder bought an acre, opposite the former school, and built a house for Thomas and Lorraine Brown. Two years later, it was sold to Henry and Shirley Robertson with children, Janet, Chris, Heather and Gordon. Since 1976, it has been owned by Richard and Lorene Wildeman who have four children, Richard, Lance, Cheryl and Lisa.

In 1973, Linda, a Hewins daughter, and her husband, Wilfred Phillips, both teachers, acquired a building lot at the north corner of the farm and built a house the following year. Now Linda Ann lives on land first settled by her great, great, great grandparents, Cornelius and Ann Hewins.

Lot 8, Concession 12   **Brock Grant**

This lot which, in time, became two neat 100-acre parcels, began as John Page's 200-acre farm, but between 1865 and 1919, it was split into 50-acre sections that were shuffled about in myriad sales. The land was in the first group of Brock lots released for sale through William H. Draper. John Page's deed for the 200 acres, dated March 17, 1837, is one of the earliest deeds of the community, with a slim margin of three months over Philip Johnson and John Revel of Lot 6, Concession 12. He had been on the land two or three years at that time.

John Page (1801-1870) married Catherine Fisher (1808-1879). Their children were: *Mary* (Dec. 1834-May 25, 1905)-married John Hallam (1820-1872), children were, Sarah Jane, John Henry and Mary Ann; *Peter* (Aug. 15, 1836-Oct. 18, 1931)-married Susannah Hurren, birth year 1835 on his tombstone is apparently an error; *Joseph* (1839-1901)-unmarried; *John* (born about 1841)-unmarried; *Jane* (born about 1844)-Mrs. Scott of Petrolia; *Sarah* (born about 1846)-unmarried; *Harmon* (1852-1907)-left Mountsberg for Hamburg, New York in the 1880s, married, had a son, Albert, later returned.

In the late 1850s John Page went to Oxford County and bought a 100-acre farm. He never returned to Mountsberg to stay with the family.

Gordon Hewins, Lot 8, southeast, has several interesting, early documents which relate to the property and people and from which quotes are taken. In October 1864, John Page wished to raise some money on his Mountsberg property. A lawyer handling the mortgage, penciled a private note to someone concerned, which said, "Page is a man of considerable wealth for a farmer. He got this money to buy more land for his family." At the same time the land was evaluated, disclosing the following information: "frame house, 18' by 28'; barn, 30' by 60'; shed 20' by 60'...115 acres, cultivated, @ $35 per acre; 85 acres woodland (hardwood) @ $30 per acre." The "occupier" was named as John Laken and rent was $250 per annum. (John Laking rented the farm from April 1858 to February 1865). The frame house mentioned stood in front of the main part of the present Gordon Hewins house.

In February 1865, John Page put his Mountsberg property in trust to Solomon Dawson, for his wife, Catherine. In April of the same year, John and Catherine sold to John Colin McNiven the 50 acres with the farm buildings, on the northwest half of the southeast hundred (south corner of village intersection). In January 1866, Solomon Dawson released land near the 13th Concession, on which to build a new school.

At this time, both Mary and Peter were married, and Peter owned 50 acres on Lot 8, Concession 13. Mrs. Page and the four youngest of the family perhaps were living in the early log house, well back from Centre Road on rising ground southeast of the stream. But, it would be about this time that a frame house was built across Centre Road from the mill site.

John Page died July 23, 1870 in Carlisle, and was buried in the Mountsberg Methodist Cemetery. His will, as it affected Mountsberg property, gave the 50 acres, southeast of the McNiven land, to Harmon and Jane. Of the northwest 100, Mary and Sarah were to get the northwest 50, and Joseph the southeast 50.

This allocation never materialized. In January 1871, a settlement took place, involving a sheaf of documents. Solomon Dawson's trusteeship came to an end. The land inheritances were conveyed back to the mother, Catherine, who, in turn, reconveyed to Harmon the northwest 100, and to John, Jr. the 50 acres southeast of McNivens. At the same time, John Jr. bought Lot 8, northwest, Concession 11; 75 acres. Catherine, who lived until April 1879, retained a life interest in all the property.

Joseph, without an acre to his name, remained in the locality. About 1930, Mr. Ernest Tansley of Hamilton located the site of the early Page cabin which stood until well into the present century. He recalled living in it a few years in the mid or late 1870s, with his parents, Mr. and Mrs. Robert Tansley, his sister and several brothers. They had arrived from England, recently, and Robert Tansley worked in the Laking Mill. Ernest, who later was associated with the Laking-Patterson lumber business in Hamilton, remembered Joe Page well.

Misfortune overtook the Page property a few months after Catherine died. There were mortgages which could not be met, and a mortgage sale took place in Revell's store on January 15, 1880, whereby the land

AUCTION SALE
OF VALUABLE
PROPERTY!

Under and by virtue of a Power of Sale contained in a certain Mortgage, which will be produced at the time of sale, there will be sold on

THURSDAY, 15th JANUARY, 1880

At the hour of 12 o'clock noon, by JAMES McMORRES, Auctioneer, at REVELL'S STORE, in the

VILLAGE OF MOUNTSBERG,

THE FOLLOWING PROPERTY.

The Northerly half of Lot number 8, in the 12th Concession of the Township of East Flamboro', in the County of Wentworth, save and except one half acre, more or less, heretofore released by the Mortgagees. Also the Southerly half of the Southerly half of the aforesaid Lot number 8, and also the North half of Lot number 8, in the 11th Concession of the said Township of East Flamboro'.

About 160 acres of this land are cleared, on which are erected two Frame Barns, one Log House and one Frame House. The property is situated about 10 miles from Waterdown.

Terms will be made known at time of sale. For further particulars apply to,

ROBINSON, O'BRIEN & SCOTT,
VENDORS' SOLICITORS, 68 CHURCH ST., TORONTO.

was transferred to the mortgagors. J.C. McNiven took over the 50 acres, southeast of his 50. In the northwest 100, William Laking obtained the northwest 50 and Peter McLaren the southeast 50 at the village corner.

Later History of Lot 8, southeast

John Colin McNiven (1834-1918) married Rachel Bates (1840-1866) of the 10th Concession and had a son, William, born in 1866. His second wife was Rachel's sister, Maria (1834-1917). After living in the old Page home more than 20 years, Mr. McNiven built the large house still there, close behind the site of the earlier dwelling. That was about 1887, but the McNivens did not use their new home long.

In July 1889, Ralph Hewins bought the McNiven farm of 150 acres, including 50 acres in the northwest hundred, bought in 1881. The Hewins family returned to Mountsberg, after living four years on the Middle Road (Q.E.W.), east of Guelph Line. While waiting to take possession of their new farm, the family lived in the former Methodist parsonage a few months. Of the buildings now standing, Ralph Hewins built the driving shed in 1890, and the large barn in 1891. He was a township councillor in 1896.

Hewins Farm. *G.A. Hewins.*

Family of Ralph Hewins (1846-1915) commonly called Rafe, son of John, and Janet Wingrove (1847-1904), daughter of Thomas Wingrove, Sr.: *John* (1872-1944)—a veterinary surgeon in Alberta, his wife, Alice, was a widow from Wales, John died while on a visit to his family and is buried in the Methodist Cemetery; *Albert* (1875-1948)—remained on the farm, married Elizabeth MacEdward (1878-1975) of Badenoch, their daughter, Margaret (Mrs. Oliver Leslie) of Strabane, son, Gordon A., unmarried, is present owner of the farm; *Richard* (1877-1950)—married Mary Ann (Dolly) Roberts who died in 1919, children Byron, Elmer and Vera, kept store at Mountsberg, later lived in Hamilton and Stoney Creek, second wife was Edna Sayers; *Ann* (1880-1961)—married William McFarlane whose farm was at Harper's Corner, as a widow, Ann lived in Hamilton and Margaret and Oliver Leslie took over the McFarlane farm; *Olive* (1886-1950)—unmarried, had A.T.C.M. in music later a registered nurse in Toronto, retired in Hamilton with Ann.

In 1969, Bert and Evelyn Page bought an acre at the east corner of the farm from Elizabeth Hewins and her son, Gordon. In the meantime, Pages had sold their village home in 1968 and rented McCarthy's red brick house for a year, while they purchased the lot and built a new home, with the unopened 12th Concession at their side. In 1979, they split the lot and sold the half with the house to Ernest and Alice Summerfield of Nassagaweya, whose family includes Alice, Jim, John, Norah, Helen and Margaret. Pages built themselves another home on the northwest side of the lot.

In 1972, Mervyn Page bought a building lot next to his parents and built a house that year. He and his wife, Bonnie Tyrrell, have two daughters, Andrea and Laura.

Later History of Lot 8, northwest

The Southeast Fifty

Peter McLaren was less than eager to own this land when it became his in January 1880. Four months later, he sold it to Emerson Bristol, the Methodist minister. J.C. McNiven bought it in October 1881 and it remained a part of the Lot 8, southeast, farm until Burdge Gunby bought it in 1919 from Albert Hewins. Since then it has been reattached to the Lot 8, northwest, property.

House built by Wm. Laking. which burned in 1927. *J.C. Laking*

Barn built by Wm. Laking. *J.C. Laking.*

The Northwest Fifty

As soon as he became owner in 1880, William Laking built a roomy, two-storey, frame house (site of present house) and moved his wife and family from across the road. A barn was built about the same time. The new house was too close to the school of 1866, so William Laking made a trade with the School Board, as recorded in a one-dollar, land transaction of November 1882. Land was added to the northwest end of the school yard in return for an equal area at the southeast end, where William planted an apple orchard between his house and the school house. A solid, high, board fence, marking the new boundary, was not completely effective in preventing forays from the school yard.

That same year, 1882, William Laking bought 50 acres on Lot 9 which touched the south corner of the land he owned. In 1885, he bought from John Hewins, the 100 acres of Lot 7 where his mill was located, most of which he had been using for 20 years.

In the early days of Laking ownership, the Page house, opposite the mill, was used by mill workers, sometimes by two families. In a period in the '80s, it was occupied by a Palmer family with children, Phoebe, Kitty, Jerry, Bella and Maggie. A Graham family, also there, had a daughter, Evangeline (Lina) who married Robert Menzies, a Campbellville blacksmith. The house was either torn down or removed sometime after the mill ceased working. William Laking was on the East Flamborough Township Council six years, 1884-1889.

As the lumber business came to an end, and William's interests took him away from Mountsberg, the land was made available to his brother, Joseph Laking and his family, arriving from England at different times. Charles, a boy of 16 or 17, came first, about 1887. He alighted at Shaw Station (Puslinch) and, in trying to find his way to the mill, the first person he met was William Stewart who walked along with him a little way. Charles spent his time with his two uncles, John and William, until his parents and family arrived from England, two or three years later.

Family of Joseph Laking (1837-1919) and Charlotte Wilkinson (1838-1896): *Sarah*—married Harry Elvin in England where their four children were born, lived in part of the John Hewins House; *William*—married Elizabeth Oliver in England, with their sons, Ernest and Harold, they were the last of the Laking family to live in the house, left in 1906 to work with William Laking at his Haliburton mill; *Charles* (1871-1968)—married in October 1895 to Margaret Hewins (1875-1963), daughter of Aaron, lived on Lot 12, Concession 14 a year or two before going to Aberfoyle; *Fred* (1874-1937)—married Mary Jane Wingrove (1877-1948), daughter of William, lived on Lot 9, northwest, Concession 13; *Elizabeth* (died in 1963)—wife of Oscar Hood, when first married lived in a house on Thomas Wingrove's farm, one son, Mervin. Last home was at Beechgrove; *Alfred* (1881-1965)—married Ada Hilborn who died in 1972, operated the grist mill at Freelton.

Joseph Laking married his second wife, Elizabeth Manary, a widow, in 1899, and lived in Freelton. In 1902, Charles Hewins bought the 100 acres on Lot 7 and in 1906, William Laking severed his last tie with Mountsberg when he sold to Burdge Gunby his two 50-acre quarter lots.

Burdge and Martha (Campbell) Gunby had owned and lived on Lot 6, Concession 14, six years when they made this move to where they spent the rest of their lives. Burdge Gunby died suddenly, November 15, 1958 in his 83rd year, while preparations were underway for a golden wedding celebration. Martha lived until Christmas Day, 1970. In her 94th year, she was Mountsberg's grand old lady. Their family follows: *John* (1899-1971)—married Vera Binkley, see Lot 7 and village; *Isabella*—Mrs. Norman Devereaux of Georgetown; *Archie* (died Dec. 1974 in his 70th year)—remained on the farm, married Lena Tansley of Carlisle, had three sons—Laverne of Georgetown who married Betty McAllister of Galt, Kenneth, married Ruth Lewis of West Flamborough village, in Dundas, Cecil and Teresa (Simon) in a new home on Concession 13, east corner of Lot 5; *Stella* (1909-1969)—of Freelton; *Grace* (died Sept. 1972 in her 60th year)—Mrs. Francis Redding of Waterdown; *Lillian*—Mrs. Albert Taafe of Dundas.

Four generations of Gunby family; John, John, Sr. holding Marion, his great granddaughter, and Burdge Gunby. *Mrs. P. Pawlik.*

Burdge's father, John Gunby (1851-1937), friend to all, lived with the family from the time his wife died in 1918, until his own death.

In her younger days, Mrs. Gunby showed infinite patience with the tribulations in living so close to the school. During most of my public school days, the school had no water supply, so every day, pupils, alone or in groups, welcomed the diversion of a stroll to the pump near the Gunby's kitchen door, for a pail of water. Back at school, we took turns in drinking from a communal "granite" (enameled metal) cup. Horrors! But we were not preoccupied with germs.

I felt the warmth of Mrs. Gunby's tolerance during a blizzard one winter of much snow. School attendance that day was limited to children who lived nearby. By 4o'clock, weather and walking were formidable. However, with a little fortitude, I could have made the half mile home without being found stiff and lifeless in a snow bank. A beguiling tragedy to consider; but discarded because I didn't like my role in the final Act.

However, overcome with the drama and excitement of the storm, I decided it would be quite as romantic and, certainly, safer to be storm-stayed in a comfortable place. So, I went home with Isabel to spend the night. I wasn't invited. But with the bland indifference of the young for adult problems, that was no obstacle, and I was treated with hospitality, undeserving a brash intruder. It was an evening of games with the parents taking part; Northern Spy apples (still my favourite) and, finally, Isabel and I tucked snuggly in the guest room bed, undisturbed by the shrieks and wails of the elements outside.

By morning, we were indeed snowed in; locked in a wasteland of white where roads were indicated by the half-hidden lines of their fences. They would not be shovelled, except where drifted, and that by hand. Horses and sleighs would make their own tracks. So, I was stranded, quite happily, most of the day until my brother, Roy, came for me with a horse. As I rode home, bareback and in tandem, I was lectured in brotherly fashion about my inexcusable lack of stamina in not facing the storm the afternoon before, and going home; on my inconsiderable imposition on the Gunbys, and mostly on his inconvenience in getting me home. All justified, of course. My conscience did prick a little bit, but not enough to hurt and to spoil what, for me, had been fun and adventure.

In her 65 years on the farm, Martha Gunby saw change aplenty. In 1907, a year after they came, a large new part was added to the barn by carpenter, Billy Kitchen, and his men. For three years, 1913-15, Burdge Gunby was a Township Councillor. In 1914, bought 50 acres on Lot 7, southeast, first owned by John Mount and in 1919, bought from Albert Hewins, 50 acres at the Mountsberg corner, which made him owner of all of Lot 8, northwest.

The frame house was burned January 18, 1927 and was replaced by the present red brick dwelling on the same site. In 1935, when 100 acres on Lot 5, Concession 13 was stripped of its forest, it became Gunby land. And the name *Woods View*, given the home farm in earlier times, already had lost some of its meaning. The school, next door, was closed in 1966 and the following year became the property of the Township of East Flamborough, as a Community Centre.

In 1975, the Burdge Gunby estate sold the home farm (Lot 8, northwest, and 50 acres at the southeast end of Lot 9, adjoining) to Linda Dunham, wife of James F. Dunham, a Hamilton lawyer, to whom the land was transferred in 1979. The house and barns have been renovated extensively and a track was made for training standard bred horses. There are four Dunham sons, David, Jason, Patrick and Mark.

Lot 9, southeast, Concession 12   Brock Grant

George Fearnley from England had a deed for this 100 acres in 1838. As he, probably, had been on the land a few years before then, he is considered to have been one of the first settlers of the area. By 1841, he had cleared 30 acres. The 1 1/2-storey log cabin served the Fearnleys many years before they built the red brick Victorian house that still graces the farm scene. Ann Fearnley (1800-1878), wife of George, is buried in the Baptist Cemetery beside her son, Charles and his wife, Phoebe. Information concerning George is lacking. Known members of the Fearnley family are listed. Two daughters may be missing: *Mary Jane* (1830-1863)—married George Wingrove, son of Charles, went to Walsingham Township in Norfolk County, both are buried in a pioneer cemetery 2 miles east of Walsingham village; *Charles* (1831-1870)—married Phoebe Sutton (See Lot 12, Concession 12); *Joseph* (born about 1837)—married Arvilla Markle (1837-1867), Arvilla and a daughter are buried in the Methodist Cemetery, Joseph left the community sometime after the death of his wife; *George* (born about 1839); *James*—stayed on the home farm with his mother while his father worked on Lot 12, northwest, bought in 1854. James had a wife, Elizabeth, and children, James M. (born1864) and Sarah Jane(born 1867).

The Fearnley farm was sold, in 1874, to Joshua Allison and his wife, Phoebe Wingrove, daughter of James. They had three sons, John, Thomas and Joshua, who married Laura Mount, daughter of Alpheus. In 1881, the Allisons moved to Nassagaweya and sold the place to Archibald Campbell, Jr. and his wife, Isabella, a sister of Phoebe Allison.

The Campbells came from a part of the original Campbell holdings on Lot 4, Concession 12. At that time Archibald (1845-1928) and Sarah Isabella (1855-1929) had just one child. Their entire family included: *Martha* (1877-1970)—married Burdge Gunby (see Lot 8 northwest); *Albert* (1882-1953)--see lot 7, northwest,Concession 13; *Alex L.* (1886-1938)—married Edith Nicholson of Lot 11, northwest, Concession 13, remained on the farm; *James* (1889-)—married Teresa Nicholson of Stoney Creek, was a druggist in Goderich until killed in an auto accident. Alex and Edith were married in 1912, and began taking over the farmland which included 50 acres at the northwest end of Lot 4. At the same time, Mr. and Mrs. Archibald Campbell bought, for their retirement, the red brick house that is now the Baptist parsonage.

Alex Campbell was a Township councillor from

1932-1938. After his death in 1938, Edith and her son, George, continued to operate the farm until April 1954, when they sold the 100 acres to Charles and Mary McCarthy. Edith went to Dundas to be near other members of her family, and now lives with George and his wife Nadine (Anderson) who are in Freelton.

Mr. and Mrs. McCarthy did not plan to live here, but until 1979, various members of their family had some involvement with the property. During the next five or six years, the house was occupied part of the time by their daughter, Margaret, her husband, Merlin Misner and children, Ann, Teresa and Gary. Janet and Ward were born later. After a couple of years on the home farm, they moved to the 5th Concession of East Flamborough. At the same time, Edward and Joyce McCarthy shared the Lot 9 house. Their children are Edward, Jayne, Kevin, Timothy and Jeffrey. They now live in Hagersville.

In the summer of 1960, Paul and Rose McCarthy bought the farm and moved from Campbellville. In their family are: Paul—married Rita Priest, in Strabane; *Brian*—married Marilyn Rolf, in Guelph; *Diane*—Mrs. Bart Uitvlugt of London; *Nancy*—Mrs. Randy Hatt of Edmonton; *Carol.*

Paul was an East Flamborough councillor, 1968-69. Latterly, he combined a real estate business with farming and in October 1979, sold the farm, now 97 acres, to a young couple, Patricia and William Orosz. McCarthys moved to the 10th Concession of West Flamborough.

Three newer houses, each on about an acre of land, now face Mountsberg Road. In 1955, Charles McCarthy separated a building lot at the north corner of the farm, for his son, Pat, newly married to Dorothy Fritz. Their house was built that year. They have four boys, Thomas, James and John, born at Mountsberg, and Eugene, born after the family moved to Burlington. They sold the house, in 1960, to Joseph and Beverly Bodnar. The Bodnars stayed until 1974, when they sold to Thomas and Heather Appleton, who have sons, Duncan and Nicholas. Heather, English by birth, now has her mother, Mrs. Kilgour, living with them.

Southwest of the Appleton home is the house, built in 1972, for Frank and Geraldine Jablonowski and their young son and daughter. Two years later it was sold to Kirk and Christine Sauer, whose daughters, Kerry and Kimberly, were born since living at Mountsberg.

Next, to the southeast, is the home of Garry and Corrie Pennings, both of whom came from Holland with their parents. They moved from Waterdown into their new house in 1975. There are three Pennings children, Martin, Mark and Laura.

The Wingrove Brothers

Six Wingrove brothers, from Northampton, England, came to Canada in the early to mid-1830s. Most of them stopped at Campden (southeast of Beamsville) for a year or two before moving on. *Charles* (1790-1853), *Thomas* (1802-1876) and *George* (1804-1865) migrated to Mountsberg, about the same time. *James* (1808-1882), apparently, came directly to our area. Among them, they owned 500 acres on Lots 9 and 10 of the 12th and 13th Concession's. Charles and George, on the 12th Concession are buried in the Methodist Cemetery; Thomas and James on the 13th are in the Baptist Cemetery. Brothers, *William* and *Richard,* remained in the Niagara Peninsula.

Lot 9, northwest, Concession 12

Although Charles, the eldest brother, was enthusiastic about their new location, he never had title to more than 50 acres at the northwest end of Lot 9, and that for only six years. George had the first Wingrove deed. It was for the southeast 50 acres of this lot, dated March 17, 1837, the same day that John Page acquired his deed for Lot 8. Two Englishmen celebrating St. Patrick's Day! George did not stay in the neighbourhood just then, but was back by 1843. In the first Township assessment, in 1841, Charles was assessed for 200 acres, including Lot 9, northwest, and the 100 acres of Clergy Reserve land in Lot 10, southeast, which he was renting with the idea of buying it when it would be released for sale. His rating of £136 was the highest in the area, the closest contender being John Page with his 200 acres of Lot 8 assessed for £132, 3 s. Both were about double the average.

The Southeast 50 acres

George Wingrove's home was on Lot 10, northwest. This 50 acres, mainly wooded, was sold by his daughter, Elizabeth Ann, to William Laking, in June 1882. Mr. Laking then proceeded to buy a tiny triangle of land at the east corner of the northwest 50 acres, in order to reach his land on Lot 8. In 1906, he sold all his Mountsberg property to Burdge Gunby. This 50 acres went along with the deal when the Burdge Gunby estate sold Lot 8 to Linda and James F. Dunham in 1975.

Always excluded from sales was about an acre at the south corner. That was where the James Ford family lived. They came from England, about 1850, to a one-storey, log house, but it was not until 1880 that it was theirs with a deed given by Elizabeth Ann, daughter of George Wingrove. Mr. Ford worked at the Laking Mill during its period of operation. With most birth dates approximate, following are the Canadian-born children of James Ford (1817), and his wife, Hannah King (1827). There were four daughters: *Mary* (1850)—Mrs. Isaac Mitchell; *Jane* (1856-1947)—Mrs. Emanuel Mount; *Alice* (1860)—Mrs. John Dent of Lowville; *Louisa* (1864)—an itinerant dressmaker, she would live in homes for several days and make clothing, mostly dresses for the mother and daughters of the family. There were two Ford boys: *James* (1855)—went to the U.S.A. and there married; *George*—much younger, married and lived in Kilbride.

In 1904, Hannah Ford sold her place back to the Wingroves and the worn out log cabin soon disappeared. Mrs. Ford and Louisa went to Kilbride where Louisa continued to sew, but custom was changing and people went to her as she worked in her home.

A half-remembered comment hints that there once

had been two houses on this lot. There is a plausible theory about the other one, said to have been somewhere near the east corner. Roger Maynard, who taught in the log school in 1862-64, left a story of his life for his family. He and his wife arrived in Mountsberg on a Saturday night after a three-day trip from Listowel, and the only house they could get was a log structure built for the Sons of Temperance. It had a small, narrow window on each side, so high that his wife, Elizabeth, had to stand on her toes in order to see out. There was no hint concerning the site of this building, but a Directory of 1864-65 placed Mr. Maynard on Lot 9. He had gone to the new Beechgrove school in 1864, but this location would be about equidistant to either school.

Joseph Fearnley, son of George, across the road, bought two acres from George Wingrove in December 1864, and, two years later, sold it back to the Wingroves; but the buying price of $220 indicates that a building was included. So, it seems reasonably certain that Mr. Maynard lived there. But, that was long ago, and who, now, ever heard of the Sons of Temperance?

Mr. Maynard's story, courtesy of his granddaughter, Ruth Hopkins of Waterdown.

The Northwest 50 Acres

This 50 acres, first claimed by James Wingrove, now belongs to his great, great, grandson, Doug, but, in the meantime, many deeds were recorded. In 1839, James Wingrove added it to his 100 acres across the road, in the 13th Concession. He sold it to his brother, Charles, in January 1841. In December 1846, Charles divided the 50 acres, northwest to southeast, into two 25-acre parcels. At the same time, the northeast 25 acres went back to James and became again a part of the main farm to move down through his descendents to the present day. And the southwest 25 acres were sold to Thomas Aiken.

The Southwest 25 Acres

Very little is known of Thomas Aiken; not even his name, for sure. In assessments and other records, it appears, variously, as Atkins, Adkins, Aitken, and even Atkinson. In 1850 he was cultivating 6 acres and had built a small storey-and-a-half stone house. A young English couple, George and Elizabeth Parnell, with two tiny girls, Martha and Emma, were living there around 1860, or later, either as tenants or co-workers.

In June 1874, Thomas Aiken and his wife sold the 25 acres to John (Sandy) McPherson (not related to John MacPherson of the 14th Concession). In the Sandy McPherson family were: Marian, Annie, Isabel and Malcolm (Mac). They sold the property in 1897 and moved to the Beechgrove area.

Mr. and Mrs. David L. Calloway were owners from March 1897 to February 1905. They had a son Haldimand, known as Haldy; and a nephew, Frank Ryan, lived with them. Following Calloways, Fred Laking and his wife, Mary Jane Wingrove, daughter of William, bought the property and lived there three years. In March 1908, sold it back to the Wingrove farm, then owned by William, and moved to Lot 9, northwest, Concession 13.

Mrs. William Wingrove (Elizabeth), a widow since 1914, made this her home for many years. She died in 1931, and in April 1933, her son, Gordon, sold the house with an acre of land to Anna H. Dickson, whom he later married. In November 1948, as Anna H. Wingrove, widow of Gordon, she sold the house and lot to Robert and Flora Cochrane, a retired couple. They stayed until October 1963, when they sold to Pansy Caswell who lived there with her school-age granddaughter, Barbara. Charles Simpson made this his home until his death; also Frank Coulter, until he went to a nursing home.

The frame house, believed built in the McPherson era, has seen many changes in its appearance. For many years it was covered with insul-stone siding. Since 1971, it has been owned by John Marshall, a teacher, and his wife, Jody, who have two sons, Richard and Andrew; and the house has been rejuvenated with new white siding and comparable improvements inside.

In 1971, Frank and Frances Szponarski bought a building lot at the north corner of Lot 9 and built their house that year. Their family is a little league of nations. Frank, born in Poland, married Frances Foley, a native of Ireland. Their two oldest children, Richard and Eugene, were born in London, England; the two youngest, Steven and Monica, were born after the move to Canada in December 1956.

Lot 10, southeast, Concession 12   Clergy Reserve
Wingrove-1830s to December 1860

The Crown deed for this 100 acres was made out to John Wingrove, son of Charles, on October 19, 1854, the year that the last of the Clergy Reserves was released for sale. It had been Charles Wingrove's chosen land and, regrettably, he died the year before it was lawfully theirs. In years to come, it was home to several well-known Mountsberg families.

On arrival, Charles lost no time in building a cabin and a barn. By 1841, his livestock included 3 horses, 4 oxen and 8 cattle. With four sons to help him, he worked not only this lot but the northwest half of Lot 9, 50 acres of which he owned.

Family of Charles Wingrove (1790-1853) and his wife, Sarah Houser (1784-1852): *James* (1813-1891)—married Lucy Jones, their two-year-old daughter, Maria, is buried in the Methodist Cemetery, moved to Walsingham, north of Port Rowan in late 1850s; Thomas—married Mary Hunt; *John* (born 1821)—married Elizabeth (Betsy) Johnson, daughter of Philip, on farm until 1860. Family—Emma (born 1845), Philip (born 1848) died in infancy, Ruth (born 1850), Ezra Charles (1854-1860), Eli (born 1857), Helen (born 1859), and Fraser, who may have been born after the family moved to Burford; *George* (1824-1903)—married Mary Jane Fearnley (1829-1863) from the next farm, moved to Walsingham with James.

Revell—December 1860 to October 1874

Charles Revell, son of John, who lived on this lot,

should not be confused with his nephew, Charles, son of Thomas. This Charles bought the farm at the time he disposed of the property on Lot 6, Concession 12, where his father had settled.

Children of Charles Revell (1827-1895) and his wife, Delilah Sutton (1832-1901) were: *Pearl* (born about 1855)—married John Henry Donovan of Moffat, both were killed at a nearby railway crossing when their buggy was hit by a train; *Orpha* (1857-1892)—married John H. Kerr, not related to Kerrs of Lot 11, moved to New Liskeard area of northern Ontario; *Agnes* (born about 1860); *Mary* (born 1861)—married John Connell, Mountsberg blacksmith who continued as a blacksmith in Burlington where he was killed by a fall from a ladder; *Levi* (born about 1863)—married Agnes Thurston; *Henry* (1868-1877).

On leaving the farm in 1874, Charles Revell owned and operated the general store, and lived in the village. In 1889, Levi took over the sto,re for 10 months. Levi and Agnes had four sons, not all born at Mountsberg: Harvey (1889-1974; Charles who died in 1944 and had been in the 173rd Highland Battalion in W.W. I; Clifford (1901-1974); and Cecil, living in Hamilton. A daughter, Laura who died in 1892, at 10 months, is buried in the Methodist cemetery.

Levi Revell continued in the grocery business in Hamilton and, later, at Hamilton Beach. He was buried in Hamilton's new Woodland Cemetery where the first burial took place in November 1921. Levi's was the tenth.

Thompson—October 1874 to May 1885

The eight-year partnership of Oron Thompson and William Laking in the lumber business came to an end in 1874, but only after a few months of shared ownership of the general store. After buying the farm, the Thompson family moved there from the mill area. As far as known, the children of Oron and Mary Thompson, born in the 1860s to the early 1870s were: Samuel, William, Sarah, George and Margaret. As a hobby, Mr. Thompson was an artist who painted local scenes. He left Mountsberg to have another fling at lumbering in Dufferin County. In later years, he spent some time with his son, George, in North Tonawanda, New York.

Emmons—May 1885 to March 1917

William Emmons (1840-1918) and Euphemia Campbell (1847-1929), daughter of Archibald Sr., were married on the first Dominion Day, July 1, 1867. They lived in many Mountsberg locations. They owned and operated the General Store, in 1873; owned and lived on the former McDougall mill property on the 11th Concession, several years, ending in 1880, and at the time of buying this farm, they also owned Lot 12, northwest, nearby.

Members of the Emmons family were: *Martha* (1870-1895)—Mrs. Thomas Gunston; *Walter* (1872-1917)—spent most of his life in the area, family listed on Lot 7; *Nellie* (1874-   )—Mrs. Charles Morton of Moffat; *Albert* (1876-1950)—unmarried, worked in Brantford, but spent later years at Mountsberg; *John* (1878-1913)—married Maybelle Cook; *Hannah* (1880-1969)—Mrs. Burnice (Bun) Page; *Aubrey* (1886-   ) —an accountant and a major overseas in W.W. I., he and his wife, Edith, lived in Brantford, Hamilton and Owen Sound.

When the Emmons family came to this farm, they lived in the old Wingrove log cabin, but soon made vast changes to their home. The roof of the log house was raised to provide a roomy upstairs, and a large new frame house was attached to the northeast side. It all tied together so neatly that a passerby on the Mounts-berg Road sees, at the end of the long lawn a comfortably large, 19th century, farm home that gives no hint of the history in its heart.

William Emmons served on the Township Council, 1899 to 1903 and again in 1908 when, in June of that year, he and Mrs. Emmons retired to the village.

John and Maybelle Emmons stayed on the farm and, in 1909 owned it. Some time later they left to try farming in Western Canada, where John was killed in a horse and wagon accident. Maybelle sold the farm back to William in the spring of 1915. Two years later it was bought by William Mount. In the intervening years, Bun and Hannah (Emmons) Page rented the farm before they bought their own place in Concession 10, facing Concession 11. Their children, born at Mounts-berg were: Lorne—married Shirley Fields and lives in Galt; *Flora*—Mrs. Albert Maltby of Rockwood; *Albert* —on Centre Road, see Lot 8, Concession 12.

Mount—March 1917 to March 1919

William Mount, son of Emanuel, was a bachelor at this time.

Leslie—March 1919 to May 1943

Mark Leslie (1876-1943) and his wife, Myrtle Ingram (1879-1955) with their young children moved to this farm from the farm at Beechgrove later owned by John Mount. Their children were: *Bessie*—Mrs. Neil O'Neil of Belleville; *Isabel*—Mrs. G. Crow of Guelph; Oliver—married Margaret Hewins, daughter of Albert, lived on the farm six or seven years, their sons, Murray and Ronald, were born there and Diane was born after they moved to Strabane; *Edith*—Mrs. James Stinson of Toronto; *Anne*—Mrs. William Farrel of Toronto, now Lindsay; *Alma* (1917-1969)—twin of Anne, Mrs. Westman Hudson; *Helen* (1922-1975)—Mrs. Hanley Gray, Freelton.

In September 1919, Mark Leslie added to his acreage by buying the northwest half of Lot 9, in the 11th Concession. This landlocked 75 acres was reached at its west corner via the unopened 12th Concession, from the east corner of the home farm. Mr. Leslie was an East Flamborough Councillor for three years, 1928-30. After his death, Mrs. Leslie sold the property and moved to Freelton.

Shanks—May 1943 to September 1972

Some years after buying this farm, as well as the supplementary land in Concession 11, Samuel Shanks took his son, Sidney, into full partnership and, together, they operated a dairy farm with Annadale

Holsteins. In June 1958, Sidney Shanks bought almost all of the adjoining Lot 11.

When Mr. and Mrs. Samuel Shanks left Belfast, County Down, Ireland, in 1923, it was not their first break with their native Isle. When first married, they spent a few years in Massachusetts, where their first child, Doris was born. On their second exodus, with four children, they left Ireland and went directly to Mr. Shanks' brother, David, living on Highway 6, near Strabane. Samuel worked in that area a year or more, then two years with Robert Wigood and, after owning the former Methodist parsonage for 17 years, he bought this farm. The grandfather, William Shanks (18391933), had come to Canada with David but, later, lived with Samuel at Mountsberg.

Following is the family of Samuel Shanks who died February 1971, in his 84th year, and his wife, Annie (1885-1970); *Doris*—Mrs. Charles Welker of Geneva-on-the-Lake, Ohio; *Ruth*—Mrs. Russell Colling; *Sidney*—living with the Collings since the farm was sold; *Isabel*—Mrs. Victor Kuran, lived in Sudbury, now Winnipeg.

In July 1960, Ruth and Russell Coiling, who had been living in Hamilton, bought a building lot southwest of the farm lane and built a new home. They have two sons, Brian, married Beryl Jeffery and lives in Waterdown; Ronald, married Marlene Dawdy, lives in Stoney Creek.

Sidney sold the home farm and the land on Concession 11 in 1972. The new owner, Dr. J.R. Kearns of Hamilton, is non-resident and the farm is rented separately from the house.

Lot 10, northwest, Concession 12

Early activity on this Clergy Reserve lot is hazy. George Wingrove was interested. His name was in the records in the mid-1840s, and he obtained a deed, dated January 20, 1851, probably as soon as the 100 acres was released for sale. However, Nicholas Jacques (or Jones) was working on the land, including George's 50 acres in Lot 9, before and after 1850 and had farm buildings near the 13th Concession. Later, in the 1850s, George used the farm himself, and the buildings, always regarded as the Wingrove homestead, were beside Mounts-berg Road.

George Wingrove (1804-1865) was married twice. His second wife, Ann Teller (1816-1870) was the mother of the children. They were: *Daniel* (1835-1913)—married four times—(1) née Hurst who died with baby at childbirth, (2) Elizabeth Emmons (1836 - 1873), mother of the family George, William, Emma, Hannah, and Phoebe Elizabeth, (3) Sarah Flowers, née Whitehead, (4) Mrs. Grant; *John Wesley* (1841-1922)—married Margaret Forsyth (1850-1932), daughter of William Forsyth, a Baptist minister, they had two sons—George Edgar, died in infancy, and Osborne (born 1881) married Etta Bradley of Carlisle; *Anthea Axie* (1842-1928)—married Henry Whitehead, moved to Muskoka, had four sons and two daughters; *Rebecca*—Mrs. Parr; *Elizabeth* (born 1856)—married William McKinney (born 1863), Elizabeth inherited the 50 acres of Lot 9 which she sold in 1882.

After George died, both sons remained on the farm several years. John W. became owner, but, after Dan left, the property was rented as John W. was not physically able for heavy farm work. William Emmons, living across the road, rented the land for some years prior to 1905, followed by Charles Galloway, whose lease called for half-yearly payments of $75.

From about 1900 to 1905, a Smith family lived on the Wingrove place. John Smith was the eldest of eight children of John (or James) Smith (died 1898) and his wife, Ann Eliza Harker (died 1918) who lived on the 10th Concession of East Flamborough. John's sister, Emily A. (1869-1896) was the wife of Robert Wigood, Lot 4, Concession 13. A brother, James, also died young, and his widow, Martha Wigood, and his daughter, Edith (Mrs. Percy Haskell), lived at the Wigood home with Robert.

John Smith (1853-1938) and his wife, Isabel Weir (1859-1940), daughter of Thomas Weir, Concession 10, went from Mountsberg back to the Smith family farm and, after their daughter Eva (1888-1961), married Hunter McCarthy in 1912, the parents, with Jane, Delmar and Merrit, went to western Canada. While there, Jane married and, as Jane Begg, was buried in the west. After several years, Mr. and Mrs. Smith and their sons returned to live at Puslinch.

Following the Smiths, a respected family of German lineage, with three boys, occupied the house a few years. At this late date, their correct name is obscure. Local people of British Isles descent could not cope with the German pronunciation and it came out as "Roadhammer".

Still in possession of the farm, Margaret and John W. bought a house in the village, next to the store, in March 1908. In April 1909, the farm was sold to Thomas Wingrove, grandson of the first Thomas, and living on the homestead, Lot 10, Concession 13. The sale included one acre at the south corner of Lot 9 which had returned to the Wingrove name when sold back to Margaret and John W. In the ten years that the farm was owned by Thomas Wingrove, as extra land, there were occasional tenants in the old log house. In the spring of 1919, Tom sold all his Mountsberg property and moved to Rockwood. This farm was bought by James Fletcher in March of that year.

James Fletcher (1889-1956) and his wife, Gertrude Trudgeon made this their home for 37 years, and here their children grew up: *Lloyd* (1914-1974)—married Evelyn Fraser and lived in Hamilton; *Mildred*—since marriage, has lived in Dundas, her first husband, Morley Hood, died in 1969 and she later married Howard Harper, but is a widow again.

The large barn burned in 1953. Mr. Fletcher replaced it with two smaller structures. After his death in 1956, his estate sold the farm, later that year, to Mary J. Springer of Burlington. The Springer family has a tie with early Mountsberg. Mrs. Springer's husband, Fred, is a grandson of Minerva Mount (Mrs. James McNiven of Nassagaweya). Minerva was a sister of Emanuel and granddaughter of Josiah.

From 1956 to 1976, Michael McKenna and his wife, Helen Priest, rented the farm and lived there with their growing family: Brian, Katherine, Earl and Paul David. From here, they moved to the Troy-Sheffield area of the former Township of Beverly.

The old Wingrove house stood vacant for a year before it went up in flames on Hallowe'en night in 1977.

In 1972, Mary J. Springer sold to Douglas and Joyce Rasberry a 1-acre lot at the north corner of the farm, beside the 13th Concession. Rasberrys built a house that year, for themselves and children, Brian, Susan and Cindy. In 1977, Paul and Elizabeth Beaudoin bought the home and moved to Mountsberg. Their family is now two daughters, Lindsay and Lauren.

Lot 11, southeast, Concession 12   Brock Grant

Abraham Purnell (1783-1856), a native of Achton, Gloucestershire, England, and one of the founders of the Mountsberg Methodist Church, held one of the earliest deeds of the area. He obtained it on March 30, 1837, the same day that his friends, John Revell, and Philip Johnson, on Lot 6, Concession 12, acquired theirs.

No record of Abraham Purnell's wife is available. She may have died in England or before Mountsberg had a cemetery. But, he did have with him a son, Joseph, born about 1810, and a daughter, Christiana, perhaps others. Arriving much later was his brother, Thomas, with his wife, Mary, and their son, Abraham, who made his home on Lot 12, Concession 11.

In 1850, Abraham Sr. sold 25 acres at the southeast end of his lot to his son, Joseph, who built his home there. Joseph and his wife, Hannah (born about 1826) had the following family, with approximate birth dates: Christiana, 1848: Hester, 1849; Samuel, 1851; Elizabeth, 1853; Elijah, 1855; Benjamin, 1857; Joshua, 1860; Hannah, 1863; Robert, 1865; and Martha, 1870.

After Abraham's death, his 75 acres with farm buildings became Joseph's, although, at the time, the land was rented to Oliver Ferrier. Other tenants followed. Later Purnell names associated with the farm were Joseph's sons, Robert L. and Joshua, whose wife was Sarah. Robert and his family lived there a few years about or before 1910. Of his family, only Shirley is recalled. Until about 1920, Samuel, a bachelor, lived in his family's house at the back of the farm. He was a painter as his father had been.

Troubled times beset the Purnell property, and when it was bought by Earl and Flossie Dougherty in 1950, it was sold from the estate of a mortgagee. The farm buildings, beyond restoration, were demolished. A new house was built for their son, Lyle, and his wife Florence Reid, who lived there about four years. Their children, Sharon, Bonnie and Wayne were born at Mountsberg before they moved to Port Credit, where Lyle was on the Toronto Township police force. Cecil Hood rented it for two years before Earl retired and he and Flossie moved there from the farm on Lot 3. It was here, in October 1966, that they celebrated their golden wedding.

In 1958, Sidney Shanks of Lot 10, bought the farm, all except half the frontage to a depth of 150 feet, which included the Dougherty home. A month later, he sold 37 acres at the southeast end to Edward and Georgina Bridle. Since about 1965, that acreage, along with 12 more acres bought in 1971, has been the location of the Four Seasons Nature Park owned by Hans and Elizabeth Stein.

The remaining 54 acres, lying behind and southwest of the Dougherty strip, were sold in 1972 to Donald and Barbara George who, that same year, built their new home, some distance from the road. With their family, David, Carol and Heather, they operate a market garden.

Three houses, newer than the Dougherty home, now are seen along Mountsberg Road. At the north corner of the lot is the home of John and Pauline Scott and children, John and Karen. Nadja Drown bought this building lot in 1970, had the house built in 1971, then sold it to the Scotts in 1972. The next place, southwest, is the home of Donald and Nadja Drown, built in 1966, the year after they bought the lot. They have a son, Daniel, and a daughter, Jacqueline, now Mrs. John Henlow of Hamilton. The Dougherty home is next. Beyond it, is the home of a German couple, Joachim (John) and Walltrant Urban who moved into the new house in 1970. Their Canadian-born children are Margarete, Rosemarie, twins Gloria and Gina, and Michael.

Note:

When Earl Ray Dougherty died on September 10, 1980, in his 85th year, Mountsberg lost its oldest citizen of the day. Earl was a true son of Mountsberg, descended from three pioneer settlers. He was a great grandson of James Dougherty; a great grandson of Joseph Page, and a great, great, grandson of John Revell. Earl never lived anywhere but Mountsberg and, with his passing, the name Dougherty also passed from the neighbourhood.   *M.H.C.*

Lot 11, northwest, Concession 12   Brock Grant

This farm has known only two names, Kerr and Woolsey.

Kerr

Robert Kerr and his wife, Isabella (Weir), apparently newly married, were on Lot 11 in 1840. By 1842, they had cleared 16 acres. Robert had left his home in Sligo, Ireland, a few years before taking up this lot. He carried with him the farewell gift of his brother, George, a Bible, inscribed and dated, July 6, 1837.

Robert's wife, Isabella Weir, also from Sligo, came with her family. Her mother, Isabella is buried in the Methodist cemetery. She died July 9, 1864, at age 78. There is no record of the father, Thomas Weir, who may have died before the family left Ireland. Weir sons, William and James, settled in Nassagaweya, and Thomas on Lot 9, northwest, Concession 10.

Robert Kerr built the sturdy, stone house, long a landmark on Mountsberg Road. He was a member of the Reserve Militia in 1864-65, and, in 1866, died at the early age of 50. He left all his land to his eldest son,

John; land which included the home farm, deeded in 1857; Lot 12 southeast, which had been bough in 1854, as well as two lots in Freelton and another parcel of land outside the locality. Along with the inheritance, John was given the responsibility of caring for his mother and providing a home for the younger members of the family. The boys were to receive schooling or training for a trade and, at age 21, a sum of money $500 or $600. The girls were to be educated, up to age 16, and receive a good outfit when they married. At age 21, each was to be given $200 and a cow.

We do not know which school the Kerr family attended. Perhaps it was the early log school at Mountsberg, or it could have been the old school at Purnell's Corner, slightly nearer, but over the line in West Flamborough. The stone school at Beechgrove was not built until 1864. The family members were active in the Methodist Episcopal Church. John was a trustee in 1875-76 and his brother, William, was on the first Board of Stewards after the Methodist Union of 1884.

Isabella Kerr died at Brantford, April 4 1892, at age 72, according to her tombstone, or age 74 on her death certificate. The family of Robert Kerr (1816-1866) and Isabella were: *Catherine* (1841-1931)'—married John McPhail—a grandson, John McPhail, still lives on their farm on Concession 10 of Beverly, with his son and family; *Henry* (1842-1848); *Thomas* (1844-1850); *Robert* (1846-1848); *John R. (1847-1921)*—was only 20 and unmarried when he inherited his father's land and assumed all family obligations. He married Annie McLean of Puslinch about 1875. Their first two children, Robert and Isabella, died young. after they had a son, John I. (1884-1962). In January 1876, the family moved to Brantford, where John owned a glove factory and ran a coal business; *William H.* (1850-1934)—after John left, William, a bachelor of 25, farmed the Kerr land, with his mother and sister, Louise, still living in the home. In 1883, he bought Lot 12, southeast, from John. In 1884, he married Jane Reid of Georgetown and, in 1886, William and Jane, with a baby daughter, Laura Bell, moved to a farm in Esquesing Township of Halton, in an area known as the Scotch Block. William had bought his farm in 1880, and when he left Mountsberg, his mother, Isabella, went to Brantford to live with John; *Thomas* (1851-1931)— was a carpenter who went to Vancouver where he became owner of a sawmill, and there spent the rest of his life. About 1880, he married Elizabeth Kennedy of Georgetown; *Louise I.* (1854-1931)—married George Henning (Hanning) in 1880's, and lived in Morriston; *Robert J.* (1856-1937)—a builder, married Mary McLean, a sister of John's wife, Annie. They lived in Freelton where their first child was born, then in Brantford where he built a brick house for himself and one for John; *Mary Ann* (1858-1935)—a dressmaker, married John H. Walkinshaw in 1888, and lived in Hamilton.

Information re Kerr family, courtesy of Ernie W. Kerr of Ottawa, great grandson of Robert and Isabella Kerr, descended through William H. Kerr and Robert H. Kerr (born in Esquesing). Ernie and his two sons are now the only male Kerrs on this family tree.

Woolsey

When William Kerr left the farm in 1886, Thomas Woolsey, his hired helper, stayed on, planning to make it his home. In 1893, he was given a deed from John R. Kerr, then living in Brantford.

Thomas' father, William Woolsey, came from County Armagh, Ireland, and married Emma (Amy) Hopkinson, daughter of Thomas Hopkinson, Sr. of Nassagaweya, who had emigrated from Derbyshire, England. About 1890, Thomas Woolsey met and married Susan Smye who had been working for Mrs. William Laking at the mill. She was a daughter of John and Jane (Sivell) Smye.

Family of Thomas Woolsey (1860-1945) and his wife, Susan (1860-1916): *Margaret* (1892-1940)—married Edmund Beaver of Morriston, lived in London; *William* (1894-1967)—married, had daughter, Susan; *Stanley* (1896-1968)—married Gladys Stone, had children, James and June (Hunter); *Robert Garnet, M.D.* (1897-1968)—known by either name, graduate of University of Western Ontario, married Beatrice Mast (1898-1966) of Concession 14; *Bertha* (1903-1975)—named for the teacher, Bertha Nixon, married Laurie Gartley of Strabane, widowed, married Alan Nicholson and lived in Nassagaweya.

Thomas Woolsey built a large barn in 1907, the year that four new barns spring up in the neighbourhood, including those of Albert Campbell, Burdge Gunby and James Rutherford. All were built by Billy Kitchen and his men.

The Woolsey family attended the Methodist Church and many are buried in the adjoining cemetery. The children went to Mountsberg School. About 1911, they were required to transfer to Beechgrove. The change affected Garnet and Bertha, a few months before Garnet graduated from public school.

Robert Garnet retired from his medical career in New York and bought the farm from his father's estate, in 1947. Stanley, who had worked along with his father, continued with the farm work. Present owners are the doctor's two daughters, Elizabeth Donatelli and Beatrice, who live in the farm's stone house.

Lot 12, southeast, Concession 12   Brock Grant

As early as 1843, and for ten or more years, John Flowers was working on this lot. At a later date, and perhaps even in the 1840's, there was a Flowers home across the creek in West Flamborough. Robert Kerr of Lot 11, northwest, bought the 100 acres in 1854. Apparently, he had a tenant on the farm. The Agricultural Census of 1861 shows James Sharp on the land with very little stock or produce; much less than Mr. Flowers had had. James Sharp and his wife, Margaret, were from Scotland with children, Isabella, John, James, Margaret and David.

After Robert Kerr died in 1866, the property went to his son, John, who sold it to his brother, William, in 1883. John B. Curry bought it from William in 1888.

Until midway in the present century, two small buildings stood well back from the road and some distance apart. Mr. and Mrs. Curry lived in the one to the northeast, and it was home to their family: William, Bailey, Robert, Mary, Emma and Margaret (order uncertain).

John Curry sold the farm in 1920. From then until 1934, it was in the name of H. Dolynuk (also written Dolenick) who lived there. He sold to a Perilli family who, some years later divided it into two parcels of 40 and 60 acres.

The Southeast Forty

In April 1946, Peter Wheeler bought the 40 acres at the southeast end from the Perillis and, in May 1953, sold it to Cecil and Myrtle Pentecost. Glen McLeod, trustee for the Pentecosts, sold to the Waterdown Sportsman's Club in 1966.

The Northwest Sixty

The Perilli group sold the 60 acres beside Mountsberg Road to William and Margaret Castleton in September 1945. One year later, Castletons sold an acre at the north corner to Alfred and Doris Pook who bought the lot with a partly-built house. In 1963, their daughter, Doreen Pook, and her husband, John McKenna, purchased the house and lot and, since then, have lived there. McKennas have a daughter, Lee Ann, married to Bill Paul of Burlington; also Dennis, Jacqueline and Patrick.

The remaining 59 acres became the property of Frank and Clara Bell in 1962. Their house is in the central part of the farm frontage. Frank is an uncle of Doreen McKenna. In 1962, Bells sold 20 acres on the southwest side. It was resold in 1968 to Renate and Herbert Lamm who built their house in 1970.

Mr. and Mrs. Bell kept 10 acres, which included their home, and, in 1963, sold the remaining 29 acres to Edward Horyn. This property at the north part of the farm is a rectangle except for the McKenna acre at the north corner.

Lot 12, northwest, Concession 12

George Fearnley of Lot 9 became the first owner of this property in 1854, but, before then it had been used as rental land. John Wingrove of Lot 10 had worked on 50 acres and James English on the remaining 50. Presumably, it was James and Elizabeth English with young daughters, Hannah, Elizabeth and Almira, who first lived near the 13th Concession in a small log house that stood there until about 1900.

Charles Fearnley, son of George, married Phoebe Sutton about the time his father bought the lot, and it became their home. They lived in a 1 1/2-storey log house, beside Mountsberg Road and, by 1866, the farm was theirs by deed.

The family of Charles Fearnley (1831-1870) and Phoebe Sutton (1827-1914) follows, with most birth dates approximate and information incomplete: *Freeman* (1855)—a builder; *Fred* (1858-1929)—married Sarah J. Smith (1854-1936), lived in Strabane; *Elizabeth Ann* (1860)—married George Walker; *Haslett* (1865)—drove a fire team in Guelph before going to western Canada; *Eliza Jane* (1867)—married John Henry Van Norman, died at Elora in 1925; *Lavina* (1868-1942) — married John Alger; *Franklin*—died at 15 months.

Charles died in 1870, but the family stayed at the home for several years. In 1877, a red brick house was built for Phoebe at the corner of Concession 13 and Centre Road, on about an acre of land bought from John Revell. In 1880, Freeman Fearnley sold the farm to William Emmons who established his parents there.

The father, Henry Emmons, was Pennsylvania Dutch. In Canada, he married Hannah Parker, born in Ireland. Their family included: *John Henry*—married, no family, lived in Guelph; *Elizabeth*—second wife of Dan Wingrove of Lot 10, lived in Muskoka; *William* — see Lot 10, southeast; *Rosalie*—married David Brown, family—John, William, Robert, Hannah and Mary; *Amelia (Millie)*—second wife of David Brown, no family, married a second time to Robert Maddaugh who had been married twice. At this home, Millie wove rag mats for people who provided her with large balls of sewn-together strips of cloth.

In December 1904, William Emmons' son, Walter, bought the property and lived there until February 1907, when he sold it to James and Alice (Kitchen) Rutherford, who had been married a year and living at Carlisle. On March 6, 1907, seven days after moving into their new home, the barn was struck by lightning and burned. It was rebuilt that spring by Alice's cousin, carpenter Billy Kitchen and his crew. One of his men was Ed Gray, brother of James on Centre Road. This second barn was burned, by mishap, around 1960-62. It, too, was replaced.

James Rutherford was of Scottish descent. His great grandfather came to Strabane from Glasgow but James' family home was in Halton County at the corner across Town Line from Concession 10. James and Alice were married in Kilbride. Alice's sister, Lorrie (Mrs. John Peacock), attended the Methodist church while living in the neighbourhood and, later, from their own home on the Town Line. Her brother, James Kitchen, and his family, for several years owned the Linn farm on Town Line, opposite Concession 13.

The old Fearnley log house stood there, undisguised, until 1930. Well built, well cared for and plastered inside, it was an exceptional early-day home. Measuring 36 by 24 feet, it was spacious as farm cabins went. Downstairs was a large kitchen, a roomy parlour and a bedroom, with three more bedrooms upstairs.

When it came time to replace the aging home, the old kitchen was moved back and the two-storey, red brick house rose on the site of the former dwelling. The maple floor of the old kitchen became the floor of the new kitchen. The log house had no cellar, but the later home has a basement on solid rock.

James Rutherford (Jan. 1878-Oct. 1963) and Alice (Oct. 1885-Jan. 1958) are buried at Strabane. Their eldest child, Olivia, died in 1913, at age four. Ruby is

Mrs. James Cooper of Hamilton. John's first wife, Evelyn Fuller, died. His second wife, a widow, was Janet (Gillespie) Tait. John was a City of Hamilton employee; they live in Hamilton.

Late surveys of farms show many variations in size from the stated 100 acres. None were found undersized, but bonus land varied from 1 to 10.2 acres on the Rutherford farm which has a branch of the Bronte Creek flowing through most of its southwest side.

In November 1960, James Rutherford sold 23.7 acres at the northwest end of the farm to Edward J. Fiddler, Nicholas Schalme, and Julia Chysik. The Fiddler share went to Tonie Fiddler from the Edward Fiddler estate in 1971. A cottage was built in the vicinity of the creek.

After the death of James, the remainder of the farm (86.5 acres) was sold by his son, John, in June 1964. The new owners, Jack and Lyda Scully, divided it into 8 lots. Resident owners of the lots, up to January 1, 1980, are listed, moving southwesterly from the east corner of the farm:

1. 10 acres—Sold in 1966 to Harvey and Donna Brown. To Raymond and Pauline Collingridge in 1975; they live in the Rutherford farm house.
2. 15 acres—Bought in 1967 by James and Marianne Hutchison who operated a riding stable. Stable and land sold to Gerald Taylor in 1975; then to William and Joan Davis in 1976.
3. 10 acres—First sold in 1967. Fourth owners, Dale and Diane Hicks, bought in 1971 and, the following year, built their home some distance from the road.
4. 10 acres—First sold in 1966. Third owners, Peter and Sylvia May, bought the land in 1968 and built the house the same year.
5. 10 acres—Sold in 1966 to U.J. and T. DeVries and resold in 1967, with a house, to Robert and June Jones.
6. 10 acres—Sold in 1967 to Reinhold and Gerlinde Hambsch. The house was built the following year. John and Eileen Bellingham bought the property in 1974.
7. 10 acres—First sold in 1967. Third owners, Thomas and Barbara Dowling bought in 1968, the year the house was built.
8. 11.5 acres—Ralph and Barbara DeBlauw bought the land in 1967 and built the house that year.

The Laking and Linn Farms

Two farms in Nassagaweya Township of Halton, across the Town Line from Lot 1, Concession 13, East Flamborough, are included. Both the Laking and Linn families had close ties with Mountsberg, with church or school and relatives in the area.

The Laking farm in Nassagaweya
Opposite Lot 1, northwest, Conc. 13

John and Lucy Laking spent the first seven years of their married life on Lot 8, Conc. 12, which 200 acres they rented from John Page. In the spring of 1865, they bought the Nassagaweya farm from Mr. Menzies and, with their four small children, moved into the log cabin on that farm.

The original barn was burned about 1875 and was replaced. A few years later, about 1881, the buff brick house replaced the log cabin which, for another half century, served as a woodshed.

The family: *John Laking* (1827-1915); *Lucy Harper* (1835-1916); *Clara* (1859-1960)—married George Cartwright (son of Edmund), lived in Progreston and Carlisle before moving to British Columbia, about 1900; *James S.* (1860-1944)—married Annie MacPherson (daughter of Peter), operated a heading mill on the 12-Mile Creek in Badenoch. They attended the Methodist Church. With their daughter, Edna, they moved to Guelph about 1910; *William Emmerson* (1862-1953) — known by both names, married Amy McFerran of Milton and operated a saw mill in Cloverdale, British Columbia; *Sarah E.* (1864-1969)—married Frank Coulson of Lowville; *John B.* (1867-1876)—died in his 10th year of appendicitis, then inoperable; *Charles* (1869-1962)—married Rachel Redpath of Mountsberg and remained on the *farm; Annie* (1872-1950)—married Charles Hewins of Mountsberg.

The family attended the Methodist Church, but the children went to school in Nassagaweya. In April 1908, a double golden wedding was celebrated at the farm, for John and Lucy Laking, and Lucy's brother, Charles Harper and his wife, Elizabeth Worthington.

Family of Charles and Rachel (Acie): *Robert*—became owner of the farm, married Gertrude Bousfield of Carlisle who died in 1972; *Clarence*—a gunner in World War I, made a career of lumber, married Helen Paterson of Toronto; *Wilfred*—in banking, for many years City Manager of Ferndale, Michigan, where he married Helen Scott; *Grace*—a childrens' nurse in Toronto, died in 1961; Myrtle—married George McPhail, living in Toronto.

This family also attended school in Nassagaweya.

Robert and Gertrude had four sons, all of whom attended Mountsberg school. They were: Orval—telegrapher in the Navy, during World War II, in the lumber business in Toronto, married Beatrice McCreath of Edmonton; *Ross*—since 1970, living on Lot 3, Conc. 12, facing the 13th Concession Road; *John (Jack)*—with the C.P.R., married a Scottish nurse, Margaret Thompson, lives in Preston; *William (Bill)*—married Ruth Brinklow of Eden Mills, a teacher, living on a stock farm in Badenoch.

After being Laking property for almost a century, in the spring of 1959, the farm was sold to Dr. Davis of Hamilton. Extensive alterations were made to the house. A few years later, Dr. Davis died and the farm is now owned in part by the Halton Region Conservation Authority and partly by John King who lives in the house. Bob and Gertie moved to Milton.

**The Linn farm in Nassagaweya Township
Opposite Lot 1, southeast, Concession 13**

Hugh Linn (1781-1861) and his wife, Jane (1781-1869) came from County Antrim, Ireland in 1835, and chose this site for a home. Arriving with them were their friends, the Agnews, who settled nearer Campbellville. Linn had two teenage sons, Joseph, who later owned the Flamborough farm across the townline; and Robert who went to the Owen Sound area.

The first Linn home, of logs, had a lane leading to the Town Line. The new red brick house (the present Rollins home) had access to the Campbellville Road. It was built by William Linn (son of Joseph) the second owner of the farm. William married Charity Johnson, daughter of Benjamin and Ann Hewins Johnson.

William Linn family. Rear—Joe, Trueman, Arthur and Russell. Front—William, Charles, Myrtle and Charity. *Mrs. W.C. Cust.*

Family of William (1854-1939) and Charity (1854-1912): *Anna Lena*—born March 28, 1883, died in early childhood; *Myrtle* (1885-1943)—not married; *Joseph* (1887-1944)—married Fanny Weir of Campbellville, no children; *Arthur* (1889-1920)—married Winnifred Hurren, a granddaughter of Edmund of Centre Road; *Trueman* (1890-1970)—married Hattie McClung, a Campbellville school teacher, lived in Florida; *Charles* (born in 1891)—married Lillian Hurren, sister of Winnifred, lives in Galt; *Russell* **(1894-1963)**—an auctioneer, married Margaret Slee, lived in Galt.

William Linn's second wife was his former sister-in-law, Emma Heath Johnson (1859-1837), widow of Trueman Johnson who died in 1905.

The Linn children attended Mountsberg school. After Arthur's death, Joe and Russell carried on the farm for a while before selling to Arthur Partridge. About 1924, it was re-sold to Mr. and Mrs. James Kitchen who had three sons. Jim married Beulah Inglis, now deceased. They lived on the home farm a while before going to a farm in Badenoch. Their son, Claire, died in his early teens. Lloyd married Doris Cairns of Nassagaweya; they live in Hamilton. Her family, including brothers Roy and Archie, attended Mountsberg church. Calvert married Anna Bell Stokes of Campbellville; he died in 1975; his wife now lives in Badenoch.

In 1933, Kitchens sold to George and Olive Rollins who are still on the farm. Olive is the daughter of Thomas and Mary Beaton of Badenoch. Her sister Velma lives with them.

Concession 13

Lot 1, southeast, Concession 13   Brock Grant

Joseph Lynn came from Ireland with his family, in 1835, and, about five years later, took up this farm, across the Town Line from his parents. His deed of May 16, 1846, is unique in our neighbourhood. It is the only one signed by a member of the Brock family in Guernsey, England wherein property was transferred directly to a person intending to live on the land and use it for himself. By 1850, Joseph had 50 acres under cultivation. The original Hugh Linn spelled his name with an 'i' as did grandson William and family. Son Joseph and grandsons Hugh and family used a 'y'.

Family of Joseph Lynn (1816-1905) and his wife, Margaret Agnew (1821-1902) also from Ireland: *Eliza Jane* (1845-   )—married Joseph Hagen, lived at Eden Mills; *Mary* (1847-1933)—unmarried; *Hugh* **(1849-1860)**—buried at Kilbride, as were his grandparents; *Janet* (1851-1897)—married Alexander Yule, lived at Harriston; *William* (1854-1939)—married Charity John- son, lived on Nassagaweya farm; *Margaret* (1856-   ) —married Andrew Yule, lived at Listowel; *Sarah* (1857-1936)—unmarried; *Joseph (1859-1887)*—killed in a farm accident; *Christina* (1863-1950)—unmarried; *Hugh* (1866-1922)—remained on farm, married Agnes Nichol.

House on Harold Small place, circa 1925. *Bruce Small.*

Harold Small holding Bruce, wife, Charlotte, holding Don, circa 1926. *Bruce Small.*

Small Barn. *Bruce Small*

Joseph Lynn bought the rear 50 acres of Lot 2, beside him, in 1854 and, in 1901 turned over all 150 acres to his son, Hugh. Several years later, Hugh married Agnes Nichol (1871-1942) in Western Canada. At that time, Mary, Sarah and Tina established a home in Guelph. Hugh's death in 1922 marked the end of the Lynn era.

Agnes and their son, Murray, moved to Guelph when, in 1923, the farm was sold to Harold Small and his bride Charlotte (Lottie) Shadwell. Lottie died in 1939, and Harold and his two young sons, Bruce and Donald, kept the farm going until 1966.

The sturdy stone farm house was built by Joseph Lynn in 1869, to replace the first small frame home. Early in this century, Hugh Lynn moved a small barn from Lot 2 to become part of the barn on Lot 1, and Harold Small built an implement shed in 1963.

Taxes on this farm followed the trend everywhere. In the 50-year period from 1915 to 1965, they more than tripled. Now, a mere 15 years later, that seems Utopian.

In 1965, 21 of the 50 acres of Lot 2 went to the H.R.C.A. The next year, Harold sold Lot 1 and the remainder of Lot 2 to William Huiskamp; all, except an acre at the corner of Concession 13 and the Town Line where he built a retirement home for himself. Bruce already was married to Jean Blacklock. Donald was with his father a short time before marrying Mary Free Wigood, widow of Lyle. Both boys live in Nassagaweya.

In the six years that Mr. Huiskamp was there, the farm was sold off in parts. In 1968, R. DeGroot bought 60 acres, that being the remainder of Lot 2 and the northwest end of Lot 1; 33 acres of this went to the H.R.C.A. The northeast side of the farm was divided into 10-acre lots. Moving northwesterly along the Town Line, they are:

1. To George Satelmeyer, less Harold Small's acre; vacant.

2. Edward and Marjorie Carter Bailey, both teachers; with children, Sara and Scott, moved from Burlington in 1977 and bought from Gerald Duncan who built the house in 1974. Gerald and Melba Duncan and children, Krista and Brent, were there three years.
3. Yngve (Slim) Kangas and his wife, Tuulikki, who came from Finland at age 15, bought the lot in 1968 and built the house which they sold to David A. and Jane Fournier Croft, in 1973. The Crofts, with children, Philip and Ann, moved from Islington.
4. The Kangas' bought this lot in 1973 as the stem part of a T-shaped property, the cross bar being 27 acres bought from R. DeGroot. A house was built on the hilltop in 1973-4. The Kangas family includes Mark, David, Karen and Michael.

5 and 6 are vacant woodlots owned by L. Dal Bello and B. Gaetan, respectively.

Twenty-six acres, including the stone homestead and farm buildings, were sold to Murray E. Brand-stater, M.D. at McMaster Medical Centre and his wife, Karen, in 1972. They and their children, Zoe, Justin and Nathan, came from Australia in 1968.

Lot 1, northwest, Concession 1

Duncan Cameron of Lot 2, northwest, formally purchased this lot in May 1885. Two years later the lot was divided lengthwise and Duncan sold the northeast side, along the Town Line, to his brother, Donald, of Lot 2, southeast. Duncan and Donald were sons of Archibald Cameron, Sr. of Lot 3.

Later, the northeast half was owned by Donald's son, Archie D., and still later, by the youngest son, John P. It was sold to Edward and Helen Dredge in 1955 and to the H.R.C.A. in 1964. No one ever lived permanently on this lot which still has much forest. However, about 1919-20, Archie D. sold lumber to Gilbertson who set up a sawmill northwest of the railway. Mr. Gilbertson put up temporary homes for himself and his employees, Lickers, 1920, Vanfleet and Thibeau, 1922. Children from this lumber camp attended Mountsberg school.

The southwest half remained with Duncan's heirs until sold by James, the last of the family, in November 1960 to John King. This, too, was sold to H.R.C.A. in 1964.

Lot 2, southeast and front of Lot 3 Canada Company

In 1840, or earlier, Joseph Dixon (1799-1875) settled on the southeast 100 acres of Lot 2. By 1850, he reduced his claim to the southeast 50 acres, at which time he had 30 acres cleared. Job Mason worked on the other 50 until it was bought, in 1853, by John White who held it a year before selling to Joseph Lynn of Lot 1, thus making it a part of a 150-acre Lynn farm.

Joseph Dixon had the deed for his 50 acres in 1853, and stayed there until June 1861, when he sold his land to Donald Cameron, son of Archibald, Sr. In 1870, Donald bought the front 50 of Lot 3 from his aunt, Mrs. Duncan Cameron, giving him a 100-acre farm with a two-lot frontage on the 13th Concession Road. In the meantime, he had married and lived for a time in the Dixon cabin before building the brick house, now the Singleton home.

Donald Cameron (1830-1900) was married twice. His first wife, Catherine Campbell, died about 1871. They had one child, Jessie (1866-1959), who married Alex MacLean of Badenoch. Annie McKenzie (1848-1925), the second wife, a sister of Mrs. Peter MacPherson, was the mother of the following family: *Archibald D.* (1874-1943)—unmarried; *Duncan* (1876-1908)—unmarried; *Annie* (1879-1907)—unmarried; *Donald (Dan)* **(1881-1969)**—unmarried, lived in Yorkton, Saskatchewan from 1905 to 1964, when he returned to the home area; *Catherine (Kate)* (1883-1943)—married William Holmes of Campbellville. Helen, eldest of their three daughters, married Edward Dredge and later owned the Cameron farm; *James* (1885-1886); *Lillie Belle* (1887-1888; *John P.* (1889-1968)—unmarried, a teacher, was in Western Canada from time to time, later lived with his niece, Helen, on the home farm.

Donald Cameron was a Township Councillor in 1891 and 1892. After his death, his son, Archie D., ran the farm during his lifetime. It passed to John P. in 1951 and, in 1955 was sold to Helen and Edward Dredge who moved there from Esquesing Township. Their family included: Elmer, married to Barbara Revell and living in a home, built in 1959, near the road; Douglas and his wife, Millie, for several years lived across the road on Lot 1, Conc. 12, moved to Campbellville; Marilyn is in Burlington.

Dredges sold the farm late in 1967 and after an auction sale in March 1968, moved to Campbellville. Helen died in 1975; Edward in 1977.

William Bebluk, the new owner, divided the 100 acres into 10-acre parcels. Most lots had one or two early buyers who merely held land. Following are the residents, moving southwesterly:

In Lot 2
- Vincenzo *DiRado*, only owner, farms the land, keeps a few animals; built a garage and barn.
- Third owners, Robert and Ann *Wignall*, bought the lot in 1974, built a house in 1975 and in 1977 put up a barn for their horses. They have two children, Bonnie and Geoffrey.
- Next is the lot and home of Elmer and Barbara *Dredge*. Their house was built in 1959 when the land was separated from the Dredge farm. They have two daughters, Michele and Cheryl and a son, Richard.
- Charles and Joyce *Head*, third owners, bought in 1974 and built a house and stable that year. Their family includes Pauline (Mrs. R. Ogden) and Barbara (Mrs. Peter Beaton).
- Francis and Rena *McGroty*, second owners, bought in 1972. Natives of New Brunswick, with children, Patrick, who married Jane Finlayson, Bernard, Stephen, Esther (Mrs. James Carroll) and Roger, they moved here from Mountsberg Road where they had lived from 1965 to 1972. They built a new house and barn.

- Well back from the road, George and Joan *Singleton* live in the Cameron homestead. In their family are: Carol, who married Michael Slacer; Howard, married to Laura Slacer; and Nicholas.

Continuing in Lot 3
- The first lot is vacant.
- Peter and Jane *Pettingill* with children, Christopher and Heather, are second owners. They bought their lot in 1972 and built the house the following year.
- Wayne and Jane *Rayner,* also second owners, bought the lot in 1973 and built their house that year. They have a daughter, Teresa, and son, Timothy.
- David and Marion *Wood* have two lots or 20 acres. They bought the land in 1973 and, in 1975, moved to their new home from the corner of the Town Line and Mountsberg Road. Access to their house is from the Cameron lane. They have two daughters, Laurie (Mrs. Garry Law) and Cindy.

Lot 2, northwest

Duncan Cameron (1827-1904), son of Archibald, Sr. was working on this lot a few years before getting his deed in 1853. He married Janet Campbell who had come from Scotland at age 10, along with brothers and sisters, to live with relatives. Romance began during the daily hike of more than a mile to and from the old log school. Duncan, being about six years older, probably attended school according to his being needed at home for farm work. There was no wedding until the mid-1850s when Janet was about 20. Their family follows: *Annie* (about 1858-1941)—the survivor of twins; *Archibald* (about 1860-1933); *Robert* (born about 1863)—killed by a fall from a tree when a young boy; *Jessie* (1865-1944)—married W.B. Cockburn of Guelph; *James* (about 1867-1962); *Duncan* (1870-1953); *Colin* (1872-1953)—a dentist in Apollo, Pennsylvania, married a Canadian, no children; *Isabel (Bella)—died* in 1925.

All, except Jessie and Colin, never married and remained on the farm.

The first house was built of logs. With a coat of plaster it stood beside and became part of the stone house of the early 1860s. The site was remote and picturesque, but the Credit Valley Railway changed all that when it pushed its way through between the house and barn, and cut off access to the 14th Concession. The barn, with no basement, was moved to the southeast side of the tracks and placed on a foundation that provided stables. And so it became a "bank barn".

Other adjustments were required when trains clattered by trailing veils of smoke. The Cameron house, on the very verge of the right-of-way, lived with the ever-present threat of fire. Its people suffered noise and smoke pollution without ever having heard of that common term of today. Since then, a long lane beside the tracks, through Lot 1, leads to the Town Line.

After living alone many years, James (Jimmy), the last remaining member of the family, sold the farm, including the 50 acres in Lot 1, to John King, in November 1960, but Jimmy lived out his days in his lifetime home. Part of the time Jessie's daughter, Margaret, stayed with him; he died in 1962.

In December 1964, the property was bought by the H.R.C.A. The stone house was vacant for a time, before becoming headquarters for the H.R.C.A. The barn is used. Outbuildings were removed to salvage boards as large as 18 feet by 18 inches. The new Wildlife Interpretive Centre is south of the house and, to the west, the man-made Mountsberg Lake laps at the railway embankment. A caretaker lives in the house. Since 1974, that position has been held by Martin Wernaart, with his wife, Toni, and three sons, Andrew, Michael and Robert.

Lot 3, all, Concession 13   Clergy Reserve

The Cameron story began here, in 1833. Two brothers, Archibald and Duncan, both young and married, left Perthshire, Scotland, and, via Dundas, found their way to Lot 3, to establish Canadian homes. Archibald chose the northwest hundred acres and Duncan, the southeast half. Their early dwellings were fairly close. In fact, Archibald built his so close to his southeast line that the re-survey of 1836 put him over the line onto Duncan's property. It didn't create a problem. Even when Archibald put up a new brick house, it was in almost the same place. But, by then, they may have mapped out changes that were to take place.

Later Cameron families all were descended from Archibald. Duncan (1793-1870) and his wife, Isabella, born about 1800, had no children. Information regarding Archibald's family is limited. He was born about 1791; his wife, Janet McLaren, about 1795. Both lived to a good old age. Several of their children were born in Scotland. The family follows but the order of members is unknown: *Isabella* (born about 1826)—married James Campbell of Lot 1, Conc. 12; *Duncan* (1827-1904)—of Lot 2, northwest, adjoining; *Donald* (1830-1900)—of Lot 2, southeast adjoining; *Janet* (born about 1833)—unmarried, kept house for brother, Archie; *Archibald* (born about 1838)—unmarried, remained on the farm, died in 1908; *Margaret*—married name was McKenzie; *Annie—married; Christina*—married a McLean of Badenoch, grandmother of Annie Clark (Mrs. George Stewart).

The Cameron brothers received their deeds from the Canada Company in August 1845. In 1870, Isabella, widow of Duncan, sold her 100 acres to her nephews, Donald and Archibald. Donald added the front 50 to the front 50 of Lot 2 where he had his home. Isabella retained for her lifetime use the quarter-acre where her log cabin stood. (Later history of this 50 acres is told with Lot 2). The rear 50 went to Archibald Jr. to add to the 100 acres of Lot 3 northwest.

In early times, the Camerons reached their homes by using the trail through the Campbell property of Lot 4. In 1908, after the death of Archibald Jr., a 33-foot lane was separated from the southwest side of the land, then owned by Donald's son, Archie D., to give access to the rear 150 acres. John Kennedy, then on Lot 4, was accorded a right-of-way over the lane.

With a concentration of four Archibald Camerons, it was inevitable that a means of identifying them would come about. Archibald Jr. was long known as "Foxy Archie". The nickname bore no connotation of cupidity, but was a tribute to his expertise in hunting foxes. Donald's son was always "Archie D." and, by reason of location, Duncan's son was "Railroad Archie". Makes one speculate on the possibilities if any one or all three of these Archies had married.

Duncan, son of Duncan of Lot 2 northwest, unmarried, owned the 150 acres from 1908 to 1939. At times the brick house was rented or used by hired men. About 1916, Henry Donovan (a great grandson of pioneer John Revel) began working for Duncan. Two Donovan boys, Roy and Clark, attended Mountsberg school. Archie was their younger brother.

David Campbell (1857-1920) who once owned Lot 4, northwest, rented the Cameron house in 1920. He had married Ellen Castell (1875-1966) a Hamilton teacher, and lived in Carlisle and Hamilton. While in Carlisle, about 1907, a daughter, Margaret, their only child at the time, died at age seven. David died soon after moving back to Mountsberg with his wife and younger children, Dorothy (now Mrs. W.F. Guenther) and Jim, both in Hamilton. They and their mother remained there a few years.

William MacLaren bought the northwest 100 plus 23 acres from Duncan Cameron in 1939 and resold to James H. MacLaren in 1945. In 1955, it was bought by Remi and Blanche Desender. They had arrived from Antwerp, Belgium earlier with family: Gabriele, Gerald and Georgette, also George and Mary who married and lived elsewhere. The family went into the turnip waxing business using a machine invented by the son, Gabriele. Also, they raised poultry on a large scale and put up a cold storage building for their products. Fire destroyed some of their buildings and they left the farm in 1962. For two years, the property was owned by George and Elizabeth Chapman (and occupied by Mr. Thibodeau, a son-in-law) before becoming part of the lands of the H.R.C.A. in 1964. Mike Pasuta of Lot 4 now owns about 25 acres at the southeast end of the farm acquired in an exchange with the H.R.C.A. for land on Lot 4.

Conservation personnel make use of the former Cameron home, the present occupants being John and Sue Hall, and son, Peter.

Lot 4, Concession 13   **Brock Grant**

Settlement of our northwesterly part of East Flamborough began here. A Campbell family with several grown sons left their home in Perthshire, Scotland, and found their way to Lot 4, in 1832. That much is known, but their story has blank spaces. Parents are believed to have been Alexander and Jane (born 1791). A son, Archibald, spent his life on this land. Two brothers seem to have been James and Peter.

A Wentworth Historical Society publication of 1892 contains a first hand account by John Glasgow of his family's arrival in Hamilton from Scotland, in 1832, and the next year, locating on Lot 5, Concession 5 of East Flamborough. They were three miles from the nearest road in untouched wilderness. In the spring of 1834, they needed a proper chimney and "had heard that a family named Campbell had settled on the 13th Concession and that one of the brothers was a mason." He decided to look him up, and made the trip on foot. "I found my way to Carlisle very well, for the trees were blazed all the way. But, from the 9th to the 13th Concessions, I had no mark to guide me." He described his return trip, much of it after dark, as a "life and death struggle."

By 1853, Archibald and his wife had a deed for the entire 200 acres of Lot 4. Family of Archibald Campbell (1808-1894) and Martha Bowman (1819-1878), also a Scot: *Archibald* (1845-1928)—married Sarah Isabella Wingrove, daughter of James; *Euphemia* (1847-1929) — married William Emmons, lived in Mountsberg area; *Catherine* (1850-1868); *Alexander* (born 1853)—married Margaret (Maggie) Gunston of Nassagaweya; *Margaret* (1855-1919)—married David McKenzie; *David* (1857-1920)—married Ellen Castell of Hamilton (died in 1966 in her 92nd year), became owner of the northwest part of the lot; *Elizabeth* (born 1860)—married George Agnew of Campbellville.

Archibald Sr. was married a second time to Catherine Lumsden, a widow with a family.

The Southeast Part

Later, in 1853, Archibald Campbell sold 50 acres beside the 13th Concession Road to Jacob Wright who had 50 acres across the road on the 12th Concession. For a few years, about this time, Solomon Dawson's family lived as tenants in a house that preceded the present Watson home.

Mr. Wright sold the timber to James Gage, in 1857, and, in 1873, sold the 50 acres back to the Campbells, along with his 50 acres across the road. Archibald Jr. lived there until 1881 when he moved to Lot 9, Concession 12. At that time, Alexander (Sandy) took over the 50 acres in the home farm, also the half-lot to the northwest, less 10 acres at the north corner, on which stood the Campbell homestead. Thus the original 200 acres were divided into two parts of 90 and 110 acres.

The Sandy Campbells had two daughters: Mina, who married Norman Mills of Carlisle where they operated a general store for many years, and Ethel who married William Bell and lived in Campbellville, then Toronto. In 1922, Mr. and Mrs. Campbell sold the 90 acres to Allan Eaton, and went to live with Mina. George Eaton, son of Allen, with his wife and three boys, Douglas, Gordon and Jack, lived there until about 1935.

In 1937, John (Jack) and Florence Watson moved there from Lot 9, bought the farm and remained. In their family are: Patricia, who married Frank Smuk of Peter's Corners; Ross, on the farm; and Bette, who married Donald Berry of Fleetwood Farms, Mount Hope. Ross and his wife, Lynn Stacey, built a new house in 1972 at the south corner of the farm. They have two children, Kelly and Kevin.

The Northwest Farm

David Campbell sold his 110 acres to John and Janet (Hunter) Kennedy in 1905. The Kennedys had come from Dumfries, Scotland, in 1881 and had lived in near neighbourhoods. Of a family of eight, only three younger members were associated with this farm: Nellie (1880-1954); (Mrs. Peter McPhail); James (1882-1941) and Elizabeth (1886-1975).

When the Campbell family owned the entire 200 acres, access to the rear part was by a trail through forest and field from the 13th Road. This arrangement continued with the Kennedys, until 1914, when they obtained an official right-of-way from Duncan Cameron on the southwest side of Lot 3, to be used jointly.

On May 18, 1933, John Kennedy observed his 100th birthday; his death occurred in August of that year. Mrs. Kennedy (1849-1937) lived out her years there with Jim and Elizabeth. Jim died in 1941.

During the following eight years, the farm was worked for short periods by the McPhails, Jack Watson, a Maitland family and Fawcett Eaton. In 1949, Elizabeth sold the place to Michael (Mike) and Stephanie (Stella) Pasuta, and lived in Campbellville until her death in 1975.

Members of the Pasuta family are: Kenneth (1950-1973); Robert, who married Elaine Smith of Mountsberg; Susannah (Susie) and Linda.

The boundaries of the farm changed in 1965 when a large acreage at the northwest end was released to the H.R.C.A. in exchange for its equivalent from Lot 5, alongside the Pasuta land. Pasutas also now own some property on Lot 3 to the northeast, giving a total of 121 acres. As well, they rent about an equal amount of land nearby.

Mike and Stella built a new house for themselves in 1976-7. It is not far from the old Campbell homestead where Robert and Elaine, with son, Robert and daughter, Brandy, now live.

Lot 5, Concession 13. The McCrae Place   Brock Grant

In 1850, this 200 acre lot was assessed as uncleared land under the name of McLean and Clark. For some years before then, these men operated a water-powered sawmill on the 12 Mile Creek, near the 14th Concession. In 1855, George Clark obtained a deed to this Brock land, through John H. Cameron, seven months after Mr. Clark had given John Thompson and Thomas Mc-Crae lumber rights to the 200 acres. In 1859, it was listed as Thompson, McCrae and Co., operating two sawmills, one water-power and one steam. That same year, Thomas McCrae bought the Thompson share and the 76-year saga of "The McCrae Place" began.

Thomas McCrae:
1820—Born in Lauristen, Kirkcudbright (Kur-coo-bray) Shire, Scotland.
1841—Came to Canada.
1842—Returned to Scotland where he married Jane Campbell on March 15.
1849—Returned to Guelph along with his wife and two small children; also his parents, David (1800-1878) and Mareon (pronounced Marron) Munro (1793-1893). Thomas became a bookkeeper in Guelph.
1853—Along with David Anderson, he established the first lumber yard in Guelph.
1855—With John Thompson, he began a sawmill business in East Flamborough.
1863—Moved to a farm southwest of Guelph, which he named Janefield Farm in honour of his wife.
1866—As the pine began to give out in East Flamborough, he went into a woollen business in Guelph, known first as Armstrong, McCrae & Co., later as Guelph Woollen Mills.
1892—Died at Janefield.

Family of Thomas and Jane McCrae: *William* **(1842-1844);** *David* (1845-1930)—succeeded to the East Flam-borough farm; *Margaret* (born 1847)—married Rev. Robert Leask, a Presbyterian; *Daughter* (unnamed) —born April 8, 1849 at sea on the "Emperor" and died 10 days later. A pathetic family story tells how Jane tried to conceal the death of the baby to prevent burial at sea, to no avail; *Mareon* (1850-1853); *William* (1853-1930)—lived on the East Flamborough farm; *Jane* (1855-about 1935)—known as Jeanie, married Alex Matthews. Her scrapbook of newspaper items, etc. relating to family, have been the source of much of the family history.

In January 1870, David married Janet Simpson Eckford, daughter of Rev. John Eckford of Bruce County; she died in 1921. Long before David became owner of Lot 5, on the death of his father, in 1892, he and his brother, William, had been assuming much of the responsibility. David's special interest was the army. He had the rank of Lieut.-Col., but was always called "Colonel". He was active in the South African War and again in W.W. I at age 70. Family of David and Janet McCrae: *Thomas*—a medical doctor, professor of medicine at Jefferson Medical College, Philadelphia. Married Amy Marion Gwyn, daughter of Col. H.C. Gwyn of Dundas, they had no children. He collaborated with Dr. William Osler, a relative of his wife, to write medical books, the last McCrae owner of the farm.

John (Nov. 30, 1872 to Jan. 28, 1918)—unmarried. Although he had a brilliant career in medicine, he is best remembered for his poem In Flanders Fields, written three years before his death. *1894*—graduated in biology at University of Toronto; *1898*—graduated in medicine with a gold medal and scholarships in pathology and physiology; *1899-t902*—served with the artillery in the Boer War, South Africa, as a major; *1902-1914*—spent some time in Toronto General Hospital and John Hopkins Hospital in Baltimore. Became associated with three hospitals in Montreal and lectured at McGill University, wrote medical textbooks; *1914*—became a member of the Royal College of Surgeons, London, England, had a second textbook on pathology published in Philadelphia, at the outbreak of war, was a medical officer at Valcartier; *1915—in* charge of the McGill Hospital unit as Lieut.-Col. with the troops in France; *1918*—appointed Consulting Physician to the British armies with the rank of full

Colonel, but died of pneumonia before assuming office, buried at Wimereux, France.

Geills (pronounced Jeels)—married Chief Justice Kilgour of Manitoba and lived in Winnipeg. Of four children, one, Katherine, married Dr. Donald Campbell of Hamilton.

William, brother of David, the only McCrae to live on Lot 5, managed the farm. He went there when first married. After four years, he left for a short time, but returned to remain for a long period. His wife was Jessie Bell Hood; born Bell but adopted by her stepfather, Mr. Hood. She died in March 1928.

Family of William and Jessie McCrae: *Mary*—married Archibald McCorkindale; *Thomas Gideon*—married Agnes Haddon, died October 1933; *Jessie*—married Robert McCorkindale; *David* (died March 1931)—married Jessie McIntosh, they had two children: Flora (Mrs. Douglas Cleghorn of Guelph) and Alex, who had two children—his son, David, the third David McCrae, became the only "McCrae".

The Lumber Era

Looking southeast in Lot 5, Concession 13 at the McCrae chimney and the railway. *Mrs. D. Croft.*

A tall chimney stands alone in a grassy meadow, south of the 14th Concession, not far from the Mountsberg Conservation Lake. The obelisk of faded brick is a fitting memorial to the once-busy site of the steam sawmill and its complement of buildings which then sprinkled the area between the mill and the 14th Concession. There were, besides the main house, three or four small houses for the 20 or more employees, and stables for the horses.

The early years were very busy. With the old water-powered mill still in use, the two mills turned out the lumber for all the stores on Lower Wyndham Street in Guelph; for the Market House and all the principal buildings that went up in Guelph at that time. When Thompson & McCrae bought Lot 5, they also took over, from McLean & Clark, timber rights on Lot 1, southeast, Concession 12, owned by John Haines. This 100 acres had an excellent stand of pine, some of which became ship masts. The Company also did sawing for local people. In 1855, when James and Adam McCurdy (Lot 10, northwest, Concession 13) replaced their log cabin with a frame house, they hauled their own logs to the mills to be sawn.

In 1861, William Moffat was the superintendent with 20 employees. Two were women; cooks, no doubt. The men were all young; five were married, and only two were over 30. Of the various lists of employees in the 1860s, only a few names were constant: Alex Sinclair, Kenneth McLeod, Robert Porter, Michael Welsh, James and William Leith.

With gruesome fascination, a neighbourhood story persists like an aura around the old chimney. Whether the years added a bit of fiction to fact, is uncertain; but the account, as handed down in founding families, is that, near the end of the lumbering business, a workman fell on a circular saw and was so horribly injured that he lived only a few hours. He managed to get to his nearby house and, knowing full well that only moments were left to him, he made and signed a will. Later, a witness of the tragedy was giving an on-the-scene demonstration of how the accident happened. He was too graphic; too accurate. He, too, suffered the same fate.

Another legend says that the brick chimney was destined to be the basis of a woollen mill. Maybe, Thomas McCrae did consider it. It was in 1866 that he established a woollen mill in Guelph. Or, it may have been just a fond hope of the local people.

Pine, for which the demand was greatest, gave out and lumbering came to a close about 1870. There followed a decade or more in which some land was cleared mainly in the northwest hundred and was used for general farming. It was probably in this period that the barn was built.

McCraes—Importers and Breeders of Registered Stock

About 1860, Thomas McCrae became interested in stock-breeding. On his Guelph farm he bred Herefords, Shorthorns, and Polled Angus cattle, as well as Cotswold and Southdown sheep and Clydesdale horses.

Besides all these there were the Galloways, placed on the East Flamborough farm about 1880, and where they remained for half a century. They represented the oldest herd of Galloway cattle to be established in North America. At first, the imported Galloways were herded from the Guelph farm during the night when the Brock Road (Highway 6) was quiet.

Early in this period a shipment of 100 cattle, "the best herd of Galloways ever to leave Scotland", crossed the Atlantic in the "Brooklyn" which foundered off Anticosti Island. The animals all milled about the sinking ship and, exhausted, only 30 were able to swim to shore. Even on shore, misery was not over for the survivors. They are claimed by salvors, had their feet tied together and were rolled down the bank into water and loaded on rafts. McCraes were forced to buy back their own cattle, but were able to get only three bulls and seven heifers; the others had gone to Nova Scotia.

A shipment the following year suffered disaster of a different kind. The cattle developed disease, were put into quarantine and 57 head had to be destroyed. Further importing was curtailed and the stock on hand was used to build up the herd.

In 1874, the Credit Valley Railway, now the C.P.R., bought a right of way through the northwest end of the 13th Concession. In Lot 5, it crowded close to the dam that had provided water for the mills. By 1880, trains were running. McCraes had their own station on a 100-year agreement. It was an open sided structure, several steps high on the north side of the tracks, and was a flag stop for anyone who cared to walk to its inconvenient location. The stock loading ramp was across the tracks from the station.

William McCrae managed the farm for many years. Other managers followed, among them, Mr. William Fisher in 1889 and Mr. Aiken. George McIntosh, the last one, was there for a long period, prior to 1931, when the McCrae epoch came to an end. That was when Archie Scott of Puslinch bought the 200 acres from Dr. Thomas McCrae of Philadelphia and lived there about 10 years.

Over the years, the many buildings on the McCrae place gradually disappeared. The unused steam mill, still standing in the mid-'80 s, left the scene in the following decade. Houses went, too. In 1917, two houses were left: one two-storey log and one frame. Charles Hewins bought the frame house and razed it for lumber. It was the place where Donald Kennedy, who had a stumping machine, lived for a time in the 1880s when there was plenty of call for his services.

When Archie Scott (1900-1953) bought all of Lot 5, in 1931, he had the barn, newest of the buildings, removed. The first McCrae flag station had been burned and its replacement was moved to a Badenoch farm and used as a chicken house. The last building, the old family home, was burned about 1940, while vacant. For years, small heaps of stone marked its site near the 14th road.

Archie Scott had disposed of the southeast half of the lot in 1935. In August 1964, his widow, Marv. sold the northwest half to the H.R.C.A. That same year, the H.R.C.A. traded almost 50 acres at the south end of their newly acquired lot to Mike Pasuta of adjoining Lot 4, for acreage at the north end of his farm.

And now, this land that has seen many changes, serenely accepts its new regime. Time has erased the symbols of its past. All but one. The faded rose shaft of the tall brick chimney still stands, remote and lonely; a little aloof from the activity around the new Mountsberg Lake. (I am indebted to Mrs. Douglas Cleghorn of Guelph, formerly Flora McCrae, great granddaughter of Thomas, the pioneer, for details of the McCrae family tree and other interesting information. Mrs. Cleghorn is custodian of the family bible and the voluminous scrapbooks kept by her great aunt, Jeanie.)

—Merle Hewins Cust

Lot 5, Concession 13, southeast half

Until recently, no one ever lived permanently on this 100 acres, although there are known to have been cabins or shacks for temporary use. Before 1934, it was largely covered with timber, mostly hardwood with some pine. The west corner had a swampy section where the 12-Mile Creek entered, and, in the high north corner, were a few acres of tilled land.

As long as McCraes owned the property, Galloway

cattle had the run of much of the 200 acres. When short of pasture, they often foraged through the forested section.

Oh, those Galloways! Black, hornless and in infinite numbers, they were an abomination in my early years on the next farm (Lot 6). It became routine procedure to check on their whereabouts from time to time, from our hilltop. With good reason.

Inevitably, the time came when the cattle paused at the sunny south fence, a much-mended barricade of stumps, stones and rails. They looked with envy at our growing grain and green pastures, and plotted their course. No fence could withstand a herd of determined Galloways.

The alarm went out, "McCrae's cattle are in!" and, away we went with dogs and sticks. They were scary, half-wild animals, and usually ran way from us, but sometimes one, either defiant or curious, would turn and stand and stare. And I froze with terror and stared back.

Usually, we called them McCrae's cattle; sometimes, the Galloways. But, in times like this when they ignored line fences, they were the black devils; an epithet first bestowed on them by my usually mild mother, in a moment of utter frustration.

The Galloways had disappeared before Archie Scott bought the property in 1931. Other changes came about, almost insidiously; changes that eventually erased a forest. Back about 1915, David McCrae gave timber rights to Murray Crawford of Campbellville, for all large trees, the diameter to be above a specified size. A camp was set up and the woods thinned out. This selective lumbering altered only slightly the character of the woodland and the overall scene.

The respite lasted until Archie Scott, in 1934, sold the 100 acres to John A. McAllister of Guelph. Then, in a few short months, a magnificent and ageless forest was stripped and reduced to a barren wasteland of brush heaps. In November of the same year, Archie Scott bought back the land, and the following year sold it to Burdge Gunby. It became Archie Gunby's grazing range as rotting stumps and scrub growth gave no hint of past dignity.

Archie Gunby died in December 1974. The following year the lot was sold from the Burdge Gunby estate to Wrentham Developments; all except the building lot of more than an acre at the east corner, sold to Lena E. Gunby (Mrs. Archie Gunby). In 1976, Cecil Gunby, the youngest son of Archie and Lena, acquired the lot and built a home for himself and his wife, Teresa Simon.

Elizabeth I. Neil bought the large acreage in 1978, and in 1979 sold to Judith A. Emmert who promptly began to build a house southwest of the creek, well back from the 13th Concession Road.

McCrae's Bush...As I Remember It

This was our forest primeval, complete with murmuring pines and hemlocks. Within its quiet gloom, it was easy to imagine the land around as our ancestors first beheld it; or even when Indians roamed the region. It was a beautiful forest, mostly of hardwoods, tall and straight in its shaded depths. But, beside the concession road, where the trees basked in the morning sunshine, they grew broad and luxuriant. There, the heavy foliage leaned to brush the rails of the snake fence. It was much the same along the southwest side where banks of leafy branches formed a handsome backdrop for our fields. And, just inside the fence, the cattle kept a path well packed.

In the south corner, pines grew in a grove, ankle-deep in soft needles. There, one could pause, breathe deeply the heady air and eavesdrop on sibilant sighs, as the pines gossiped with the passing breeze.

The Twelve-Mile curved through the heart of the woodland. In it we saw, not a foot of water, but one hundred foot trees in reverse, reaching for a fathomless sky, where little clouds of pure white fluff moved lazily across the bluest of blue heavens. For games, small outcroppings of dark, mossy rock, deep-shadowed even at noon, served as story-book caves.

When tired, we could sit on a fallen log, in silence, and watch frisking squirrels, scampering chipmunks, nervous brown cotton tails and darting birds. If we were lucky, a fox with streaming brush, flashed a red-gold streak through a maze of the tree trucks. If we were very lucky and very quiet, we might see some of the forest children; fat young groundhogs or juvenile foxes frollicking like puppies, in a sunny glade.

Seen from our hill, the expanse of tree tops made a resplendent picture that varied with the seasons. In May, it was the Spirit of Springtime in fresh, variegated greens, with accents of dark pine. In autumn, the blazing red and gleaming gold, heavily pencilled with the pines, fairly took one's breath away.

However lovely to look at from afar, spring also meant a forest floor carpeted with trilliums; hepaticas to be found around decaying logs and tree roots, and water cress in the creek. And, in the fall, we knew where to find two butternut trees.

So well remembered; memory aided by a living souvenir from my Enchanted Forest. A maple that had its roots in McCrae's Bush, was transplanted to our small, city lot in 1924.

It was many years before I read John McCrae's sad but profoundly beautiful sonnet "The Dying of Pere Pierre." I saw the tall trees of McCrae's Bush as a "cathedral nave". I like to imagine that, perhaps, John McCrae, too, thought of those same stately tree trunks when he wrote:

> "..they made his grave,
> *Below the altar of the hills; and night*
> *Swung incense clouds of mist in creeping lines*
> *That twisted through the tree trunks, where the light*
> *Groped through the arches of the silent pines."*

Lot 6, southeast, Concession 13   Clergy Reserve Lot
Maple Bank Farm

In 1867, John Hewins purchased this 100 acres in Concession 13, across the road from his own farm buildings on Concession 12. Francis Kerr, a land surveyor of Guelph, had bought it from the Crown in April 1850, with no thought of using it himself. At that time, surveyors, who knew the land better than any one since the Indian era, were encouraged to promote and assist in the sale of lots.

This seems to have been the case with the farm's original settler, John Gant (also seen as Ghent) who had gone there about 1840 or earlier. In May 1850 he was issued a deed from Francis Kerr. John Gant and his wife, Elizabeth, lived in a small cabin near the road, on the northeast side of the present lane, and had a log barn near the site of the present horse barn. They cleared about 30 acres and owned horses, cattle, pigs, and sheep. In 1853, the Gants sold their land to James Hurren of Centre Road who, in turn, passed it on to his son, Philip, in 1863.

During the Hurren ownership, John Borer, Sr. and his wife moved from Guelph and lived there eight or 10 years. Mr. Borer set up a whip saw (pit saw) in the middle of the farm and produced much of the lumber for early buildings on this and nearby farms.

A whip saw requires a deep hold dug in the ground, preferably on a hillside. The log to be sawn is placed across the pit in a holding device. One man stands below the log, another man above, and the two pull a long rip saw up and down, to slice a log into boards.

The Borers lived in a new log cabin which stood about 100 feet west of the present house. It was the birth place of some of their family. They moved to the Rock Chapel area in 1861.

John Hewins' son, Aaron (1847-1905) married Christine Falconer (1852-1943) of Morriston, in September 1870, and the Borer cabin became their first home. Their children were: *Charles* (1873-1941)—married Annie Laking (1872-1950), daughter of John; *Margaret Ann* (1875-1963)—married Charles Laking, son of Joseph; *Georgina* (1877-1946)—un-married; *Mary* (1881-1944)—married James Spring of Toronto.

There was still much forest on the farm and in the surrounding area in 1870. Christine told of an incident when she was a bride in the log cabin. One dark evening she answered a knock on the door to find her brother-in-law, Ralph, who acted so strangely she thought he was joking. But it was no joke. Ralph has lost his way in the bush, and wandered for hours. At night he made his way to a lighted window. Thinking he was miles away, he was too dazed to recognize either the cabin or his sister-in-law. He could scarcely believe that he was but a few hundred feet from his own home.

Back of the cabin was a dug well, 50 feet to rock. As was common then, it had a roof, and water was drawn by a windlass and an oaken bucket attached to a long rope. The second well, nearer the brick house, also 50 feet to rock, was never satisfactory. It was hard to get water on the hilltop. Early in this century, a well-driller, Mr. Mooney of Freelton, attempted unsuccessfully to improve the well by drilling into the rock. Power was provided by a team of horses moving in a tight circle around the capstan. For years thereafter, a water supply was obtained from a 6-foot well at the base of the hill to the north. A windmill forced the water up 100 feet to a storage tank in the hayloft of a horse stable. From there it went by gravity to the house and barn. Now, water is pumped electrically to the buildings from a well, drilled to 129 feet, and located about 20 feet from the unfortunate second well.

The present 90 by 54 foot barn was built in 1909, using lumber from trees on the farm, sawn at Crawford's mill in Campbellville. The barn-raising was in June. All the neighbourhood men came to help, most of them bringing wives and children to present a scene as festive as a church garden party. Supper meant three settings at trestle tables the length of the lawn. This barn replaced a U-shaped complex of buildings, built in the period of 1855 to 1880, near the site of the early Gant barn. Some of this group were razed when the new barn went up, leaving two sections which still remain. At the base of the U was the main barn, its ramp now marked by the 1974 horse barn.

In 1874, Aaron and Christine, with one-year-old Charles, vacated the log cabin and moved into their new, one-and-a-half storey frame house which became the nucleus of the present home. A veranda almost encircled the house, to enter, from either way, a one-storey kitchen and woodhouse, at the rear.

To enhance the outlook, about 1880, a row of maple trees was planted beside the lane and the lawn. The maples were the inspiration for the name "Maple Bank" which Christine then chose for their farm. It was not until 1972 that a second row of maples was planted on the northeast side of the lane.

Hewins' Maple Bank Farm. *Mrs. W.C. Cust.*

The house saw change in 1884. The veranda was taken away. The kitchen was moved aside to become a summer kitchen and, in its place, a red brick, one-and-a-half storey wing was attached to the rear of the main house which was then bricked to match.

Charles and Annie were married in March 1895, and a few alterations were made to accommodate two families, Aaron keeping the front, older section. Thus it remained throughout the lifetime of Charles and during

Family of Charles and Annie Hewins; Morley, Charles, Merle, Annie, Roy and Reg sitting in front. **Mrs. W.C. Cust.**

the tenure of his son, Roy (1896-1968), a bachelor, and oldest of the family which included Merle who married William Cust of Hamilton; Morley, now of Warren, Michigan, who married Irene Hood (1901-1968) of Freelton, and Reginald, present owner with his wife, Violet Holloway of Toronto.

There was a day in November 1914 when the house barely escaped a flaming exit from the hilltop scene. It was Sunday morning. Charles and Annie were at church, while Roy was doing the morning chores at the stable, and keeping an eye on young brother, Reg, toddling about with him.

Roy happened to notice a man walking out the lane, wearing what looked suspiciously like his father's new overcoat. He went to the house to investigate and, on opening the kitchen door, was met with a small but fast-developing fire. A smoldering stick of wood had been taken from the kitchen stove and placed on the floor. Roy doused the flames, not a second too soon, then checked on the overcoat. It was gone.

Thus, time was lost; but in less than an hour, several concerned neighbours were helping to scour the local roads, looking for a strange man in a new overcoat. By mid-afternoon, they found him at Guelph Junction. No one had ever seen the black man before. While they guarded the two doors of the waiting room, their man escaped through the baggage room and was seen disappearing east along the track. The sheriff of Milton was notified, and the capture could have been a excerpt from a comic opera. The thief-arsonist actually went to the Milton jail to seek a night's lodging. He was, eventually, accorded three years of free bed and board in Kingston Penitentiary.

Reg and Vi became owners in 1960 and moved from Port Credit. For several years, Reg continued his work with Ontario Hydro in the System Supervisor's Office. They completely renovated the farm house and had a 3-car garage attached to the rear. There are two daughters, Linda, who married Wilfred Phillips and lives across the road on Hewins land (see Lot 7, Concession 12), and Dawn, who married David Sehl in 1973, a professional motorcycle racer. They live on the farm with Dawn's parents and breed thoroughbred horses.

Mixed farming best describes the work done by the various family owners. In 1867, when John Hewins bought the farm, most settlers could afford horses, although many still kept a team of oxen to help out at times. Though slow, oxen proved to be satisfactory work animals. It was not until the early years of the 20th century that they disappeared entirely from the farm scene. And about that time, it became popular to own a "driver", a lighter and faster horse to pull a buggy or a cutter, according to the season.

Early cattle on the farm were of a mixed breed, to supply beef, milk and butter. After Charles took over the work, he obtained some purebred Shorthorn (or Durham) cattle, and built up a quality herd. During the depression of the '30's, purebreds were allowed to fade into grade cattle, when the value of prime beef sank to five cents a pound. When Roy, son of Charles, ran the farm from 1940 to 1960, he bought Western beef calves and grazed and fed them for the beef market. Reg continued to do this when he took over the farm. By 1970, he chose to raise Herefords. Now, a herd averaging 60 head, grazes on land of this farm, and also on 45 acres of land originally settled by Cornelius Hewins on Lot 7 of the 12th Concession. This quarter lot has been annexed to Maple Bank farm since 1902.

In 1925, 3 acres of rocky land, beside the McCrae line fence, were planted with Norway pine seedlings. Additional plantings in 1964 filled in the empty spaces.

During most of the lifetime of Charles, the adjoining farm was owned by Col. David McCrae of the second generation and father of Thomas and John. In the late 1870's, when the Credit Valley Railway was pushing through the northwest parts of Lots 5 and 6, Charles, then 6 or 7, and curious, went back as often as permitted to watch the activity. Occasionally, an engineer would take Charles on the engine, when they went back towards Campbellville for a fresh load of construction material.

That was when Charles first knew the McCrae boys. He was two months younger than John. David McCrae's family never lived on their Flamborough farm, but during vactions from school, the boys were there from time to time, and Charles played with them, often in the bush. Even in his early years, John liked to express his thoughts and ideas. In those make-believe times, a certain rock served as his pulpit or stage, depending on his current interest. That rock still remains just where it was a century ago.

Lot 6, Concession 13, northwest

Francis Kerr held this half of Lot 6 until 1855 when he sold it to James Martin, one of a Badenoch family. In 1868, it was sold to Matthew Burns who, in turn, sold to James Scott in 1874. At that time, trees had been cut for lumber but very little farming had been done.

James Scott and his wife, Mary Murrison, with a growing family, had left their home in Aberdeenshire, Scotland, a few years previously. After a sojourn in St.

Thomas and two years in Hamilton, they bought the farm in East Flamborough. Their family included Alex, James, George, Jonathan, William, Margaret, John, Andrew and Mary. Alex and Margaret died in Scotland. *James*—a shoemaker, married and remained in St. Thomas; *George*—lived in St. Thomas, also Australia for a few years, but died at home; *Jonathan* (1850-1937)—married Janet Revell (see Lot 8, southeast, Concession 13); *William* (1852-1940)— unmarried, retired to the farm after being a section foreman for C.P.R.; *John* (1857-1932)—unmarried, remained on farm; *Andrew* (1862-1941)—married Mary McGeachy. For a period which included 1889, Andrew rented Lot 5, Conc. 14, later, owned and lived on a farm in Badenoch. In 1936, he was given title to the home farm. His family of boys (order uncertain) were William, George, Donald, Edward, John, James, Archie (later on Lot 5, Conc. 13) and Hugh, a medical doctor who practised in Morriston until his early death in 1941; *Mary* (1869-1935)—unmarried, remained on farm.

William was the last surviving Scott on the farm. After his death, the stone house, built by his family about 1875, had little use until the Andrew Scott estate sold the farm to Clarence (Barney) Warner and his wife, Lillian Pasel, in 1950. The Warners carry on mixed farming. Attached to their barn is the former drive shed of the Baptist Church. Family members are: Marie—married Stanley Kobylinski, lives in Dundas; James—married Doreen Proud, lives in Kitchener; Gerald—married Lois Kitchen, lives in Morriston.

Lot 7, Concession 13, southeast   Brock Grant

Thomas Revell left Lincolnshire in 1840, five years later than his family, and went directly to his chosen lot. Ten years later, he held title to his 100 acres, which would remain Revell property until 1968.

On his way to Canada and East Flamborough, Thomas made friends with the Bush family, fellow travellers planning to settle in Caistor. He fell in love with the daughter, Anne, eldest of a family of eight. He said he would need a year to establish his farm and build a cabin. At the end of the year he would return and marry Anne.

So a year passed with not so much as a note passing between the young lovers. Six acres were cleared around a new log cabin when Thomas set out for Caistor. He found a minister along the way, and the two arrived at the Bush farm. Mr Bush came in from the field where we was working and, with no further fuss or bother, Anne married Thomas and left for her new home, where she spent the rest of her long life.

Family of Thomas Revell (1816-1889) and Anne Bush (1821-1903): Many birth dates approximate: *Mary Anne* (1842-1882)—married William Dougherty; *Martha* (1844-1892)—married William Laking; *Elizabeth* (1845-1871)— married George Allison; *Susan* (18461848); *John* (1847-1910)—unmarried; *George* (1848-   )—married Bella Anderson; *Delilah* (1850-   )—married Andrew Wise; *Emma* (1852-1874)—un-married; *William* (1854-   )—married Nellie Cole; *Evangeline* (1855-   )—married Judson Barlow;

Thomas and Anne Revell. *Mrs. H. Rennick.*

Matilda (1857-1911)—married John Cartwright; *Job* (1859-1926)—married Margaret Jane Haines; *Charles* (1862-1946)—married Phoebe Jane Hurren; *Janet (1865-1932)—married* Jonathan Scott.

The large brick house (now Rintoul's) was built about 1860 from the same basic plan as the John Hewins house. It replaced the log home which stood a short distance to the north. Later, this became the home of Charles, and his parents lived out their lives in the home they founded.

Thomas passed his lot on to his two youngest sons, Job and Charles, dividing it lengthwise into two 50-acre farms, facing the 13th Concession. Job had the northeast side without a house, but when he married Margaret Jane Haines in 1889, his bride designed her new home, the red roughcast house at the foot of the hill.

In 1904, Job sold his 50 acres to Charles and moved to Badenoch and, some years later, to the Fergus area. When William, son of Charles, married Mildred Dawson, in 1925, the Job Revell house became their home. In the meantime, it had been rented at intervals. Percy and Edith Smith lived there when first married in 1914, the year that Percy worked for Charles Revell.

Family of Job Revell (1859-1926) and Margaret Jane Haines (1869-1952): *Marshall* (1889-1962)— overseas in World War I, married an English girl, lived north of Guelph; *Annie* (1893-

Job Revell family; Margaret Jane, Annie, Marshall, Lillian and Job. *Wm. Revell.*

1959)—married Albert Pinkney, lived north of Guelph; *Lillian*—married W.J. McEvoy, lived in Woodburn, later in Dundas.

Family of Charles Revell (1862-1946) and Phoebe Jane Hurren (1869-1962): *Clara—married* Charles

Phoebe Jane and Charles Revell in front of Baptist Church, 1942. *Lloyd Gunby.*

Gunby, lived in Ottawa until retirement, later in Mississauga; *Lena—married* Albert Campbell, at Mountsberg until 1953, then Waterdown, now Mrs. H. Rennick; *Earl* (1903-1904); *William—married* Mildred Dawson, owned the farm until 1967; their family—William—married Elenore Neil of Chatham, Bill Jr. is a manager for International Harvester and lives in Burlington; Alice—married Ernest Ellis, in Westover; Elizabeth (Betty)—married Ronald Wilson, in Dundas; Barbara—married Elmer Dredge, see Lot 2, Concession 13.

Following the death of Charles Revell, Mrs. Revell lived alone in her home until the spring of 1954, when she moved to Waterdown to live with her daughter, Lena, a widow. At that time, the house and about 5 1/2 acres at the corner of the 13th Concession and Centre Road, were sold to Roy and Dorothy Rintoul of Dundas. Roy, a veteran of W.W. II, was married overseas to Dorothy Chambers of West Dalwich, South London. They have three sons: Ralph, a dentist in Burlington, married to a university classmate, Cheryl Kemp, D.D.S. and two younger boys, Richard and Raymond, at home.

The remainder of the farm was sold in the fall of 1967 and the following spring Bill and Mildred moved into their new home in Freelton.

The new owner, W. Bebluk, divided the property into 10 lots of similar size, for resale. Two parcels faced the 13th Concession. One, containing the red house and farm buildings, went directly to William and Renee Velke who moved in, with children Thomas and Vanessa, as soon as the house was vacated. The Velkes had left Germany about five years earlier.

The lot at the east corner of the farm, after a resale, was bought in 1969, by Murray and Sally Whibley who have three sons, Christopher, Michael and Timothy. A secondary building in the rear, a combination house and kennel, is occupied by Sally's sister, Patricia (Patti) Elliot and son, David; also their father, Cliff (Happy Gang) McKay; Mrs. McKay died in 1978.

Eight long, narrow lots facing the Centre Road are as follows, numbering from the Rintoul corner lot, north-westerly:

1. Bought by Anton and Kathleen Szelei in 1969. They built a house near the road the same year. Their two grown sons are away from home.
2. After passing through two ownerships, George and Anna Biegerl and family bought the lot in 1978 and began building a large house on high ground at the rear.
3. Stanley Hughes, an artist, bought the lot in 1968 and built his house himself, providing for a large studio. Living there also, is Joan Van Damme with children, Heidi, Laird, Anjel and Val.
4. Elio Mancini, a hair stylist, and his wife Thelma bought the lot in 1968 and built their house in 1972. They have two married daughters.
5. Owned by L. and P. Mazzucco; vacant.
6. Owned by S. and M. Mazzucco; vacant.
7. After two brief ownerships, the lot went to Greig Hand and his wife, Mary, a pharmacist in Freelton in

1970. They have two daughters, Anne Marie and Courtney, and a son, Greig. Their house, built in 1972, is set well back in the lot.

8. Dr. William T. Kellington, of the Freelton Family Medical Centre and his wife, Ena, were the third owners of this lot, bought in 1971. Since 1974, they have lived in their new home on high wooded ground near the north corner of the former farm. Their family: Elizabeth (Beth) married Cecil Buttenham, in Carlisle; Timothy married Mary Whetstone, in Freelton; Anne married Raymond Kearsley, in Freelton; Alan, at home.

Lot 7, northwest, Concession 13

William Johnson, son of Philip, chose this lot for a homestead when he married, about 1842. His first home was a one-storey log cabin. By 1857, he had his deed, and, in 1866, built the stone house still in use after many additions and changes.

Family of William Johnson (1819-1886) and his wife, Charlotte (1822-1896): Their first two children, Elizabeth and John, died before the others were born. They are buried in the Methodist Cemetery, as are the parents. Sarah Ann (born 1848) became Mrs. Green; Susan (born 1851) became Mrs. Inglehart of Stoney Creek; Philip (born 1852) a tinsmith in Morriston; George (born 1854) remained on the farm; Martha (born 1856) became Mrs. Hershiser of Lansing, Michigan; and Robert (born 1860).

When Mr. and Mrs. William Johnson retired at the home of their daughter in Michigan, George and his wife, Carrie, took over the farm. They had no children and, at times, shared their large home with other families. Mr. Vanderburgh, a teacher, lived there a while in the nineties, with his wife and family, including Stanley, Louella, Blanche, Laura and Eva. Later when William Moore married Katie MacPherson, daughter of Peter, they lived in this house a year or two. Here, their eldest child, Russell, was born.

George Johnson planted a large grove of English walnut trees southeast of the house. They flourished and for several decades were a landmark on the hilltop.

Some years after the railway went through, the township procured a right-of-way near the northwest end of the lot, to lead from Centre Road to the northeast, thus leaving a strip of land cut off from the main part of the farm.

Archibald Campbell of Mountsberg Road bought the property in May 1901. It became the home of his son, Albert E. (1882-1953) when he married Harriet E. Gunby (1881-1923), sister of Burdge. In their family were: John who married Beatrice Bousfield of Carlisle, and died in 1959; Olive, Mrs. Robert Hurren of Campbellville, died in 1962, and Irene, Mrs. Brock Howard, who lived a few years on Lot 3, northwest, Concession 12.

In 1906, Albert Campbell bought Lots 7 and 8 on Concession 14, to add to the strip of land left isolated by the new road. In the following year, the present barn was built on the home farm.

Albert Campbell, whose second wife was Lena Revell, died in March 1953 in the midst of plans to sell the farm and retire in Waterdown. Lena and their son, Bertram, went to Waterdown, and the combined properties went to Kenneth Wright. In a brief two-year ownership, two Wright children, Fraser and Martha attended Mountsberg School.

In 1955, John Easterbrook Q.C. and his wife, Edythe, bought the farms and made further changes to the house. Raising horses is the main farm interest. Mr. Easterbrook, who died in 1977, served on the township council from 1952 to 1967, beginning before they moved to Mountsberg from their former home, also in East Flamborough.

In the Easterbrook family are Terrence (Terry), Cheryl and Brock. Terry built a castle style house in an attractive woodland setting on the strip of land on Concession 13, near where the Centre Road branches to the northeast. A fire in 1977 left only the sturdy walls of the five-year-old building. It was rebuilt. Cheryl and her husband, Stewart Moon, live at Puslinch (See also Lot 7, Concession **14**). Brock and his wife, formerly Debbie Lemon of Burlington, and their two daughters, Ten-ille and Jacqueline, live in the stone farm house with

Mrs. John Easterbrook.

Lot 8, southeast, Concession 13 **Brock Grant**

Sometime in the 1830's, James/ Wheeler, an Englishman, settled on this 100 acres. As proof of his industry, by 1841 he had 60 acres under cultivation and owned two horses, as well as oxen, at a time when only eight other local farmers could afford the luxury of a team of horses.

Mr. Wheeler did not have a deed until 1854, but, by private arrangement, John Page took over the northeast 50, along Centre Road, thus dividing the farm lengthwise. Mr. Wheeler kept the southwest part with his 1 1/2-storey log house.

The Southwest Fifty

Set well back from the 13th Road (Regional Road 18) is the Wheeler's frame house which James Hurren helped build in the 1860's, its wooden walls now hidden under aluminum siding.

In 1841, there were, on the farm, James Wheeler (1794-1880) and his wife, Sarah Fowler (1797-1876) with two boys and four girls, not all of whom can be traced. *James Jr.* farmed on Lots 10 and 11 on Concession **11**; *Rachel*, born about 1834; *Harriet* (1836-1917), and *John* born about 1841, apparently left the area before he was 30.

After the death of her parents, Harriet, unmarried, ran the farm as long as her years permitted. Latterly, she was assisted by her niece, Mrs. Harriet Swim (18731924) who came to live with her.

Patrick McCarthy bought the 50 acres from Harriet Swim in 1919 and he, his mother and sister, Christina, lived in the Wheeler house a few years. In 1924, Pat sold the farm to his brother, Charles, who, four years later, sold to James Scott, then owner of the northeast 50. From time to time the house was rented. The Golden family went there about 1931, followed by Stan

Pat McCarthy. *Mrs. Lloyd Campbell.*

Woolsey. Jack and Florence Watson lived there two years before they bought part of Lot 4, Concession 13, in 1937, and switched dwelling places with the Legg family. The old Wheeler barn burned in the early 1940's.

In April 1946, James Scott sold 10 acres which included the house, to George and Frances Hambleton, the first of many changes of ownership. It went to Hermano and Maria Battjes in 1953; to Andor Szitas in 1961, and was rented to Peter Nantais; to Mr. and Mrs. Paul Schmitz in 1967. The present owners, Edward and Ruth Chechalk, came in 1969. Ruth's daughter, Ruth McDonald, lived with them until her marriage. Chechalks sold a building lot near the road, in 1974, to Ryck Van der Meulen, a builder. A house was built and sold the following year to Geoffrey and Rosemarie Edwards.

The Northeast Fifty

John Page worked this land for many years after the agreement with James Wheeler, but it was his son, Peter, who acquired a deed in 1863. In 1867, he sold the 50 acres to Philip Hurren who passed it on to Thomas Revell that same year. A son, John Revell, was assigned to this farm and had full title in 1873. The house, still there, was built in 1886. The first barn was burned by lightning, about 1904, and was replaced at that time. John, a bachelor, lived there alone until his death in 1910.

Jonathan Scott (1850-1937) and his wife, Janet Revell (1865-1932), a sister of John, had been living on Concession 10, East Flamborough, for many years. They bought the farm from John's estate and moved there in February 1911. Their three daughters later married and remained in the Mountsberg area. *Mary* married Fred Mast, *Nellie* married Clarence Wingrove, and *Annie* married Hugh Wigood. The only son, *James,* remained on the farm many years before moving to Mount Forest in late 1951 where he married Mary Ferguson, became a widower in 1962, and died in 1965 in this 65th year.

In the meantime, Hector and Flora Law of Flamborough Centre, bought the Scott farm from Charles McCarthy, in January 1953. With two daughters, Mary and Marjorie, they remained there until 1967.

John D. Campbell, retired President of Canadian Westinghouse and his wife, Ina, bought the farm from the Laws that year. In 1970, they divided the property, keeping 40 acres at the northwest end for themselves. A son, Colin D. and his wife, Lois, became owners of the remainder of the farm. They live in the renovated farmhouse of 1886, with two daughters, Robin and Tamara, and son, Ian. Doug Wingrove farms the land.

The John Campbells built a large, new home on the rising ground, west of the entrance to the farm. Thirty five of the 40 acres are planted in pine and black walnut, and two acres in apple trees. Another Campbell, son, Ian C., lives in Hamilton.

This Campbell family is not related to the earlier Campbells of Mountsberg.

Baptist Church Property

The red brick Baptist church stands on the hill facing the 13th Road. The first church of 1852 was on the same site when John Page was using this 50 acres of Lot 8. However the first Page deed, dated February 1863, was in the name of John's son, Peter. In September of that year, the Baptists had full title to their land. In June 1918, the church obtained additional land from Jonathan Scott to enlarge the cemetery. In 1979, it was further enlarged by land donated by Colin and Lois Campbell.

Baptist Parsonage, 1981. *Mrs. D. Croft.*

The Parsonage

In 1877, Phoebe (Sutton) Fearnley whose husband, Charles, had died 7 years earlier, moved from her farm on Mountsberg Road into her new brick house. The lot, bought from John Revell, was on the east corner of the 50 acres at the road intersection, and abutted the church property.

Mrs. Fearnley remarried and, in May 1907, as Phoebe Maddaugh, twice a widow, sold her home to William Dutton. Mrs. Maddaugh, then about 80, already had been away from Mountsberg a few years, living with a son, and the house had been rented to Mrs. Easterbrook of Nassagaweya, and her unmarried son, Mark. An Easterbrook daughter, Isabel, was married to Archibald Robertson Jr., formerly of the 14th Concession, near the north corner of East Flamborough.

Mr. and Mrs. Dutton, parents of Mrs. Emerson Carton, lived here until both families moved to Rockwood. Mr. Dutton built a small barn at the east corner of the lot. The stone foundation was just large enough to provide shelter for his horse and buggy and had a hay loft. Later, the building became a garage and remained standing many years.

In 1912, Mr. and Mrs. Archibald Campbell bought the house and retired there from their farm on Mountsberg Road. Mr. Campbell died in 1928 and his wife in 1929 and, in 1930, their heirs sold the house and lot to the Baptist Church for a parsonage. When not needed for a resident pastor, the house was rented at times.

Lot 8, northwest, Concession 13

The first record of activity on this 100 acres was in the late 1840's, when it was assessed to John Wingrove, son of Charles. By 1850, he was cultivating 70 acres. He held no deed and returned to this father's farm on Mountsberg Road when James Hurren came along wanting to buy. The Hurren deed is dated April 1851. Susannah Heaton, born in Pennsylvania and mother of Mrs. James Hurren, lived with them.

Family of James Hurren (1810-1871) and his wife, Ruth Heaton (1821-1901): *Susannah* (1841-1920)—married Peter Page; *Edmund* (1843-1921)—remained on the farm, married Jane Wingrove; *Philip* (1844-1876)—his son, James, was superintendent of Mimico School for Boys in early 1900's; *Alpheus* (born

Hurren Home. **Wm. Revell.**

Family of Edmund and Jane Hurren. Standing—James, William and Phoebe Jane. Sitting—Rebecca, Edmund and Jane. **Wm. Revell.**

1847)—died in infancy; *Charity* (1849-1874)—first wife of William Wingrove on Lot 9, southeast; *William* (born 1851); *Alpheus* (born 1854)—lived in Erin; *Moses* (born 1855); *Francis* (born 1858).

The first Hurren home was a storey-and-a-half log house, replaced by the present stone house in 1869. InDecember 1863, at a youthful age, Edmund becameowner of the farm and soon after, married Jane Wingrove. Their family was: *James* (1867-1961)—married Annie Clark, sister of Mrs. GeorgeDougherty, farmed near Harbor Beach, Michigan; *Phoebe Jane* (1869-1962)—married Charles Revell, see Lot 7; *William* (1871-1949)—married Mary Jane Wise, lived on Guelph Line, southeast of Campbellville; *Rebecca* (1878-1949)—unmarried, remained at home.

The year 1886 marked the beginning of improvements to Centre Road and the 13th and 14th Concession Roads. For this, Edmund Hurren supplied 62loads of gravel at 8 cents a load, but John McNiven was paid 10 cents a load for 313 loads. However, in 1888the price was steady at 10 cents a load to both these gentlemen. This was at the time of Statute Labour, which continued until after 1900, and meant that each farmershould keep the road in front of his property in passable condition. Road masters were appointed from local residents, three or four to a Concession.

After the death of Edmund Hurren in 1921, the farm was sold. John Howard had it for less than a year before selling, in April 1922, to Clarence and Nellie (Scott) Wingrove who had been living on Concession 9.Members of their family: *Ivan*—married Elsie Spracklin, in Galt; *Lloyd*—see Lot 9, northwest, Concession13; *Lorne*—died in infancy; *Earl*—married Mary McAllister of Crieff; *Leona*—married Morris Scott, in Galt; *Audrey*—married Robert Johnson, in Galt.

Since Clarence died in 1958, Earle and Mary have owned and operated the farm, assisted by their son, Bradley. Nellie lives in Galt (Cambridge).

A triangle of about an acre, at the north corner of the lot, became isolated 100 years ago, when Centre Road branched to the west. In 1973, Alexander and

Shirley Smith bought this piece of bushland, amid more bush, and, two years later, had a family home for children, Derek and Melissa.

Lot 9, southeast, Concession 13   Canada Company

James Wingrove (brother of Charles, George and Thomas) settled on a Clergy Reserve lot that had been bought by the Canada Company. Now, over a century and a half later, this lot has the unique distinction in Mountsberg, of being a one-family farm. There are no land transfers, excecpt as it passed down the line from father to son.

Family of James Wingrove (1808-1882) and his wife, Sarah Bell (1815-1889): *Eliza* (1836-1875)—married Aaron Peer; *Mary Ann* (1837-1897)—married Edward Hirst (Hurst); *William* (1839-1914)—remained on the farm; *Lucy* (1841-1916)—married Charles Lambier; *Daniel* (1842-1914)—married Elizabeth Gunston of Nassagaweya, sister of Mrs. Sandy Campbell; *Jane* (1845-1918)—married Edmund Hurren of Lot 8, Concession 13; *Maria* (1847-1932) —married Parker Allison, lived at Moffat; *Phoebe* (1850-)—married Joshua Allison; *Sarah Isabella* (1855-1929)—married Archibald Campbell Jr., see Lot 9, Concession 12.

Family of William Wingrove who was married three times:

Wife 1: Margaret MacIntyre (1841-1865), sister of Janet (Mrs. Jonathan Wingrove)—Margaret (1865-1891).

Wife 2: Charity Hurren (1849-1874), daughter of James—*William* (1874-   )—went to Alberta and married there.

Family of William Wingrove. Rear—Gordon, George, William, Jr., Mary Jane and Clarence. Front—Sarah, William, Margaret, Elizabeth and Clara. *Wm. Wingrove.*

Wife 3: Elizabeth Cartwright (1851-1931), daughter of Edmund—*Mary Jane* (1877-1948)—married Fred Laking, son of Joseph, see Lot 9, northwest; *George* (1879-1962)—married Carrie Grummetts; lived in Alberta; *Sarah* (1881-1956)—married George Sockett, lived in Guelph area; *Clara* (1885-1942)— married

Selena and Gordon Wingrove. *Mrs. A. Page.*

Lawrence Huether, kept store in Hamilton, and later in Morriston; *Gordon* (1888-1948)—married Selena Purnell, daughter of Alfred; *Clarence* (1892-1958)—married Nellie Scott, see Lot 8, Concession 13; *Margaret* (1895-1971)—married Asahel Bates of Carlisle.

Family of Gordon Wingrove and Selena Purnell (1888-1945): *William A.*—married Marjorie Robinson of Waterdown, remained on farm until 1961; *Evelyn*—married Albert Page, son of Burnice, lives at Mountsberg.

Family of William A. and Marjorie Wingrove: *Allen*—married Milene Chipman, Vice-President of IBM in Toronto; *Douglas*—married Evelyn (Babs) Clarke of Puslinch, living on the farm with children, Kimberly, Stephen, Suzanne, Brian and Julie.

The Wingrove Heritage

Early in 1838, James Wingrove and his wife, the former Sarah Bell, along with their two tiny daughters, Eliza and Mary, left Northampton, England, to establish a new life in Upper Canada. Obviously, they crossed the Atlantic by sailing ship, possibly by cattle boat. Today, it is difficult to comprehend the faith and the fortitude exemplified by this man, his 23-year-old wife and his young family.

We can only surmise as to the clothing, furniture

Wingrove Homestead. *Wm. Wingrove.*

and utensils which they brought with them. We do know that, among the furniture brought, was a full "parlor" suite, including a love seat and a throne chair. This suite was divided among the surviving children at the time of Sarah's death in 1889. The throne chair is now in the possession of James' great-great-grandson, Douglas, who owns the original homestead.

The first land purchased by James was the north quarter of Lot 9, Concession 12, for £32 3s 6d, in 1839. In addition to this original 50 acres, another 100 acres, being the south half of Lot 9, Concession 13, was purchased for £ 81, 5s, in 1845. This 150 acres forms the present farm, less two building lots from the 50-acre parcel. The farm buildings are in Concession 13.

The first house was a log cabin, situated 30 yards due northwest from the present barn. In 1855, possibly because the farm had increased to seven girls and two boys, the present house was built. It is of frame construction with hand-hewn beams and square-cut nails. Two fireplaces were in use; one in the basement and one on the main floor. The house was constructed in such a way that two entrances were provided. After William, the oldest son, was married, two families lived in the house for many years.

Both the house and the main barn, built about the same time, were covered with a crude clapboard siding. Some of the timbers, or "sleepers", of the ceiling of the stable of the original barn are black ash, which must have been plentiful in the area. Although over 40 feet in length, they are the same size at one end as at the other. The ell on the front of the barn was added in 1902.

The hardships of this era are difficult to imagine. It is said that Sarah, on many occasions, walked from Mountsberg to Dundas to purchase some of the necessities of life. Clearing land, which, in this area, included moving large boulders as well as stumps into fence-rows, must have been a formidable task.

The prime purpose of the entire operation, in those early years, was to provide the family with food and clothing. This need dictated that the farming be of a mixed nature, to include a few cows, a sow, some sheep and, of course, some hens. Milk, meat and eggs were of prime importance, as was wool for clothing and hides for leather.

James continued to own the farm until his death in 1882. His oldest son, William, who was born in their second year in Canada, took over the operation. Little change was made in the type of farming during this period. Implements were improved, production increased and, gradually, provision of food and clothing took second place to produce offered for sale. Shearing sheep by hand; carding and spinning wool; churning butter; butchering and "frying down" and curing meat were still chores for William and his family of four boys and four girls.

In early times, cattle were permitted to pasture on the roadsides, where they mingled with neighbours' herds. Obviously, traffic was light on the 13th Concession (now known as Regional Road 18) at the turn of the century in pre-automobile days.

While William never did own a car, he took a special pride in always owning a spirited driving horse. On one occasion as he and his wife, Elizabeth, were driving down the old Brock Road to Freelton, the horse's ears went up and, yes, coming down the rough road toward them, sputtering and backfiring and going at least 15 miles an hour, was a dreaded Model T Ford. The horse went crazy with fright, jerking the buggy off the path which was the road. The man stopped the car and took the horse by the bridle to try to lead it past the car. William looked at his wife hanging on to the side of the buggy with terror in her eyes, turned to the man holding the horse and stated rather forcefully, "If you can get the old lady past, I'll manage the horse."

In 1911, James' grandson, Gordon, took over the farm and farmed it until 1938. During this period farming was becoming more specialized and, in 1926, Gordon purchased for $200, the first purebred Holstein cow to come to Mountsberg. Many of his neighbours questioned his sanity. Subsequent purchases were made and in 1932, the first milk was shipped from the Wingrove farm. This move necessitated selling the sheep and all the evidence we have of almost 100 years of having a flock of sheep on the farm, is the remains of a dam where the sheep were washed each spring.

Old traditions die hard, and Gordon did not believe in life insurance or borrowing money. During the Great Depression, in the fall of 1933, the taxes were due and there was no money. Gordon sent three of his purebred Holstein yearling heifers out for slaughter. They averaged 600 pounds each and the price was 2 cents a pound, a total of $36.00. The taxes were paid.

The first great-grandson of James, another William, had the farm from 1938 unti1.1962. Hydro had been installed in 1935. The telephone had been in use for many years and labour saving devices became the order of the day. During this period the herd of Holsteins were expanded. The cows were placed on test for butter-
fat and milk production. The name Allangrove Holsteins was chosen for the cattle. They were entered in the show ring with moderate success. Water was installed in the house in 1949. Power machinery lightened the load of farming, and productivity of both the land
and the Holsteins increased. William's two sons, Allan and Douglas, were active in 4H clubs, winning several showmanship awards.

In 1962, the younger son, Douglas, took over the farm and is still very active as a Holstein breeder. With land available to rent in close proximity, the operation has been expanded. In the herd of over 100 head, between 40 and 45 are milking. A pole barn and silos with automatic unloaders have been built. A pipeline milker and stable cleaner are part of a completely new stable.

In 1972, Douglas received the highest award that the Holstein fraternity can give to a member, the Master Breeder Shield. He is the youngest man ever to receive it.

If James and Sarah were to walk in what now is Regional Road 18, we are sure they would be amazed. We hope they would be proud.

Note:

W.A. (Bill) Wingrove was on Township Council for 10 consecutive years. He took office as a councillor in January 1952. In January 1956, he became deputy reeve and, in January 1958, reeve. He had the honour of being County Warden in 1960. In June 1961, he resigned from council to accept an appointment as Superintendent of Wentworth Lodge on July 1, a position he still holds (1980). He lives in Dundas.

M.H.C.

Lot 9, northwest, Concession 13

The name of James Dougherty, an Irishman, appears in 1848 when assessed for this 100 acres. However, in December 1854, the deed obtained from the Canada Company was in the name of James Dougherty and Daniel Chambers. The following March, the farm was divided lengthwise. Daniel Chambers took the northeast side, which he sold a few months later to William Hunter, who, in turn, sold to William Hurren in August 1859.

map of 1859 has the name of John Kennedy on the northeast 50. Presumably, he was a tenant. James Dougherty had the southwest side. His family lived in a one-storey log house. Following is his family as far as known:

James Dougherty (born about 1808) and his wife, Joanna (born about 1812): *William* (1834-1905)—married Mary Anne Revell, daughter of Thomas, see Lot 3, southeast, Concession 12; *Elizabeth* (1838-1881)—married Page Mount, see Lot 6, southeast,

Family of Fred and Mary Jane Laking; Fred, Ivan, Alma, Mary Jane, Harvey and Edwin with dog, "Jack". **Mrs. Wm. Wigood.**

Concession 12; *Daniel* (1844-1884)—killed in an explosion of Dakota Powder Mill near Kilbride.

Between 1860 and 1919, various divisions of property took place in both 50 acre farms.

The Northeast Fifty

In 1860, William Hurren sold 10 acres at the southeast end to William Dougherty and, in December 1871, sold the remaining 40 acres to William A. and Sarah Ann Forsyth (both born about 1844). In their family were: Wilhelmina (born 1867) and Elzira (born 1870). Mr. Forsyth died in the late 1870s and, in March 1880, his executors sold his land to Richard Nelson Moore. In January 1890, Mr. Moore sold to Richard Tief (Taafe).

The Southwest Fifty

Meanwhile, James Dougherty had died leaving his 50 acres to his sons, William and Daniel, each getting 25 acres. Along with his 10 acres, William then had 35 acres which he sold to Daniel in November 1874. The following year, Daniel sold his 60 acres to Alexander Bannatyne. Following Alexander's death, Hector, his son, continued on the farm. Apparently Hector died in the early 1900s and his sisters, Mary, Elizabeth and Janet, sold the 60 acres, in March 1903, to Daniel McCurdy and his wife, Maud Marshall (of Lot 10, Concession 14). They built the house still in use and lived there until March 1908 when they sold to Fred Laking and moved to Guelph.

In October 1919, Fred Laking bought the 40 acres from Richard Tief, thus erasing the various divisions the land had known in the previous 65 years.

Family of Fred Laking (1874-1937), son of Joseph, and his wife, Mary Jane Wingrove (1877-1948), daughter of William: *Harvey*—married Eileen Wigood, daughter of William, lived in Morriston. Harvey died in December 1965, and Eileen earlier in the same year; *Edwin*—married Emma Land, they live in Guelph; *Ivan*—married Myrtle Watson, see Lot 9, Concession 14; *Alma*—married William Wigood, brother of Eileen, and lived on Lot 11, Concession 11 and now is a widow living in Morriston.

After the death of Fred Laking in 1937, his son, Edwin, owned the farm until April 1940, when he sold to Clarence and Nellie Wingrove of adjoining Lot 8. In 1958, it passed on to their son, Lloyd and his wife, formerly Hazel Wise of Carlisle. In their family are: *Linda,* who married David Walker, lives in Hamilton; *Donald,* married Anne Crow, lives in Mississauga; and *Katherine,* at home.

In 1973, Charles and Linda Cyopik bought 8 acres at the north corner of the farm and built a house that year.

Farm Divisions 1855-1919

```
                    1855    Daniel Chambers 50 acres
                    1855 to William Hunter 50 acres
                    1859 to William Hurren 50 acres

1871 to William A. Forsyth         40 acres
1877 to William Forsyth            40 acres
1880 to Richard N. Moore           40 acres      1860 William Hurren to
1890 to Richard Tief               40 acres      William Dougherty
1908 to Fred Laking                40 acres                  10 acres

                    1855 James Dougherty 50 acres

Daniel Dougherty 25 acres    | William Dougherty 25 acres |
                             | 1874 to Daniel Dougherty 35 acres |

                    1875 to Alexander Bannatyne 60 acres
                       to Hector Bannatyne 60 acres
                    1903 to Daniel McCurdy 60 acres
                    1919 to Fred Laking 60 acres
```

Thomas Wingrove, original settler. *The late Miss J. Wingrove.*

Wingrove Homestead, now the Dryden Farm, about 1963. *Mrs. C. Dryden.*

Lot 10, southeast, Concession 13   Brock Grant

Thomas Wingrove, brother of Charles, George, and James, settled on the 100 acres next to James, and by January 1839, had his deed. Before this, he had lived, briefly, at Campden where he met and married Catherine Griffin of Smithville. They established this home in the mid 1830s. According to the first assessment, in 1841, he had 45 acres under cultivation and owned two horses, three cows and two young cattle. In 1861, they were still living in their one-and-a-half storey log house. Soon after, the sturdy stone house, still in use, was built.

Family of Thomas Wingrove (1802-1876) and Catherine Griffin (1805-1867): *Mary* (born 1935)—married Rev. William Forsyth, see Lot 9, Concession 14; *Martha* (1837)—married Patrick O'Neil, see Lot 12, Concession 14; *Sarah* (born 1839)—married Henry O'Neil, both O'Neil families moved to Hanover, Ont.; *Jonathan* (1841-1911)—married Janet MacIntyre, sister of William Wingrove's first wife, Margaret, daughter of Alexander MacIntyre of Nassagaweya, who arrived in Dundas at the time of a cholera epidemic. Three young MacEwan men died—and Alexander later married the widow of one of them; *Huldah* (1842-1921)—married Alpheus Mount of Mountsberg; *Agnes (1845-1938)*— married Tilman Houser of Campden; *Janet* (1847-1904)—married Ralph Hewins of Mountsberg.

A small, weathered, frame house once stood near the road, at the east corner of the farm. The family built it about 1880, for their daughter, Mary, after the death of her husband, Rev. William Forsyth. It was a pretty, little house surrounded by lilacs and trees. Mary had $1,000 which, invested at 6%, provided a comfortable living for herself and two tiny sons, Thomas and Albert. What a difference a century makes! The house remained on the *site* about 30 years. Betsy Laking, daughter of Joseph, with her husband, Oscar Hood, and son, Mervin lived there for a time in the early 1900s.

Family of Johathan, who inherited the farm, and his wife, Janet (1847-1918): *Thomas* (1872-1946)—married Nettie Page (1878-1958) daughter of Peter; *Mary Adina* (1876-1901)—unmarried; *Herbert* (1881-1934)—unmarried; *Janet* (1883-1978)—Jennie, unmarried.

After their marriage, Tom and Nettie stayed on the farm and, in time, took charge when the parents and Herb and Jennie moved to Freelton.

Family of Thomas and Nettie Wingrove: *Charles* (1900-1919)—drowned in Guelph; *Viola*—married Cameron Kitching, lived in Acton and Milton, died in 1979; *Edna* (1904-1912)—died of diabetes, several years before Drs. Banting and Best discovered insulin; *Robert*—married Mae Flewelling, in Florida; *Elsie* (born 1913).

In the spring of 1917, the large barn on the farm was destroyed by lightning, and on July 5, 1917 a hot sunny day, the usual barn-raising took place with the entire neighbourhood present. Two years later, the farm was sold to William E. Stewart, on adjoining Lot 11 and the Wingrove family moved to the Rockwood area. After Tom Wingrove died, Nettie lived in Hamilton with her daughter, Elsie, a teacher.

The farm became the home of David Stewart, son of William, when he married Jane Pinkney of Morriston. Members of their family: *Isabel*—married Allan Elliott, see Lot 6, Concession 12; *Allan*—married Helen Winer, in Preston; *Waiter*—unmarried, employed at University of Guelph; *Eleanor*—married Howard Winer, in Morriston; *Gordon*—married Mary

Jane Hill of Waterdown, was Township Clerk, now in Tax Department, lives in St. George.

The Stewarts sold to Thomas D. and Marion Livingston, in 1953, and lived in Morriston until 1957, when they were displaced by Highway 401, and moved to Guelph. David died in 1959.

For a brief period from October 1962 to December 1963, the farm was owned by Phyllis Browning who sold to the present owners, Clifford and Theresa (Terry) Dryden. Their two sons, Alexander and Glenn, help on the farm.

Lot 10, northwest, Concession 13

For 116 years this was the McCurdy place. In 1846, members of the McCurdy family left their Irish home beside the Giant's Causeway, in County Antrim, and set sail for unknown Canada. It was a three-generation exodus, the group including, as far as known, elderly James McCurdy, his wife and two sons, James and William, with their wives and children.

In crossing the Atlantic, they had the misfortune to be driven back 200 miles by gales. Nevertheless, they completed the voyage in the average six weeks. Thence, they made their way to Burlington via Lake Ontario.

The brothers took their time to choose a home site. It was 1848 when James settled on Lot 10, while William went on to establish himself in Puslinch township.

James McCurdy (1792-1855) and his wife, Rose Curry (1800-1855) had a family of five: Eliza and Daniel, their fate unknown; also John, James and Adam.

The first McCurdy home was made of logs, and built far back, near the southeast end of their 100 acres, despite the fact that they got their drinking water from a spring near the 14th Concession Road. A shelter for oxen stood in the same general location as the cabin.

John and Adam helped their father on the farm while James went out to work. In September 1850, John, then 26, met a tragic death. A logging bee was in progress at Ned McCarthy's (Lot 9, Concession 14) as preparation was underway to build a log house. The oxen started up with a rush, and a handspike (a logging tool) flew off and struck John in the temple. Adam Darling, huge and strong, who lived on Lot 10 beside Ned, carried John to the far-back McCurdy cabin, but John had died.

James, working in Milton, was called home where he remained, and for a time, he and Adam were joint owners of the farm. In 1855, the cabin was replaced by a frame house, built much nearer their access to the 14th Road. The lumber used was cut on the farm and sawn at McCrae's mills. About the same time, a barn was built near the new house.

The parents did not live to enjoy the new home and by 1860, Adam too, had died at age 30. For about 10 years, James was alone, except for casual help, until he married Elizabeth Monkhouse, a near neighbour.

Family of James McCurdy (1829-1899) and Elizabeth Monkhouse (1842-1927): *Annie* (1872-1893); *James* (1874-1949)—unmarried, the fourth James McCurdy in Canada; *Daniel*—married Maud Marshall from across the 14th Road, first lived on adjoining Lot 9, then Guelph and area, died in British Columbia in 1955; *Mary* (born about 1879)—the last of the family, in Hamilton; *Rose* (1881-1970); *Elizabeth (Eliza)* — married Harry Trantor, Hamilton, died 1958; *George* (1889-1977)—for several years, including the 1920s, he owned a farm at Puslinch and Rose kept house for him. When a farm accident cost him a hand, both returned to the home farm.

In 1890, the present barn was built near the site of the former barn and, in 1907, a large, new two-storey house was built of stone quarried on the farm, its site a short distance north of the frame house. In the past, a wing with a large, stone fireplace had been added to the old house. At this time it was removed to the barn area and the older part was placed beside the new house to continue in use as a summer kitchen.

A springtime task on most farms, in early years, was making maple syrup. It was done in the old way with the sap boiled in a huge iron kettle suspended from a pole, slung between two trees. McCurdy's tapped 1,000 maple trees each year.

Mary, Rose and George retired in Morriston, in fall of 1964, after selling the farm to Marvin and Ruth Groves. Two years later, the Groves sold to William and Inga Barlow, who moved there, in 1967, when Mr. Barlow retired from the Barlow Tool and Machine Ltd., Hamilton. The house has been extensively renovated and the barn, outbuildings, and surroundings improved. Part of the land is rented. The Barlow's family of six helped celebrate their Golden Wedding in June 1979.

Lot 11, southeast, Concession 13   Brock Grant

From the time this lot was settled, in the mid-1840s, through to 1966, it was a one-family farm. John Stewart (1773-1856) whose wife died in Perthshire, Scotland, came to Canada with his grown children, four boys and two girls, a few years before he and his son, Alexander, chose this location. Together, they built a one-storey log cabin and established a home. Alexander married Catherine Kennedy of Badenoch who had come with her parents from Badenoch in Invernesshire, Scotland. His sister, Ann (1802-1885), married an ancestor of the Organs of Concession 6, East Flamborough. Alexander had a niece, Agnes (1830-1915), who married Peter Davidson of Freelton.

Following is the family of Alexander Stewart (1806-1889) and Catherine (1817-1904): *John* (1845-1923)—married Penelope Hanning, lived on Concession 10, Beverly; *Charles* (1851-1941)—married Janet MacBeth, lived on Concession 7, West Flamborough; *William* (1852-1932)—married Mary Jane Currie, remained on the *farm; Margaret* (1855-1907)—married John Philpott; *Robert* (1858-1949)—married Janet Ross (1857-1934) whose family operated the toll gate on the Brock Road (Highway 6) just northwest of the intersection with Concession 13; *Lochlan* (1862-1944)—married Lillian Kidler, was an architect in Buffalo, New York.

The William Stewart Family. Rear—Russell, Joseph, Katherine, Charles and David. Front—Margaret, William, Mary and George .circa 1930. *Mrs. A. Elliott.*

The family included triplet daughters, born in 1855, but, apparently, one did not survive at birth. Another one, Agnes, died in April 1860, the victim of a virulent scarlet fever epidemic that scourged the neighbourhood that spring, and a month earlier had taken her sister, Jane, one year younger than Agnes.

Other neighbours suffered a similar, heart-breaking tragedy that spring. Now, with communicable diseases under control, one cannot comprehend the terror that devastated parents years ago, at the very thought of an epidemic flaring up in their community.

In February 1854, Alexander Stewart had a deed for his farm. The property passed on to two sons, William and Robert. The lot was divided lengthwise, giving Robert the northeast side and William the southwest side. About this time, the frame house was built for Robert and Janet. William and Mary continued to live in the earlier home which had been enlarged and, later, was coated with "roughcast". In 1906, Robert sold his 50 acres to William and the newer house became the home of William's family.

Family of William Stewart (1852-1932) and his wife Currie (1862-1948): *David* (1888-1959)—married Jane Pinkney, see Lot 10, adjoining; *George* (1890-1964)— married Annie Clark of Puslinch Township, remained on farm; *Charles* (1891-1941)—married Olive Wyse who died in 1947; *Joseph* (1894-1978)—married Gertrude Playfair, lived in Toronto, Brantford and Galt; *Margaret* (1896-1960)—married James W. Dainard, in Hamilton; *Russell* (1898-1968)—married Olive Wyse Stewart, widow, lived near Strabane; *Katherine*—married Nile Finch, lived on Concession 10, Beverly, now Dundas.

All children, except Katherine, were born in the farm's first abode.

When George (Geordie) and Annie Clark were married, they lived in the renovated pioneer home. They had two sons, William and Donald. In 1957 they moved into the frame house and rented the old place to the Flynn family who had five school age children: Pamela, Patricia, Sheila, Jane and Kevin. However, when their son, William, married, he was assigned the frame house and George and Annie returned to their earlier home. William's wife was Audrey Haskell, daughter of Ross and Doris Bates Haskell; granddaughter of Percy and Edith Haskell. Their children, Margaret and Lynda, were the fifth and last generation of Stewarts on the homestead. The second son, Donald, married Florence Swanson and went to Guelph. George died in October 1964, and, in June 1966, the 100-acre property was sold.

In the following 12 years there were three non-resident owners, and the farm was rented to a Bosma family. In 1978, it was James R. Barrow who sold the 100 acres to Bruce and Susan Durrant who have two children, Graham and Nancy. They are interested in general farming.

Lot 11, northwest, Concession 13   Brock Grant

The pioneers of this lot were Edmund Cartwright (1805-1883), earlier known as Edward, and his wife, Margaret Dixon (1817-1903), who came from England about 1845. In their family were: *Sarah* (born about 1845)—Mrs. Dickson of Mount Forest; *Ellen* (born about 1847)—married Andrew Miller of Strabane—as a widow, Ellen later went to the vicinity of Mackinac, Michigan and there married a member of the State Legislature; *Thomas* (1849-1895)—married Mary Anne Monkhouse, a neighbour; *Elizabeth* (1851-1931)—third wife of William Wingrove; *John* (1854-1940)—married Matilda Revell, lived at Strabane; *George* (1856-1932)—married Clara Laking, daughter of John, ran a sawmill at Progreston for 8 years, lived at Carlisle for 10 years, to British Columbia about 1901; *Isabella* (born about 1859)—married Joe Alger of Progreston; *Margaret Ann* (1862-1937)—married Richard Tief, lived on Concession 14.

The first Cartwright home was a one-storey log cabin. This was replaced by the present frame house, set well back from the 14th Road.

It was not until 1870 that Edmund Cartwright held the deed to his farm. When he died in 1883, the eldest son, Thomas, remained on the land. He and his wife had no known family. He died in 1895 and his wife, Mary Ann, went to Hamilton, while Isabella and Joe Alger took over the farm work. Some of the four Alger children, Harold, Orval, Elva and Bertha attended Mountsberg School.

Mrs. Cartwright died in 1903 and the following year, George F. Nicholson bought the farm from the Cartwright estate. Mr. and Mrs. Nicholson moved there from the 7th Concession of East Flamborough. Of their family of 11, only the four youngest came to Mountsberg. They were: Ethel—married Arthur Binkley, lived on Concession 4, West Flamborough, died 1974.

The Dennis McKenna Family, July 1961. Rear—Joan, Marie, Dennis, Jack, Michael, Kenneth, James, Joe and Bob. Front—Patricia, Frances, Helen, Bernice, Joyce with Gerald, Shirley and Margaret. *Mrs. R. Geraghty.*

Her daughter, Doris, taught at Mountsberg School, 1929-34; *Edith*—married Alex Campbell, lived on Mountsberg Road, Lot 9, Concession 12; *Ruby* (1891-1963)—attended Mountsberg School; *Elmer* (1893-1960)—with Ruby, ran the farm after his father's death, about 1919-43.

These four all retired in Dundas. Another sister, Mrs. Cummins, lived in Dundas 61 years. A sister, Amy Patton, moved to Mountsberg later than her parents and lived on Lot 6, Concession 12. A brother, William J. Nicholson and his wife, Annie, celebrated their 70th wedding anniversary in 1972 in St. Catharines.

Dennis McKenna and his wife, formerly Frances Player, bought the farm in April 1943 and it remained their home until 1968, when they retired in Freelton. Dennis died in December 1970 in his 79th year. Later, Frances moved to Waterdown. Their family follows: *Marie*—Mrs. Raymond Geraghty, Hamilton; *Bernice*—Mrs. Edward Giavedoni, Stoney Creek; *Tom*—killed on Highway 6 when 10 years old; *Margaret*—Mrs. Carl Glass, Dundas; *Helen*—Mrs. Joseph Oilman, Waterdown; *Michael*—married Helen Priest, lives in Troy; Jack—married Doreen Pook, is on Lot 12, Concession 12; *Kenneth*—married Barbara Schults, lives in Waterdown; *Anna* Mae—died of lockjaw (tetanus) when 6 years old; *Patricia*—Mrs. Gerry McCulligh, Milton; *Joan*—Mrs. Glen Wigood, Lot 10, Concession 11; *Joseph*—married Donna Hasting, lives near Guelph; *Joyce*—Mrs. Edwin Hinds, Guelph; James—married Dolly Robinson, lives in Dundas; *Robert*—married Marilyn Burns, lives in Waterdown; *Shirley*—in Hamilton; *Gerald*—has a home base with his mother in Waterdown.

It is a large and a close family. No house will hold all the children and grandchildren, but they have two reunions in a year. Every summer they hold a family picnic in the Mountsberg Community Park and in December they have a Christmas party in the Community Centre, formerly the old school they all attended.

James and Sheila Mullins owned the farm from 1968 until 1978, during which period they made extensive renovations to the house. Present owners are Neil and Robin Vowels who moved there from Burlington in 1978. From a previous marriage, Robin has a son, Kenneth, and a daughter, Karen, who attend Parkside High School in Dundas.

Lot 12, southeast, Concession 13   Clergy Reserve

This lot seems to have been James Dougherty's first choice of land. He was assessed for it in 1843, but before 1848 abandoned it for Lot 9, northwest Concession 13. Thomas Monkhouse who had land in West Flamborough took over and, in 1862, had a Crown deed. Eventually he sold the entire 100 acres, part by part, to Alexander Stewart, of Lot 11, for his sons. The northwest 50, bought in 1869, became William's. The southeast half, bought in two transactions, 1875 and 1878, was for Robert, who sold it to William in 1906, along with his part of Lot 11.

William's son, Charles, owned it for a few years, beginning in 1931; later it went to his brother, George.

In 1958, George sold a building lot of an acre or more, at the south corner, beside the road, to Doris Smith who transferred it to John A. Smith in 1962. John, of Morriston, and his wife, Judith, built a house for themselves. A son was born in 1964. The present owners, Albert Turner from Campbellville and his wife Colleen, bought the property in 1966 and live there with their three sons, Glenn, Kenneth and Jeffrey.

Anthony Doveika bought 4 acres which straddled the Creek. He put up a shed and reforested part of his land which he owned from 1960 to 1975. Two land sales followed in 1975. A house was built for Gordon and Ilene Vince who bought in 1976 and, the following year, they sold to Joseph and Alice Mykytiuk.

The farm acreage, sold by Stewarts in 1966, still is owned by non-residents.

Lot 12, northwest

John Maddaugh settled on this lot about 1843 after Benjamin Hurst had had the use of it for a year. The Maddaugh deed was dated July 1853, one year before all Clergy Reserves were released for sale. A two-storey frame house made a home for the large family of John Maddaugh (1816-1901) and his wife, Catherine Watson (1823-1877): (years of birth approximate) Stephen, 1844; Archie, 1846; John, 1847; William, 1849; Robert, 1850-1927; Mary, 1852; Ben, 1853; Isaac J.A., 1855; Charles H., 1855; Ellen, 1857; Elizabeth, 1859; Joseph, 1860; and Jacob, 1865.

It is assumed that the older members of the Maddaugh family were educated at the old school at Purnell's Corner. After 1864, they would attend the new school at Beechgrove, which was more convenient than Mountsberg. The family attended the local Baptist Church.

In 1904, James MacEdward bought the farm from the Maddaugh estate. He and his wife, formerly Mary Doyle, had rented the place a few years before buying. Their family included: Bert; Andy, a carpenter; Alex, who had a store in Freelton; Jean, married Walter Ward; Annie, married Charles Gumbert; Bob, married Hazel Bell of Aberfoyle, lived on Highway 6 near the old home; Margaret, married Robert Boyd; and William.

James MacEdward sold his farm in 1916 to a nephew, William MacEdward, who, in turn, rented it to Jean (daughter of James) and Walter Ward for about five years. During this time, the owners, William and Beatrice MacEdward, and children, Florence, Alex and James A., were living on Manitoulin Island.

Ezra Howlett, a bachelor, bought the property in April 1931. Living there with him were relatives, Mr. and Mrs. James W. Bernard and their daughter, Violet. Mr. Howlett sold in October 1952, lived in Campbellville for a time, then went to Arizona. The buyers, Joseph B. and Maryetta Martin sold, the following August, to the present owner, Graham L. Wright, who operates a sheet metal business on adjoining land in West Flamborough.

Early in the 1960's, the farmhouse was occupied by

Gordon Rayner and his wife, Edith Pickett, who died in 1966. Their family included Gordon Jr., Robert, Kenneth, Clifford, David, Bruce, Nancy and Mary. Younger members of the Rayner family were the first from that farm to take advantage of the High School facilities of East Flamborough when school bus service began in 1954.

Gordon Rayner died February 14, 1973, exactly seven year after his wife, leaving sad Valentine memories for their children. In 1971, Gordon and family members, still around, had moved into West Flamborough and some of the boys worked for Graham L. Wright from time to time. Since then the farmhouse has been vacant and allowed to deteriorate, but the barn is good. Wrights planted hardwood trees over a large area, with pine near the road. The farm is posted "Grouse Sanctuary".

Concession 14

The lots in East Flamborough's most northwesterly Concession have but 45 acres each, and lie between the partly-open 14th Concession Road and the partly-open Town Line between East Flamborough and Puslinch.

Lots 1, 2, 3, and 4

Although Archibald Robertson, Sr., a Scotsman, was not the first person to own any of these lots, he might be called the pioneer of the north corner of East Flamborough, as he was the first true settler, and at one time or another, owned all of lots 2, 3, and 4 and part of lot 1. He settled on Lot 2 in 1860, and the Robertson homestead was the only permanent early home on the four lots. Lots 1, 3, and 4 were Brock lands, and were among the last of their many properties to be sold. In January 1853, John D. Uttermark (also written as Uttermarck) was appointed trustee of all Brock land then remaining. That he carried out his duties indifferently well is indicated by the fact that, in 1856, 3 acres in Lot 1 and 8 acres in Lot 3 were sold for taxes. At the same time, 8 acres were sold off Lot 4 to Charles Slade, but were bought back by John D. Uttermark in 1860.

This was fifteen years after the Township was organized with annual assessments, and was the first record of such drastic measures in the Mountsberg area. Previous to then, these low-lying, wooded lots, apparently, were ignored and it seemed to be the tax sale that first stirred interest in this far corner of East Flamborough.

Lot 1   **Brock Grant**

The 3 acres sold for taxes in January 1856, went to William Burness, who resold in November 1863 to Archibald Robertson, Sr. Mr. Robertson held it for ten years, then sold to William Nicoll. Archibald D. Cameron, unmarried, son of Duncan, who lived across the road in Lot 2 of the 13th Concession, bought it in 1884. As far as is known, no one ever lived on this or any part of Lot 1.

In the meantime, John D. Uttermark had sold the lot, less the 3 acres, in August 1864, to John McLean. In October 1873, it was bought by James McMonies who had a sawmill in Waterdown and was, at one time, a member of Parliament. Archibald Cameron obtained the property in 1882, two years before getting the 3 acre parcel. Thus, in 1884, the entire lot was Cameron property and remained so in passing on to a niece, Margaret Cockburn, in 1960. Late in 1964, it became part of Conservation Authority land.

Lots 2, 3, and 4   **Brock Grants**

John White obtained a Crown deed for the former ClergyReserve Lot 2, in April 1852, but did not keep the property long. It passed to Francis Campbell in December 1854; to Andrew Gage in November 1856, and to Archibald Robertson, Sr. in December 1860. Lot 2 was the first Robertson land and was the site of the Robertson home, well back in the lot, north of a later house beside the 14th Concession Road.

In 1872, Mr. Robertson agreed to buy Lot 3, less the 8 acres sold for taxes, and all of Lot 4. When he got his deed in 1877, his total holdings comprised 127 acres, which remained intact until 1946.

Family of Mr. and Mrs. Archibald Robertson: *Archibald, Jr.*-married Isabel Easterbrook of Nassagaweya, who had been the first baby baptized in St. John's Anglican Church. Their children were: Annie, who died quite young; Lottie; Georgina; a second Annie; Florence; and Stanley; *Robert*-married and lived in vicinity of Guelph; May-married William Easterbrook, brother of Isabel, lived in Hamilton; *Charlotte*-lived in Pasadena, California; *Florence* - known as Flo.

Archibald Robertson, Jr. took over the property in 1885. About 1890, he left to live in Toronto and later, in Hamilton, where he operated a livery stable. From then until 1908, the 127 acres were rented, first to William and May Easterbrook.

Another tenant recalled was John Mayhew who, for reasons of health, moved there with his wife and family, about 1900 and stayed until 1908. They attended the Baptist Church. A daughter, Martha, was baptized in the creek at Alpheus Mount's, where many such rites were performed at that time. Another daughter, Lottie, was married about 1905. The two youngest members of the family, Gordon and Chester, attended Mountsberg School. Chester, who died in 1965, was an officer in World War I and, later an assistant superintendent at Steel Co. of Canada, Hamilton.

In April 1908, Edric and Emily Winder bought the 127 acres and moved from Hamilton. Their family of sons and daughters were past public school age. Mr. Winder is best remembered for a drain which the Township opened up in the northwest end about 1912. It was known locally as the Winder Drain because it involved all the Winder lots, and Mr. Winder was an enthusiastic promoter of the project.

Neil Stewart owned the group of lots from 1916 until bought by Allan Eaton in 1920. During Mr. Eaton's ownership, the property was rented. The only tenants recalled were the Brillinger family who lived in the house beside the 14th Road; the house that burned a decade or so after Mr. Eaton became owner.

In 1946, Mr. Eaton sold the lots separately. Lot 2, from that time until 1963, when it became part of the 12-Mile Creek Conservation Authority (later the Halton Region Conservation Authority in 1963), passed through the various hands of Mervin and Marion Harrison; Charles and Gladys Smith, 1951; Edward H. Farley, 1955; Hans J. Kallman, 1957, and John King, 1957.

The 8 acres of Lot 3, sold for taxes in March 1856, went to George Brock Rousseau who sold to Edward Brown in 1861. The land was resold to John Smith in 1874; to Richard Attridge in 1878, and to Archibald Robertson, Jr. in 1887. David McCrae, of Lot 5, Conc. 13, took it in 1909 and it remained McCrae property until sold to Archie Scott in 1932, a year after Mr. Scott had bought the McCrae place.

Charles and Gladys Smith who had bought Lot 2 in 1951, added this 8 acres to their land in 1952. From then on, its story paralleled that of Lot 2.

The 37 acres of Lot 3 and all of Lot 4 were transferred from Allan Eaton to Archibald T. Eaton in 1946. John Smith bought the parcel in May 1951. Subsequently, it went to Roscoe Drumm in October 1952; to Esther Cohen in May 1954; to Robert and Thelma Lewis in May 1958; to H.R.C.A. in 1964.

Archibald Eaton sold Lot 4 in two parcels. In September 1949, John Smith obtained a deed for a strip of land 40 feet by 600 feet. This was before he obtained the adjoining part of Lot 3. But, from 1951 until it became Conservation land, it was included in sales concerning Lot 3.

The main part of Lot 4 was sold to Edna P. Hunter in 1948; to Margaret M. Martin in 1951; to Stanley and Dorothy Parks in 1957; to Wallace Ament in 1958. In October 1960, it was bought by the Twelve-Mile Creek Conservation Authority, before it became part of the Halton Region Conservation Authority.

The 12-Mile Creek bisects Lot 4 diagonally. Apparently, long ago, a cabin stood in the west triangle, with access to the now unused Puslinch-East Flamborough Townline and just room to exit, also, to the 14th Road. The only information regarding the dwelling is that it had been the scene of a murder. Although probably true, the story cannot be confirmed as to time, personalities or provocation.

The 14th Concession in front of these four lots was open until partly submerged by the Mountsberg Conservation Lake. However, its rough, single track was safe only for horses, cycles or trucks. The creek was spanned by a plank deck. No railings.

Lot 5   **Clergy Reserve**

The Canada Company held the Crown patent for this Clergy Reserve lot, in September 1838. It was first settled, about 1842, by James McDonald, a Scotsman. At that time it was completely wooded. James died about five years later and his heir, Robert (father, brother or son?) took over and in November 1854, bought the property.

Three months later, the land was transferred to another relative, William McDonald (born about 1813) and more recently arrived from Scotland. William and his wife, Isabella, and son Robert (born about 1850) lived here until 1868.

The new owner was Alexander Sinclair (born in mid-1830's) who married Isabella MacPherson of Lot 6. Their children were: George, Annie, Edith and John. The house on this lot was near the Puslinch line, and access was by way of a short section of the partially open Town Line to the Badenoch Road.

Sinclairs also owned property across the Town Line in Puslinch Township. In 1889, Andrew Scott was listed as a tenant of Lot 5.

Thomas Beaton, who had a farm nearby in Puslinch, bought Lot 5 from Alex Sinclair in 1903; and, in 1907, sold it to Andrew Gilmour who, the year before, had acquired Lot 6, thus combining Lots 5 and 6 into a 90 acre farm. Lot 5 was included in the Township drainage work being done in 1912. The combined lots were sold to J.G. Law in 1950. As of 1964, 25 1/2 acres of Lot 5 became Conservation Authority land.

Lots 6 and 7   **Brock Grants**

The early story of these lots concerns, mainly, the MacPherson family. John MacPherson and his wife, formerly Ann MacPherson, were born in Badenoch, Inverness, Scotland, and married there. John was loath to leave his homeland when, in 1833, a group of friends left to found a new Badenoch in Puslinch Township. He was a sheep farmer. The following winter was unusually severe in the Highlands, and he lost most of his flock. Faced with having to make a fresh start, he decided to do so in Canada. So, with his wife and year-old son, Peter, he joined his friends in Badenoch, Ontario. Arriving with them were Mrs. MacPherson's several sisters, some of whom were married.

The family moved into East Flamborough about 1842 and, for a time, lived in a log cabin of Lot 7. John Gallagher already was working on the lot and remained there for several more years, but seemed to have no plans to buy. In fact, John MacPherson never held a deed, either. It was not until 1867, about three years after John's death, that his son, Peter, held full title to Lot 6; and, in 1869, Lot 7 also. Both were acquired through John H. Cameron of Toronto.

By the spring of 1843, 3 acres of Lot 6 were cleared for tilling. For this family, clearing land was serious business as well as hard work, for Mrs. MacPherson's brother had been killed in Badenoch while felling trees. In due time, a one-storey stone house was built on Lot 6. Many years later, John's daughter, Annie, told of winters in the Gallagher cabin, when snow blew in through chinks in the logs, and wolves howled in the encircling forest. The larger stone house, still in use, was built in a vague period around 1870.

Family of John MacPherson (1798-1864) and his wife Ann (1808-early 1900's): *Peter* (1833-1899), married Catherine McKenzie, sister of Donald Cameron's second wife; *Annie*—born 1836, Mrs. William Milne of Hamilton, no family; *Penelope*—Mrs. Alex McLean of Hamilton, two daughters, Ida and Eva, became orphans and made their home with the Milnes; *Isabella* (born 1845)— married Alex Sinclair of Lot *5; Mary* (born 1848)— unmarried, was a dressmaker in Morriston; *Angus* (born 1857)—went to California where he died as a young man.

Peter and Catherine MacPherson had a family of four who attended Mountsberg School. *John* (born 1866)—married Sarah Burden of Puslinch; *Annie* (1868-1941)—married James Laking, son of John; *Catherine (Katie Mary)*—married William Moore; *Jessie*—Mrs. George McIrvine of Calgary.

As Peter grew old, his son, John, planned to continue on the farm. John and Sarah had three daughters, Margaret, Katherine and Anne, but only Margaret was born on the East Flamborough farm. About a year after Peter died, John had an unfortunate accident that cost him a hand. It was winter. It was difficult using the outside cutting box in icy conditions; and his hand slipped. Farm help became a necessity at all times and forced his decision to buy 200 acres about a mile north in Badenoch, and sell the property on Concession 14, which, at that time, included, besides Lot 6 and 7, about 20 acres in Lot 8, making a total of about 110 acres. It was bought in 1900 by Burdge Gunby (later of Lot 8, Concession 12).

After 1906, Lots 6 and 7 went their separate ways when, in January, Burdge Gunby sold Lot 7 to Albert Campbell and, in March, Lot 6 to Andrew Gilmour.

Lot 6 (later)

Before he became a farmer, Andrew Gilmour (1881-1976) had been working at the James Laking sawmill, about a mile upstream, in Puslinch. He married Effie Ord of Aberfoyle. Following is their family: *Kathleen*—Mrs. John F. Mooney of Hamilton, died in 1972; *Richard*—married Vanora Wyse, lives in Aber-foyle; *Doris*—Mrs. Lloyd Cummins of Beechgrove; *Helen*—Mrs. James Martinson, Hamilton; *Jean*—Mrs. Reginald Collard, Burlington; *Douglas*—married Doris Butler of Guelph, lives in Puslinch; *Evelyn*—Mrs. Roy Winer of Puslinch; *John*—married Norma Gardner of Clappison's Corners, lives in Puslinch; *Wylda*—Mrs. Jerry Billings of Owen Sound.

James Garnet Law, brother of Hector on Lot 8, Conc. 13, from the Flamborough Centre area, and his wife, the former Ida Roelofson, bought Lots 5 and 6 from Andrew Gilmour in March 1950. They have a family of five: *James*—of Toronto; *John*—married Nancy Dearing of Waterdown; *Janet*—married Roger Stark of Ottawa; *Robert; Jean.*

Garnet and Ida Law in Centennial costume beside their house.
Mrs. J.G. Law.

Lot 7 (later)

After the MacPherson family had a home on Lot 6, the old cabin on Lot 7 had tenants. Only two families are known. In the 1860's, James and Margaret McIntosh, a Scottish couple, lived there with their family, Elizabeth, Margaret, John and Isabella.

James Waggood (1862-1922) (Wigood), brother of Robert, Jr., and his wife, Rhoda Hambleton (18601937) and their older children were there in the 1880's. They moved to Mt. Brydges in 1894. Entire family members were: *Mildred*—Mrs. Holborn; *Lillie May* (1882)—died in infancy; *Charlotte* (1884-1910)—Mrs. James Kellestine of Melbourne, Ontario; *William Robert*— married Annie Newton and lived in Alberta; *Phoebe*— Mrs. H. Player, who moved to Freelton in 1944, now in Dundas.

The Waggood family returned to the home area and in 1912, James was a section foreman when the C.P.R. put a line through from Guelph Junction to Hamilton.

In passing through Lot 7, the Credit Valley Railway isolated the south corner.

After Albert Campbell bought the lot in 1906, it followed the fortunes of his home farm, Lot 7, northwest, Conc. 13 until 1971. That year, when owned by John F. Easterbrook, a building lot at the north corner was separated for Stewart Moon and his wife, Cheryl Easterbrook. They built a house near where once had been an old barn. In 1974, they sold that place to Wayne and Shannon Smith and moved into another new home in Puslinch village.

(Information re MacPherson family, courtesy of Miss Margaret MacPherson, Hamilton)

Lot 8   **Brock Grant**

In all the Mountsberg area, this 45 acres is the most irregularly sliced up piece of property. The first division was made about 1850, or earlier, when Abraham Forest settled on the northeast 22 1/2 acres, and William Stewart on the southwest half. In the late 1870's, the Credit Valley Railway ran their line through both halves, angling in a westerly direction into Puslinch Township. It was probably then that the Centre Road, to avoid two level crossings, stopped short of the 14th Concession and followed a new course to the west, south of the railway, to meet the East Flamborough-Puslinch townline.

The Northeast Half

William Hurren, believed to have been a brother of James on Lot 8, northwest, Conc. 13, took over from Abraham Forest who had no deed, and bought the half-lot. William and his wife, Charlotte, may have lived in the Forest cabin, briefly, but they were mainly interested in Lot 9 which their son, Francis, was renting from James Hurren, and made their home there.

After accommodating the railway and the new road, the log house was isolated on a 1 1/2 acre triangle at the south corner of the lot, while the land to the north was left in two sections of diverse shape. However, four years before trains were running, William Hurren had sold to Peter MacPherson. The house remained standing for many years. That was where Peter and Susannah Page lived for a while following their marriage in 1860.

The Southwest Half

In 1861, William Stewart sold his log house and an acre of land at the south corner of his lot. The new owner, John Lewis, probably was a son of George Lewis of Lot 3, Conc. 12. John and his wife, Mary, lived there for six years with their children, Abraham, Samuel, Elizabeth, William, John L. and Mary. A 7-month-old daughter, Ann Jane, had died in 1855 and

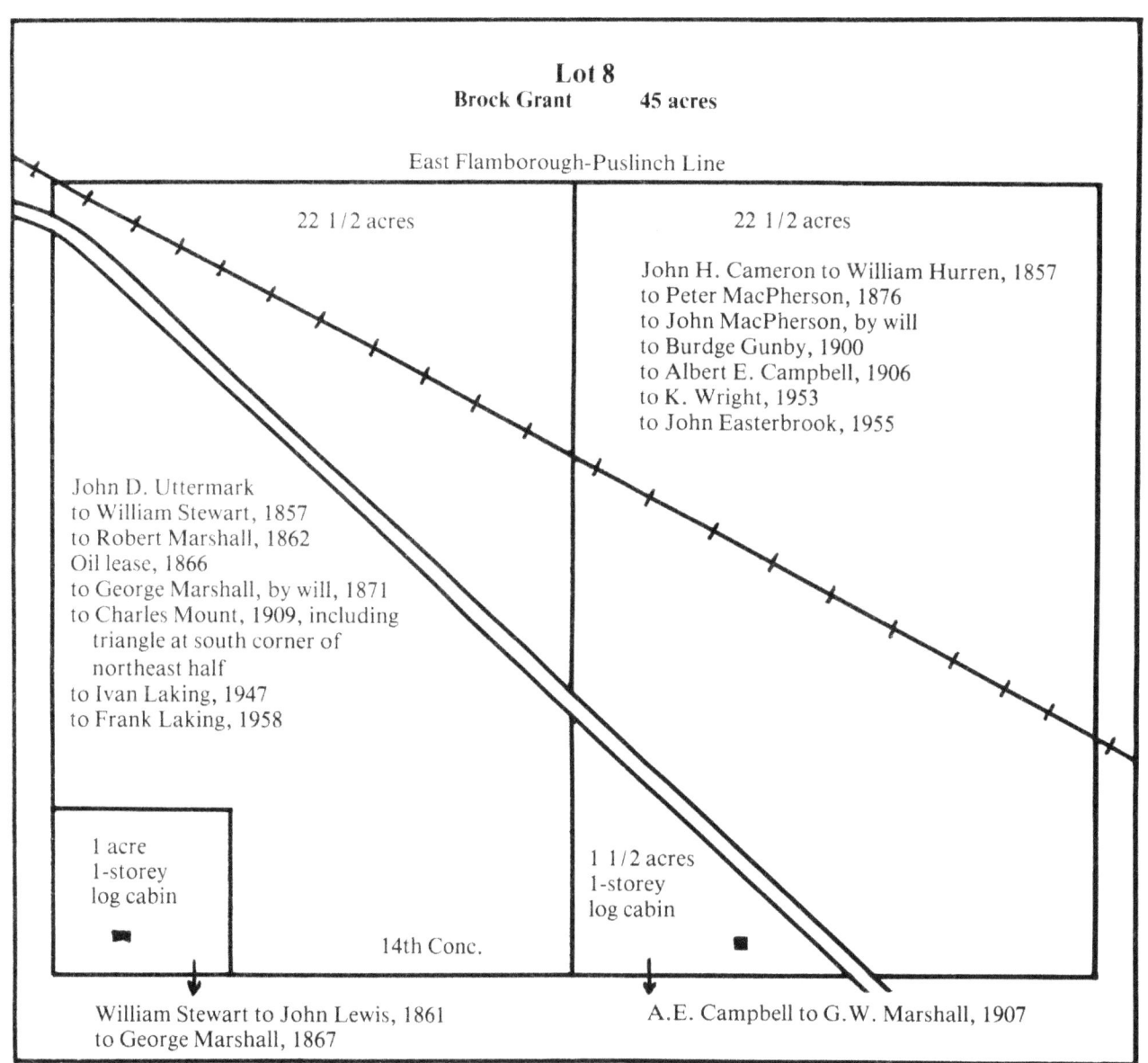

was buried in the Methodist Cemetery.

Mr. Stewart sold the remainder of his property, a year later, to Marshalls of nearby Lot 10, who owned it when Lot 8 took on the appearance of an oversize jigsaw puzzle.

Lot 9   **Brock Grant**

James Hurren of the Centre Road held the first deed to this lot, dated August 11, 1857; the same day that William Hurren and William Stewart received their deeds for halves of Lot 8. However, for about 11 years before then, Edward (Ned) McCarthy had been clearing and working on Lot 9 and, in 1850, had built a 1 1/2 storey house.

In the early 1860's, and perhaps earlier, the farm was occupied by Francis and Harriet Hurren (both born about 1829) and their children, Lila and John. Francis' parents, William (born about 1809) and Charlotte also lived there. This Francis Hurren should not be confused with James' son, Francis, an infant at the time.

David Anderson bought the property in 1866 and sold to William H. Forsyth in 1869. The initial "H" must have been an error, since it was William A. Forsyth who negotiated with the Credit Valley Railway when they took a bite out of the north corner of the lot; and William A. who in 1877, sold to William Forsyth who had been a tenant most of the time since the Hurren ownership. This latter William was the Baptist minister from 1860 to 1869 (see Lot 9, N.W., Conc. 13, re Forsyth).

The Rev. William Forsyth was married twice. A known daughter, Margaret (Mrs. John Wingrove) was born in 1850 and is presumed to have been a sister to "Joseph (1852-1865), son of William and Amelia", buried in the Baptist Cemetery. The second wife was Mary Wingrove (daughter of Thomas). She had two sons, Thomas and Albert. The Rev. William died in 1878 and, in 1880, his estate sold the farm to Richard Nelson Moore. In 1890, it passed on to Richard Tief (Taafe) who was married to Margaret Ann Cartwright, a neighbour. They had no children, and continued to live there until selling to George F. Smith in 1919. Mr. Tief had been a Township councillor for 4 years, 1916-1919.

The Laking era began in April 1923, when the farm was bought by Fred Laking who lived across the 14th on Lot 9, Conc. 13. It became the home of his son, Ivan, who married Myrtle Watson of Freelton. The house which had burned was replaced in 1928. Family of Ivan and Myrtle Laking: *Murray*—of Millgrove, who married Marian Downing; *Elsie*—Mrs. Clival Silver-thorn of Lynden; *Evelyn*—Mrs. Wilfred Wurr of Aberfoyle; *Shirley*—Mrs. James Graziotto of Arris.

Ivan died in 1978 and Myrtle sold the farm and moved to Waterdown. The new owners, John R. and Claire Tigchelaar, with children, Peter, Sharlene, David and Marcie, moved from their home on Lot 1, Conc. 12. In their first season, 1979, they planted a large apple orchard at the new location.

Lot 10   **Clergy Reserve**

Although the Crown patent for this Clergy Reserve lot is registered to Robert Marshall, in 1855, it is known that Adam Darling, with his wife and son, settled there in 1837 or 1838. The Darlings began clearing the land and, in 1841, had 10 acres under cultivation and had built a 1 1/2 storey frame house. All that is now known about Adam Darling is that he was a giant of a man with strength to match his stature.

In 1855, or a year earlier, Robert Marshall came to East Flamborough from New York City where he had been a newspaper publisher. He and his wife, Margaret Paxton, were native Scots who were married in Berwick-on-Tweed, Scotland in 1822 and he was a printer before going to the U.S.A. They arrived at Lot 10 with two children, Margaret, then 12, and George Washington, a few years younger. Margaret later married Thomas Haines of Conc. 12 and George W. married Margaret (Maggie) Simpson of Badenoch. After the death of Robert, about 1865, George continued working the farm until 1909.

Children of George and Maggie were: *Thomas*—owned and operated Lots 11 and 12 for three years until 1902, went to Saskatoon and, much later, returned to Guelph. He and his wife, Annie, had a son and daughter, and lived to celebrate their 65th wedding anniversary; *Bob* and *Jim*—both married and went to Alberta; *Jack* and *Wesley*—never married, they later lived in Aberfoyle with their father after he retired; *William*—unmarried, lived in western Canada; *Eveline*—(Eva) Mrs. Alex McCuaig of Guelph; *Maud*—married Dan McCurdy and lived for some time across the road on Lot 9, Conc. 13, adjoining the McCurdy home farm.

Charles R. Mount (son of Alpheus) and unmarried, bought the Marshall place in 1909, and lived there alone until age and poor health forced him to sell in 1947. He had been a Township councillor for four years, 1924 to 1927.

Charlie was well-known in the community as a thresher, succeeding his cousin, Len. In later summer and during the fall, his 3-unit caravan plied the Mountsberg roads regularly. In the vanguard, puffed the wood-burning steam engine with its immense black smoke stack. Following were the horse-drawn water tank and the separator. The almost-round wooden water tank had a flat top where the driver perched. The separator was a long machine of wood, featuring shiny, metal chutes, about twice the diameter of stove pipes. Their purpose was to blow the straw into inside mows or to outside straw stacks. Known as straw-blowers, they were an improvement over slatted straw-carriers, and saved on manpower. From an opening, low on the machine, the separated grains of wheat, oats or barley poured a golden stream into wooden boxes with two hand-holes. Usually two men were assigned the task of carrying the heavy grain to bins in the granary. All told, twelve or more men were kept busy. Charlie and his two helpers often stayed overnight. The others were neighbours who came to help, and no one worked harder than a lady of the farm who served two big meals a day for one, two or sometimes three days.

Ivan Laking, of Lot 9, bought the farm from Charles Mount and, 11 years later, in 1958, sold it to his son, Frank (employed in agriculture research at University of Guelph). Frank and his wife, formerly Donna Tweedle, niece of Mr. and Mrs. Oscar Pegg, live there with their grown children, Erwin and Loreen. They live in the orginal home on that farm. However, changes and improvements made at times, during almost **140** years, would make it unrecognizable if Adam Darling could see it now.

Lots 11 and 12 **Brock Grant**

These two lots, a total of 90 acres, always have been regarded as one farm. About 1840, Charles Buchan, a retired soldier, was living there with his wife, Agnes, a son Charles Jr. and a daughter. By 1842, he was cultivating 25 acres of Lot 12 and by March 1850, held his deed. It is not known how long the Buchans remained there, but Donald McLeod was listed as a tenant in 1859.

For a lengthy period in the 1860's and into the 70's, Pat O'Neil rented the farm. Mrs. O'Neil was formerly Martha Wingrove, daughter of Thomas. In 1861, the O'Neils had two children, Jonathan, 5, and Janet, 2. In 1871, their family was listed as Johathan, 7, Agnes, 4, and Viola, 2. This meagre information hints at an all-too-common family tragedy when the young children were wiped out in an epidemic. Is that what happened to the first Jonathan and his sister, Janet?

Charles Buchan, Sr. died about 1874, and, in 1876, his heirs sold to William Mast of Morriston, son of a German pioneer. In 1879, William sold the farm to John Winard (Winer) Sr. It passed to John Winard, Jr. in 1883, and to Peter Winard in 1889. Marshall Haines bought it in 1894. It was during Marshall Haines' five years of ownership that Charles Laking (son of Joseph) and Margaret Ann Hewins (daughter of Aaron) were married in October 1895, and rented the farm for about two years. Here, their eldest child, Jessie, was born before they moved to Aberfoyle.

Thomas Marshall, of adjoining Lot 10, owned the farm from March 1899 to December 1902, when it was sold back to William Mast. Family of William Mast (1845-1922) and his wife, Rosina Stein (1860-1942) of Morriston: *William* (1881-1967) and *Frank* (1884-1968—both married and lived in Alberta and British Columbia; *Elsie* (1886-1973)—Mrs. Perce Johnson of Woodstock; *Regina*—unmarried, of Woodstock, later British Columbia; *Sarah*—Mrs. David Blair of Alberta; *Frederick*—*married* Mary Scott (daughter of Jonathan); *Hilda*—Mrs. Archie Black of Orangeville; *Beatrice* (1898-1966)—wife of Dr. R.G. Woolsey; *Clarence. Two other children died in infancy.*

Clarence Mast owned and operated the farm from 1942 to 1949. He later married and lived in Hamilton, after selling to Fred and Mary who kept on until 1963 when they sold to Calvin and Doreen Arnold and moved to Morriston. Arnold children: Peter, Susan and Debbie.

New owners in 1968 were Helen and Alexander Kendrick. Mr. Kendrick died the same year, but Russian-born Helen, in Canada since 1911, stayed on alone. She has three daughters with homes elsewhere.

III

Life in the Community

Early Religion and Education

Churches

The English settlers, most of whom were Methodists, lost no time in erecting their log church or Meeting House, across the road from the later church and cemetery. The congregation, which became known as the Mountsberg Episcopal Methodist Church, is included in the Methodist archives, under the date of 1836, in a grouping of three circuits: Nelson, Dumfries and Flamborough. As such, they would be visited by ministers, though perhaps infrequently, at that early stage. In the meantime, they would carry on with lay preachers and prayer meetings.

This church sufficed unitl 1854 when Charles Mount, fifth son of Josiah, built the frame church on the southeast side of Mountsberg Road; which church was given to Wentworth Pioneer Village in 1969. It was officially closed at the time of the Church Union of 1925, but, through local efforts, services continued to be held, twice a year, at first; in later times, just once a year on the third Sunday of June.

The Baptists built their first church in 1852, but before then they had Sunday morning Bible readings at the home of Thomas Wingrove and Sunday afternoon services in the old log school.

Methodists and Baptists were about equal in numbers before 1925. Since then, the red brick Baptist church, which, in 1922, replaced the earlier church of 1852, has been the only neighbourhood church with regular services.

Scottish families held to the Presbyterian Church. A few, near the Halton line went to Campbellville, where they met in homes before their first church was built in 1869. Others, and those in the west corner of East Flamborough, joined with other Scots of Badenoch and Morriston in Duff's congregation.

McCurdys, from County Antrim, Ireland, living on Lot 10, northwest, Concession 13, were about the only Church of England representatives, and they journeyed weekly to St. John's Anglican Church, northwest of Campbellville.

Roman Catholics went to Freelton. Their number included nearly all the Irish settlers on the 1 1 th Concession who came in the 1840's.

The History of the Mountsberg Baptist Church

Although a decision was made in September, 1844 to leave the Dundas Baptist Church and set up a new church in the Mountsberg-Freelton area, it was not until December of that year that thirteen men and women met and organized themselves into a church, known as "The Brock Road Church". Elder Joseph Clutton, who would remain as their minister until 1850, was in charge of this service. At this meeting Alexander Robertson and Thomas Wingrove were chosen to be the first deacons. In February, 1845, George Fearnley, Thomas Wingrove and Loammi Sutton were chosen trustees and were given the responsibility of finding a location for the meeting house. The trustees received a deed from Mr. Craig Haggis for land in Freelton on March 22, 1845. The original site of this church has long disappeared due to changes in the direction of the Brock Road. In fact, it seems that it was these changes in the direction of the road that led to trouble with Mr. Haggis in 1847-1848 and caused dissension in the church. Prayer meetings were called for, and by 1849, Freelton was abandoned as a place of worship.

After leaving Freelton, "Bible Readings" were held every Sunday in the home of Thomas Wingrove, with a preaching service at the Mountsberg School. On September 28, 1850, a Service of Recognition was held, at which time the members accepted a Declaration of Faith and changed the name to "The Regular Baptist Church, Flamboro East". (It was not until the 1930's that the name became "The Mountsberg Baptist Church".) Delegates from the churches in Dundas, St. George, Sheffield, and First and Second Beverly shared in this service. At the same meeting an Ordination Council set apart for the ministry, Mr. Job Moxom. (The actual ordination service, however, would not take place until March 24, 1852, the first of many for Mountsberg.) In October 1850, monthly Covenant meetings were established and the Psalmist was adopted as the hymn-book. Elder Clutton continued to come at certain intervals to conduct the ordinances, and some thirteen persons were baptized by him during a two year period. At this time discipline was strict and public admonishments and confessions characterized many of the Covenant meetings.

1852 marked a milestone in the life of the Church. A framed meeting house was built on the site of the present church, at the cost of 116 pounds, eight shillings and nine pence sterling. The opening of this new building was an occasion for rejoicing. The inaugural service began on Saturday, November 6, and continued over Sunday, with Elder Clutton as the speaker. The pews of this church are still being used in the present church school auditorium. In January, the first recorded tea meeting was held to defray the debt of the new building. Two hundred tickets were requested at two shillings and six pence each. At this time, despite death and removal, the membership had grown to twenty-seven.

Baptist Sunday School Class, 1930. Teacher, Mrs. Lena Campbell, in back. Left to right, Merv Elliott, Earl Martin, Ruth Shanks, Bill McEwan, Anabelle Brooks, Bill Wingrove, Mildred Fletcher and Sid Shanks. *Wm. Wingrove.*

In 1854, Elder Moxom resigned and for several years the church was without a regular minister, except for a short period when Elder Hoyle served. Church affairs, until 1859, seem to have been in a very unsettled condition. However, in March, 1858, the congregation met for prayer and agreed to commence a Sunday School. Owing to the dissension among the members, the Ordinances had been neglected, but on March 6, 1859, Elder Clutton agreed to come from Dorchester once a month, so that the congregation might observe communion.

In March, 1860, Mr. William Forsyth became pastor. He was ordained on February 26, 1862. A few months later, in May, it was "unanimously resolved" that a collection be taken up every Communion Sunday to cover the costs of the Communion Service, with the balance to be used for the Church. At this time, morning and evening services were also begun.

In 1865, Beverly (Westover) Church desired to share the services of the minister. It was agreed to, on a three month trial basis. Elder Forsyth would alternate Sundays between the two congregations. However, this union did not materialize. The church at this time entered a low period of growth, even though the monthly Covenant meetings continued. The record book vividly expresses the minister's frustration at this turn of events. For example on September 1, 1866, he writes simply, "No meeting. Members labouring for the meat that perisheth". However, on November 11 of the same year a special day of prayer and humiliation was held with services commencing at 9:30 a.m. and at 6:30 p.m. Thereafter, according to the record, an improvement in the spiritual state of the church became evident.

On June 21 and 22, 1867, the church had the honour of hosting the Guelph Association of Baptist Churches. In preparation for this the church was re-roofed and painted. That Sunday, three services were conducted, with the Revs. John Gerre, John Sole and I.J. Rice speaking. In August, Elder Forsyth resigned and until April 1874 the church was served by the short pastorates of Elders Mackie and James Samis and the Revs. W.S. McDermand and Archibald Warren. In 1872, effort was made again to unite with Westover, and in 1873 with Waterdown, but both attempts were fruitless.

In 1874 Mr. William Grant, a student, became pastor, preaching fortnightly for fifteen dollars a month. He was ordained in 1875 and shortly thereafter resigned. In his place the Rev. Daniel Wright became the minister. He was better known as "Daddy Wright". During his ministry, sixteen baptisms took place on one Sunday. Included among these new members were Mr. and Mrs. Edmund Hurren, Mrs. William Wingrove, who was a member for fifty-five years, Mr. and Mrs. John Cartwright and Mr. and Mrs. Alpheus Mount. In 1877 a second attempt at union with Waterdown was successful under the ministry of student-pastor G. Ever-ton. The following year, under the pastorate of H.A. McConnell, the church was painted and renovated and a special re-opening was held. From 1880-1884, except for a few months when the Rev. J. Mackie supplied, the pastorate was under the ministry of the Rev. W.P. Hazelton. During this time, cooperation with Water-down ceased and work began in Freelton to set up another church. Mr. Robert Hopkins, as pastor, was instrumental in the setting up of this new church in Freelton. In May 1886, a new building was built, with student pastor A.R. Gregory serving both charges. He was followed in 1887, by James Bracken, who added thirty new members to the Mountsberg church. They included Mr. and Mrs. Job Revell, Mr. and Mrs. Charles Revell (Mrs. Revell was a member for seventy-four years) and Mr. Archibald Campbell.

While the Rev. Alexander Gay was minister, thirteen members withdrew from the church to form the nucleus of the Freelton church, which, in 1891, became independent of the mother church at Mountsberg. Mr. Charles N. Mitchell, a supply pastor in 1892, later became a missionary to Bolivia. He was followed by the Rev. William Peer, who was fond of children and gave them treats such as oranges, which were rare then, and pictures of interest. The Rev. William Spencer, who followed Mr. Peer, held revival meetings. In 1899, plans were made to ordain Mr. H. G. Gurney, but he suddenly took ill and died on August 23. During the next pastorate, the Rev. T.A.P. Frost held a baptism at a stream where ice, 4 to 5 inches thick, had been cut away. The record book says of that particular day, "The morning was bright and calm but quite frosty." After Mr. Frost, the Rev. R.G. Blundell came to Mountsberg in 1902.

On July 9, 1905, the Rev. E.J. Haines, the father of long time member Miss Eba Haines, became pastor of Mountsberg, Westover and Freelton. In 1907, the church was repaired and decorated. Due to illness in 1911, Mr. Haines resigned and, for that summer, the field was served by student-pastor John Linten. At the end of three months, Mr. Haines was approached and consen-

Mountsberg Baptist Church, 1959. *Wm. Wingrove.*

ted to supply until a permanent minister could be secured. For Mr. Haines, this meant another six years at Mountsberg and Westover. The Freelton church was closed in 1911 because death and removal had depleted its membership. In April of 1917, Westover went on its own and Mountsberg joined with Flamboro Centre. At this time, the church became part of the Home Mission Field. Mr. Haines was asked to become full time pastor of both churches. He accepted and remained their minister six more years. In November of that year, the church celebrated its seventy-fifth anniversary with Professor Kierstead of McMaster University as guest speaker.

In 1922, plans were started for a new building under the guidance of Trustees Albert E. Campbell, Charles R. Mount, Gordon Wingrove and Charles Revell. On December 3 of that year a dedication service was held for the present church building. The seats and pulpit were donated, as well as the communion table and chairs. The lights were also a gift. The cost of the building, about seven thousand dollars, was all pledged or paid for, so that the church began debt free. On July 1, 1923, Mr. Haines concluded his eighteen years of service with the Mountsberg church.

During the remainder of 1923, pulpit supplies were had until May 1924 when student-pastor Sidney Lawrence came and took over the field, which now included Mountsberg, Flamboro Centre and Westover. A parsonage was rented in Freelton and was presented free to the pastor. In July 1927, Mr. R.D. Campbell became the minister. In the fall of that year Mountsberg and Flamboro Centre became affiliated with the Union of Regular Baptist Churches of Ontario and Quebec. Mr. Campbell resigned, in 1929, and was succeeded by the Rev. R.K. Gonder, a one time missionary to China. The present parsonage was purchased in 1930 for fourteen hundred dollars. The church also, at this time, allied itself with the Fellowship Baptists. From August 1931, the church was served by supply ministers until April 1933, when the Rev. E. J. Pudney came.

At the annual meeting of 1934, it was decided to return to the Regular Baptist Convention, at which time, under the advice of the Home Mission Board, Mr. John Ward became the student-pastor. A Baptist Young Peoples Union (B.Y.P.U.) was begun at this time. During the following pastorate of A.S. Roblin, the present Ladies Aid had its beginning and electric lighting was installed in the church. In 1938, Mr. Elmore Williamson became pastor, staying until May, 1940. In June of that year, Mr. Frank Rice came as the new student-pastor. At that time, the church re-united with Westover. In May 1942, Everett G. Ward succeeded Mr. Rice.

On June 25, 1944, Mountsberg celebrated its one hundredth anniversary in a newly decorated building. In the morning the congregation was so large that seats were placed on the lawn, where the service was heard over a loud speaker. The Rev. Dr. H.S. Stewart was guest speaker in the morning with the Rev. P.P.W. Zieman of James Street Baptist Church, Hamilton, speaking in the evening. The ladies of the church served about 300 persons for the noon meal. A huge birthday cake was cut by Mr. Charles Revell, who, with Mrs. Revell, was the oldest member of the Church. He had been baptized fifty-six years earlier. The organist for the day was Mr. Osborne Wingrove, a former resident of the community.

In May 1946, Mr. Ward left the charge and was succeeded by Mr. A. G. McDowell. Mr. McDowell, in January 1948, presented Mr. Charles Mount with a gold initialled wallet in recognition of twenty-nine years as church clerk. In April of that year, Mr. John E. Thomas became the new student-pastor. Under his ministry, the defunct B.Y.P.U. was reorganized as a joint endeavour with Westover. This very successful group, under Mr. Thomas' leadership, brought new life to the congregation. In 1952, Mr. Thomas resigned and Mr. Rubin Bonney became the minister. During his pastorate, improvements were made to the parsonage. Mr. Bonney left in May 1954, following an appointment by the Foreign Mission Board to service in Bolivia. William Bidewell became the next student-pastor. Improvements were continued on the parsonage, with a bathroom and a water system being installed. During his stay, Vacation Bible School was begun and open communion was introduced.

In May 1956, Mr. Roland Glendinning came to the Mountsberg-Westover charge. The church was redecorated again by members of the congregation. In January 1959, Mountsberg incorporated Associate Membership into their constitution. While Mr. Glendinning was minister, an electric organ was purchased for the sanctuary. Mr. R. F. Coupland followed Mr. Glendinning in the spring of 1959. However due to health reasons, Mr. Coupland was obliged to resign in October of 1961. At that time Mr. George Rath became the pastor. During his ministry a new oil furnace was placed in the church, and extensive improvements were made to the parsonage.

Mr. Don Misener was minister May 1966 to June 1970. During this time, the church was completely redecorated and a beautiful illuminated wooden cross was donated to the church. In 1967, it was agreed to attempt the hiring of a full-time minister. This move was not successful.

An event of some significance occurred at the 125th anniversary service in 1969, when a plaque indicating the 13 Charter Members was unveiled in the sanctuary. Their names are as follows:

Alexander Robertson Sr.   Ann Robertson
George Fearnley   Julia Fearnley
Sarah Titmas   Loammi Sutton
Alexander Robertson Jr.   Thomas Wingrove
Catherine Wingrove   James Wingrove Jr.
Lucy Wingrove   Ann Fearnley
Margaret Robertson

Following Mr. Misener's resignation, one saw an excellent example of the sacrifice and dedication of the student ministers, when Mr. Thomas Caldwell, rather late in life, gave up a very lucrative teaching position to train for the Christian ministry. He was student pastor between June 1970 and September 1971. Mr. Robert Poole was next to serve, between September 1971 and June 1973. Mr. Poole was followed by Mr. Thomas Brelsford from September 1973 to June 1975 and by Mr. David Elliott from September 1975 to July 1976.

The present minister, Mr. Terry Dempsey, began his student ministry in October 1976 and will begin a

Officers of Mountsberg Baptist Church—December 1979

TRUSTEES	Mr. William Wingrove
	Mr. Roy Rintoul
	Mr. Earl Wingrove
DEACONS	Mr. William Wingrove
	Mr. William Revell
	Mr. Roy Rintoul
	Mrs. A. (Evelyn) Page
	Mr. Peter Pawlik
	Mr. Brian Colling
CLERK	Mr. Roy Rintoul
ASSISTANT CLERK	Mrs. J. (Grace) Bell
TREASURER	Mr. Brian Coiling
SUNDAY SCHOOL SUPERINTENDENT	Mrs. M. (Shirley) Hogg
ASSISTANT SUNDAY SCHOOL SUPERINTENDENT	Mrs. A. (Evelyn) Page
ORGANIST AND CHOIR DIRECTOR	Mr. Douglas Dredge
ASSISTANT ORGANIST AND CHOIR DIRECTOR	Mrs. P. (Marion) Pawlik

full-time ministry on January 1, 1980, as a result of a decison made by the Mountsberg-Westover Churches during 1979. An event of some importance was the re-alignment of the Regional Road No. 18 during 1977 which was something less than unanimously accepted by the church membership, since it required lowering the road some fifteen feet in front of the church. On a more pleasant note, in 1978, the Dofasco Choir taped their Christmas T.V. Special at the Church, and in 1979, Mr. and Mrs. Colin Campbell donated almost one acre of land to the church for cemetery purposes.

During the period from 1934-79, student pastors served the Mountsberg-Westover field extremely well. It should be stated in this history that without its close proximity to the McMaster Divinity College and the availability of these students, this church may not have survived some of the lean years.

As one reflects on the life of the Mountsberg Baptist Church, one is impressed by the faith, dedication and determination of those ministers and members who have been mentioned. Many of more recent time have also exhibited these admirable qualities. Heading the list of members must be Miss Eba Haines who passed to her reward on March 22nd, 1979, after 62 years a member-60 years a Sunday School teacher, 14 years a Sunday School Superintendent, and 19 years as head of the Mission Band. One thinks of Miss Jennie Mount and her years of service as the organist of the church. One remembers Mr. Albert E. Campbell and his contribution for so many years as a trustee, deacon and treasurer. We recall Mr. Charles Bryant and his efforts as the clerk for 12 years.

It is a long time from the candle light of 1844, through the coal oil lamp and the Coleman lamp eras, to the electric light of the present day, but through dark years and times of rejoicing, each of the above has attempted to make a contribution to the spiritual life of the community and therefore to the history of Mountsberg.

Ministers of the Mountsberg Baptist Church

1844-1850	Elder Joseph Clutton
1850-1854	Elder Job Moxom
1854-1859	Elder Hoyle and supplies
1859-1860	Elder Joseph Clutton
1860-1869	Elder William Forsyth
1869-1870	Elder Mackie
1870-1872	Elder James Samis
	students from Woodstock College
1872	The Rev. W.S. McDermand
1872-1873	The Rev. A. Warren
1873-1875	Mr. William Grant
1875-1876	The Rev. Daniel Wright
1876-1878	Mr. G. Everton
1878-1880	The Rev. H.A. McConnell
1880	The Rev. J. Mackie
1880-1884	The Rev. W.P. Hazelton
1884-1885	Mr. Robert Hopkins
1885-1887	Mr. A. Ronald Gregory
1887-1889	Mr. James Bracken
1890-1892	The Rev. Alexander Gay
1892-1893	Mr. C.N. Mitchell
1893-1895	The Rev. William Peer
1895-1897	The Rev. William Spencer
1898-1899	Mr. H.G. Gurney
1900-1901	The Rev. T.A.P. Frost
1902-1905	The Rev. R.G. Blundell
1905-1923	The Rev. E.J. Haines
1924-1927	Mr. Sidney Lawrence
1927-1929	Mr. R.D. Campbell
1929-1931	The Rev. R.K. Gonder
1931-1933	Supplies
1933-1934	The Rev. E.J. Pudney
1934-1935	Mr. J.M. Ward
1935-1938	Mr. A.S. Roblin
1938-1940	Mr. J.E. Williamson
1940-1942	Mr. B. Frank Rice
1942-1946	Mr. Everett G. Ward
1946-1949	Mr. Arthur G. McDowell
1949-1952	Mr. John E. Thomas
1952-1954	Mr. Rubin Bonney
1954-1956	Mr. William Bidewell
1956-1959	Mr. Roland Glendinning
1959-1961	Mr. Ron F. Coupland
1961-1966	Mr. H. George Rath
1966-1970	Mr. Donald G. Misener
1970-1971	Mr. Thomas Caldwell
1971-1973	Mr. Robert Poole
1973-1975	Mr. Thomas Brelsford
1975-1976	Mr. David Elliott
1976-	Mr. Terry Dempsey

The Mountsberg Ladies Aid

The Mountsberg Baptist Church Ladies Aid was founded during the pastorate of Mr. A. Roblin (193638) by Mrs. Roblin and other ladies of the congregation. Its purpose was to create a Christian service organization not only for the women of the church but for all those who would be interested, in the community, as well. From its inception, it has offered the ladies of Mountsberg a group for worshipping and studying, for missionary activity, for times of fun and fellowship and for the maintenance of the Baptist Church and parsonage.

Throughout its existence, the ideals of the founders

Ladies Aid of Mountsberg Baptist Church, 1940. Rear—Myrna Bryant, Mildred Revell, Allan Wingrove, Selena Wingrove, Doreen Dougherty, Nellie Wingrove, Eva Robinson, Vera Gunby, Grace Dougherty and Phoebe Jane Revell. Front—Marjorie Wingrove, Annie Wigood, Lena Gunby, Elizabeth Hewins, Lena Campbell, Isabel Stewart and Anna Dickson. *Mrs. A. Page.*

have been upheld. During the Second World War the ladies offered their services to the Red Cross and since then have supported various missionary activities, including the Leprosy Mission Board and the Canadian Bible Society. Both the Baptist church and parsonage owe much of their physical appearance to the Ladies Aid. Their quilting bees, bazaars and delicious church dinners and lunches are justifiably well known and widely supported. Members of the Ladies Aid over the years have taken part in local World's Day of Prayer services, in Sunday morning worship at the Baptist Church and have been involved in the Church's Sunday School and Vacation Bible School activities. The records of the Ladies Aid reveal a group of women who, through their widely diverse concerns, have been, and continue t., be, an influential force not only at the Baptist Church but in the community as well.

Quilting at annual Ladies Aid Luncheon, March, 1978. Left to right—Olive Rollins, Terry Dryden, Muriel MacAulay, Stella Pasuta and Grace Bell. *Mrs. D. Croft.*

Mountsberg Methodist Church

Early Methodism: As it Developed in the Flamboroughs

1808—Elder William Case, 27 years old, came from Pennsylvania and established his headquarters at Ancaster. He was a Methodist Circuit Rider and it became his duty to cover Beverly, East and West Flamborough, Nelson, Trafalgar, and Barton.

1816-20—British Wesleyans arrived and disagreed with the Episcopal nature of the Upper Canada Methodists, and deplored their unrestrained, emotional meetings. Later, the Wesleyans retired to Lower Canada.

1823—A Meeting House was established at the home of John Eaton, Carlisle, as part of the Dundas Circuit. Their first church became known as The Chapel on the Twelve. The Methodists overcame the opposition of the Church of England and obtained the right to hold church property, and share in the Clergy Reserves.

1824—Upper Canada Methodists had their own conference.

1828—Upper Canada Conference separated from the United States body.

1829—At a conference in Ancaster it was decided to publish the "Christian Guardian", to be edited by Egerton Ryerson.

1832—First Methodist Church, Hamilton, built in 1824, was selected as headquarters. Guided by Egerton Ryerson, the Upper Canada Methodists united with the Wesleyans who had arrived from Britain in the previous decade, along with some who had returned from Lower Canada.

1833—Union was in name only. Although not formally dissolved until 1840, it was never a reality. Former Upper Canada Methodists accused the Wesleyans of wanting to share in the Clergy Reserves. They held a new Conference and organized as the Methodist Episcopal Church, which was more often called Episcopal Methodist.

1836—Recently arrived English settlers on the 12th and 13th Concessions of East Flamborough were Methodists of the Episcopalian persuasion. They built a log church, opposite the present cemetery on the Mountsberg Road.

1854—Clergy Reserves were abandoned and the proceeds went to public education. The frame Methodist Church was built at Mountsberg.

1859—Weleyan Methodists built a church at Beechgrove, on the north corner.

1861—A new parsonage was built at Mountsberg.

1862-63—A church known as New Connection Methodist was built southeast of Freelton (Carmel Cemetery).

1866—Brock Road Methodist Church was built; not on Brock Road, but near, on the Concession road south of Strabane.

1872—Carmel Church (New Connection Methodist) united with the Wesleyan Church at Beechgrove.

1882—The Beechgrove group moved the Carmel Church to Freelton, to be known as Freelton Methodist. This building, north of the present parsonage, continued as a church for seventeen years and later became a residence. The former Beechgrove Church also remains in use as a private home.

1884—For ten or twelve years, encouraging progress had been made towards union. On July 1, 1884, it became an accomplished fact, and the Episcopal, Wesleyan and New Connection Methodists, as well as a few splinter groups, henceforth, were known as the Methodist Church of Canada.

1889—A new parsonage was built at Freelton and the Mountsberg manse was abandoned.

1899—The new red brick church was built in Freelton.

Mountsberg Methodists Before 1854

The English group that came from Lincolnshire in 1835 were devout Methodists, and, before a year had passed they put up a log building on the northwest side of the Cross road (Mountsberg Road) on Lot 6. There they worshipped and became part of the newly-organized Methodist Episcopal Church. As such, they were visited as often as possible by a Circuit rider who had to cover long distances on horseback.

Between visits, local members would take charge of regular meetings for prayer and study. Men who were willing to preside and proved to be capable, became known as lay preachers or class leaders.

As soon as it could be afforded, a new church was planned, and arrangements made to buy property across the road on the southeast side. Trustees were appointed. August 20, 1852, is the date recorded when "Philip and Ann Johnson, for the sum of five shillings of lawful money, granted to the church trustees, one-half acre of land for the site of a church and burying ground." The deed was registered August 28, 1852.

The fact that John Revel, a church trustee, had died July 4, 1851 at age 71, and had been succeeded by his son, Charles, suggests that the deal had been in process for some time. Also, the cemetery had been in use for seven years.

The first burial in the cemetery was that of Ann Barnes, wife of John Haines, who died February 1845, aged 38. Mrs. Haines had borne six sons. Tragically, the long-awaited daughter was buried with her. Her funeral was, not only the first, but the most unusual one ever held there. A February blizzard had made the roads impassable. Only a log boat could meet the emergency. This "boat" was a crude device made from a sturdy but slim tree, carefully chosen to have two forked branches, slightly curved and matching. Completed, the boat resembled a giant wishbone.

The coffin was lashed inside the fork. A team of horses was hitched to the single branch, or "tongue" and led the small, sad procession through bush and clearing, across the Twelve-Mile Creek and over two steep hills to the first open grave.

Thus, dramatically, was the cemetery dedicated to the pioneers.

A white slab tombstone, beside that of Mrs. Haines, is in memory of her nephew, Emmanuel, 2 months, son of William and Jane Barnes, who died January 14, 1839. The story is that the baby was buried on the Barnes' farm and later moved.

The cemetery, still in use, has been increased iii size, at least twice; in 1869 and again in 1906. A few early burials were of persons not associated with the local Methodist Church, but who were from nearby congregations which had no cemetery; one being a church of the latter 1800s, on the 10th Concession, near the Halton line; another, the church at Beechgrove.

For many years the cemetery was not fenced. Fanny Mount recalls a local, legendary witticism, telling that when a fence was first suggested, the reply was, "Why build a fence? Those inside can't get out, and those outside don't want to get in."

Mountsberg Methodists 1854-1925

Charles Mount, fifth son of Josiah, and only 22 in 1854, was given the task of building a new church. No doubt he had assistance at times either by individuals or a few Methodist "bees". When the congregation moved into their new frame church, the old log building became a shelter for horses during the service.

The following is a list of heads of families who were members or adherents during the first decade of the new church:

Jacob Allison John	John Laking
Barnes George	John Lewis
Henry Chambers	Robert Marshall
J.K. Crooker	Roger Maynard
Solomon Dawson	John Millman
James Dougherty	Isaac Monkhouse
Oliver Ferrier	Josiah Mount
John Flowers	William Murray
John Haines	John Page
John Hart	Joseph Page
Cornelius Hewins	Abraham Purnell
Thomas Hopkinson	Charles Revel
Benjamin Johnson	Robert Wigood, Sr.
William Johnson	Charles Wingrove
Harness Kelk	George Wingrove
Robert Kerr	Jacob Wright

Episcopal Methodist Church, 19??   *Mrs. A.R. Hewins.*

As the list of ministers will show, conferences and circuits were being changed constantly as the population increased. By 1861, circuits were becoming more localized. That was the year that Mountsberg had its first resident minister, J. McLean, in the newly-built parsonage.

When the frame church was built in 1854, the Board of Trustees newly-formed in 1852, included Abraham Purnell, William Johnson, John Revel, Josiah Mount, and Joseph Page. This amounted to a lifetime appointment and there was no rush to replace a member who died or resigned. In this case, nothing was done until the Board was reduced to two members, William Johnson and Joseph Page. In 1875, these two, with the Rev. E.L. Clement in the chair, appointed Charles Revel to replace his father, John, who had died in 1851; Thomas Haines to replace Abraham Purnell who died in 1858 and John Kerr to replace Josiah Mount who died in 1873.

Further changes took place at a Board meeting in March 1882, with the Rev. B.L. Cohoe presiding. John Kerr, who had moved to Brantford in January 1876, was replaced by Leonard Mount. Trueman Johnson replaced Joseph Page who resigned in May 1880. The Board members then were William Johnson, Charles Revel, Leonard Mount, Trueman Johnson and J.C. McNiven, who, at a previous meeting had replaced Thomas Haines who resigned. Leonard Mount was appointed Secretary.

The Methodist Union of 1884 caused considerable change at Mountsberg. For a period preceding that date, Mountsberg had shared a minister with Aberfoyle and Nassagaweya. A new circuit was formed, grouping Mountsberg with Beechgrove and Brock Road. In 1889, a further circuit change combined Mountsberg with Freelton and Brock Road. Freelton had service every Sunday afternoon. Mountsberg and Brock Road alternated with service one Sunday morning and the next Sunday evening. The Brock Road church was not on the Brock Road, just near that early route to Guelph on the first concession road south of Strabane. In 1889, a new parsonage was built in Freelton, a more convenient site for the new circuit. Four times a year, the circuit held what was known as the Quarterly Conference when representatives of the three churches met to discuss topics of interest to all.

At the first Quarterly meeting after the Church Union of 1884, the minister, Rev. John Stewart, had his annual salary increased to $600. And, henceforth, trustees were known as stewards; members at that time being William Laking, William H. Kerr, Trueman Johnson, Aaron Hewins and J.C. McNiven. Named to a special Sunday School Committee were William Emmons, William H. Kerr and J.S. Sparks.

And so, a Sunday School was organized, an institution that continued until the church was closed, officially. It was always held at 10 o'clock Sunday morning. A feature of its early years was a Bible Class conducted by J. Cohn McNiven. Officers no doubt were mustered from the ranks of the diligent church workers. Superintendents of the present century include Marshall Hunt, George Dougherty, Emerson Carton, Charles Hewins, Dr. John Page, Mr. Adamson and George Bogle. Many of these men also served on the Board of Stewards. Sunday School teachers were important, especially to the young children. I remember my favourite, Hannah Emmons, before she became Mrs. Bun Page.

At a meeting in 1893, William Emmons was ap-

Mountsberg Methodist Episcopal Church Conferences

Year	District	Circuit	Ministers
1836	Niagara	Nelson, Dumfries, & Buck Townships	D. Griffin, C. Sutherland, and one to be supplied
1837	Niagara	Dumfries	Barnabas Brown
1838	Niagara	Dumfries	Barnabas Brown
1839	London	Dumfries	Henry Gilmore
1840	London	Dumfries	Henry Gilmore, Robert Lyman
1841	London	Dumfries	Leonard D. Salsbury, one supplied
1842	London	Dumfries	Barny Markle, one to be supplied
1843	London	Dumfries	William McKeeley, one to be supplied
1844	London	Dumfries	E.L. Koyle
1845	London	Dumfries	W.D. Hughson, J.B. Richardson
1846	London	Dumfries	W.D. Hughson, Sylvester Karr
1847	Niagara	Dumfries	B. Browne, George Lawrence
1848	Niagara	Dumfries & Rainham	B. Browne, two to be sent
1849	Niagara	Dumfries	L.P. Smith, one to be sent
1850	Niagara	Dumfries	L.P. Smith, J. Wood
1851	Niagara	Dumfries	N.A. Fraser, one to be sent
1852	Niagara	Dumfries	Emerson Bristol, J. Kurtz
1853	Oxford	Dumfries	W.F. Lowe, J. Kurtz
1854	Oxford	Dumfries	W.F. Lowe, one to be sent
1855	Oxford	Dumfries	J. McLean, one to be sent
1856	Brantford	Flamborough	R. Service
1857	Brantford	Dumfries	W. Cope, Burnell Bristol, J.H. Mclean
1858	Brantford	Dumfries	M.D. Archer, P. Smith, Jr.
1859	Niagara	Dumfries	W. Cope, T.P. Bradshaw
1860	Niagara	Dumfries	T.P. Bradshaw
1861	Niagara	Flamborough	J. McLean
1862	Niagara	Flamborough	J. McLean
1863	Niagara	Flamborough	Eli Bartram
1864	Niagara	Flamborough	Eli Bartram
1865	Niagara	Flamborough	Eli Bartram
1866	Niagara	Flamborough	W. Yokum
1867	Niagara	Flamborough	W. Yokum
1868	Niagara	Flamborough	F.M. Smith
1869	Niagara	Flamborough	F.M. Smith
1870	Brantford	Flamborough	F.M. Smith
1871	Brantford	Flamborough	M. Dimmick
1872	Brantford	Flamborough	M. Dimmick
1873	Brantford	Flamborough	C. Burdett
1874	Niagara	Flamborough	C. Burdett
1875	Niagara	Flamborough	E.L. Clement
1876	Niagara	Flamborough	E.L. Clement
1877	Niagara	Flamborough	E.L. Clement
1878	Niagara	Flamborough	Burness Bristol
1879	Hamilton	Flamborough	Burness Bristol
1880	Hamilton	Flamborough	Burness Bristol, Walter McIntosh
1881	Hamilton	Flamborough	Benjamin L. Cohoe, W.P. Kennedy, supply,
1882	Hamilton	Flamborough	Benjamin L. Cohoe, D. Kearns
1883	Hamilton	Flamborough	Benjamin L. Cohoe, J. Lucy
1884	Hamilton	Flamborough	Benjamin L. Cohoe

Ministers of Mountsberg Methodist Church 1884-1925

Names of ministers taken from Minutes of Conference, held annually in June, as stationed for the ensuing Conference Year.

Years of	Conference	Circuit	Minister Stationed
1884,1885,1886	Niagara	Mountsberg	John Stewart
1887,1888,1889	Niagara	Mountsberg	Charles Deacon
1890,1891,1892	Niagara	Mountsberg	Benjamin L. Cohoe
1893	Niagara	Mountsberg	Samuel W. Holden
1894	Niagara	Freelton	Samuel W. Holden
1895,1896,1897	Hamilton	Freelton	Harry E. Hill
1898,1899,1900	Hamilton	Freelton	Andrew Hamilton
1901,1902,1903	Hamilton	Freelton	Adam I. Snyder
1904	Hamilton	Freelton	James Charlton
1905	Hamilton	Freelton	Supplied (J. Charlton superannuated)
1906	Hamilton	Freelton	William A. Fortner
1907,1908,1909,191	Hamilton	Freelton	George W. Smitherman
1911,1912,1913	Hamilton	Freelton	Thomas R. Todd
1914,1915,1916	Hamilton	Freelton	Benjamin Eyre
1917	Hamilton	Freelton	George Stacey Cassmore
1918,1919,1920	Hamilton	Freelton	Herbert B. Storey (Capt. G.S. Cassmore military chaplain)
1921, 1922, 1923	Hamilton	Freelton	Burdge F. Green
1924, 1925	Hamilton	Freelton	Roscoe H. Smith

List of Ministers, courtesy of Dorothy Farquharson, West Flamborough, who obtained the information from the Methodist Archives in Toronto.

pointed to fill the vacancy caused by the death of William Johnson, last of the original Board, which occurred in December 1886, and John Laking took the place of Leonard Mount who had moved away. Board members, as of 1893 were Charles Revel, Thomas Haines (previously reappointed), Trueman Johnson, William Emmons, and John Laking.

It is doubtful if the church had an organ in 1854, when the frame church was new, but for many years a reed organ stood against the back wall. It and two rows of choir chairs were one step up from the pulpit and fur ther separated by a short, red curtain about two feet high. In the 1880s, William Laking was an able choir leader with Margaret Jane Haines (Mrs. Job Revel) as organist. Elizabeth Laking, daughter of William, had a term as organist, as did Nellie Emmons in the early 1900s and Mrs. E. Carton at times prior to 1912. Olive Hewins, a serious student of music, very capably handled the organ for several years around 1910. Undoubtably, there were many others. In fact, almost anyone who could play a hymn had to substitute at times.

Mountsberg Methodists After 1925

Following the Church Union of 1925, the Mountsberg Church was closed, officially. Its members were meant to be absorbed by the newly-named Freelton United Church. But Mountsberg Methodists did not absorb that easily. It was a great disappointment to many to have their church closed, since they had never failed to meet their allotted share of the financial load of the Freelton Circuit. To be sure, some went to Freelton. Some who had Baptist ties simply turned to the Baptist Church nearby. Others, who just preferred at attend a community church, also went to the Baptist Church, as associates. A few chose the Presbyterian Church and went either to St. David's at Campbellville or to Duff's at Morriston. Some went nowhere.

There was imminent danger of the church being torn down or removed. Regardless of post-union affiliations, all former Methodists were steadfast in the common purpose of keeping the old church on its foundations. Their efforts won a reprieve that lasted until 1970.

During those first years of near-anonymity, two Sundays a year were set aside for services in the old church; the third Sundays of June and November. At each time there were services both morning and evening. Music usually was provided by a choir or singing group from a not-too-distant church. Over the years, ministers came from many places. On at least two occasions, the late Rev. Dr. George Williams went out from Hamilton and several services were conducted by the Freelton minister.

For a great many years, the November services were followed on Monday or Tuesday evening by an old fashioned tea-meeting. As the church had but one room, supper was served in the pews. When the food was cleared away, a two-hour entertainment was forthcoming. Next morning came the "pay-off" when ladies returned to wash great stacks of dishes and clean up the church.

In 1933, under the authority of the Freelton United Church, a series of eight summer services was held between mid-June and mid-September. Mr. Osborne Wingrove of Toronto supported and aided this project. Ministers were the following reverend gentlemen: J.M. Crawford, Freelton; W.B. Caswell, Oakville; S.H. Greenslade, Toronto; and R. McCormack (two Sundays); Dr. Graham, Charles C. Murray, H.S. Dodgson, all of Hamilton.

The old Methodist Church faced its second mortal threat in the spring of 1938, when one of two sheds, the one nearer the church, burned. Only the favourable quarter of the wind saved the aged wooden church. At the time of the fire, the lectern was stored in the enclosed woodshed section, and was lost. The Baptists, who had built a new church in 1922, still had the lectern from their old church. They presented it to the Methodists, and so for a time, a fitting memorial to the pioneer Baptists stood in the church of the pioneer Methodists.

In 1937, members of the Methodist Church put on a play entitled, "Eyes of Love" by Lillian Mortimer, a comedy-drama in three acts. This play, directed by Mrs. Earl Dougherty and Mrs. Alexander Campbell, was presented, later, at several nearby communities; the proceeds given for church maintenance.

About 1939, local ladies formed a group known as the Good Deed Club, which remained active for five or more years. Their aim was to raise funds to add to the proceeds from tea-meetings and the offerings at church services. All money was used for church maintenance and cemetery care. Except for installing electricity, there was no renovation or change.

Donations were received, occasionally, so that, in time, there was enough in the treasury to establish a modest trust fund. Bert Emmons, who died in 1950, spent many years, in his later life, looking after the cemetery and keeping the grass cut. For many years, Calvin Wigood has carried on with the work.

Along about 1950, McMaster Divinity students went out to preach at the semi-annual services and on more than one occasion, Mr. Roth of the Baptist Church moved into the old Methodist Church for the day, along with his choir and congregation. For several more years, the Baptist choir assisted with Myrna Bryant as organist or pianist.

The reed organ in time, succumbed to its years and was replaced by a piano, which served for a few years more. For several of the later meetings in the 1960's, Myrna Bryant had her electric organ moved in for the day with gratifying results.

As years went by and the ranks of former Methodists decreased, activities lessened. Tea-meetings had been dropped, as they became too much work for too few workers. November services were the next to be abandoned, and, for many later years, the third Sunday of June marked the one day of the year when the old church was open.

In June 1954, the church celebrated its centennial with special recognition of the Methodist settlers of 100 years earlier. On June 21, 1964, the church was 110 years old. It was a beautiful day and the pews were filled as Methodist descendants and friends rallied to the call of the aging church. L.S. Cust of Hamilton was the speaker; music was provided by the Baptist choir with Myrna Bryant at the organ, and Robert Laking of Milton as soloist.

Annual Service, June 20, 1965. Mrs. Sarah Coulson, Mrs. Albert Hewins, Charles Laking and Mrs. Hannah Page. *Mrs. C. Bryant.*

The June 1965 service paid tribute to the four oldest former members present: Mrs. Sarah Coulson of Burlington, 101; her cousin, Charles Laking of Aberfoyle, 93; they outdistanced by many years the other

Centennial Dress at Annual Service, June 18, 1967. Donna Page, Mrs. C. Wigood, Mrs. P. Pawlik, Peter Pawlik, Karen, Kerry and John David Pawlik in front. *Mrs. C. Bryant.*

two, Mrs. Albert Hewins of Mountsberg and Mrs. Hannah (Emmons) Page of Arkell.

The centennial service of June 18, 1967 was made memorable by some families who dressed in costumes of 100 years ago.

Postscript

Forty four years after the Methodist Church ceased to exist, officially, the Methodists of Mountsberg sang their final hymns and offered prayers for the last time in the 115-year-old frame church.

The great, great grandchildren of the Methodist pioneers, still living in the community, were becoming fewer. Those remaining could foresee a time when interest in the old church would all but vanish, leaving the building to inevitable decay. In this mood, they agreed to donate the church to Mr. G. Kilmer and his Westfield Pioneer Village (now Wentworth Pioneer Village).

A deconsecration service was held on Sunday, June 15, 1969, led by the Rev. J.H. MacCallum of Brantford. It was well attended by the many who were conscious of the finality of a life-long institution and a taken-for-granted landmark. Early in 1970, the church was moved in sections to its new location, to be completely restored for a new epoch of its history.

Early settlers of Mountsberg might not recognize the exterior as the plain, little church they built in 1854. A spire, in the fashion of New England churches, has been added, creating a more affluent and picturesque quality, but not truly representative of the struggling and frugal early congregation. The little porch, strictly for protection, was removed to unveil the pleasing architecture of the door.

Its quaint beauty, enhanced by its rustic surroundings, stir in one a feeling of reverence and romance; a feeling that has drawn several young couples to its altar for a wedding that is different and memorable.

Inside, the metal panelling, that was added about 1907-1908, was removed, and the Biblical quotation from verse 1 of the 84th Psalm, that once graced the wall facing the pews, again saw the light of day. Only a very few people, now, can remember, as a child, pondering the mysterious meaning of "How amiable are thy tabernacles, 0, Lord of Hosts!"

Methodist Memoirs

Mrs. Frank Coulson (1864-1969), formerly Sarah Laking, remembered well the church in the 1870's. Clearly, she recalled the weekly walk with others of her family, from their home in Nassagaweya, on the Town Line, near the north corner of East Flamborough; more than two miles, even with short cuts across fields. Their route meant a stop at the home of Mrs. Page Mount, a widow, who lived in John Revel's original log house. For the last, short lap, they had the company of the Mount children; Carrie Mount was the same age as Sarah.

In winter, when they reached the church, they were welcomed by a roaring fire in the big box stove, standing just inside the door. In summer, they arrived hot and dusty, but comfort awaited them. Every Sunday, all summer long, Mrs. Peter Page carried a pail of water and a cup from her home on the hill, for just such weary walkers.

Camp Meetings

In the two or three decades before 1900, camp meetings were common among Methodist congregations. Mrs. Coulson attended those held in the woods on the north-east side of the Centre Road, between the Laking Mill and the village corner.

Meetings lasted two or three weeks, with religious assemblies both day and evening, whilst the forest echoed the amens and the hallelujahs. Ministers, numbering 12 or more, visited from time to time, and sometimes, a noted evangelist came for a few days.

Tents were put up by the local people and furnished with beds, stoves and non-perishable foods. The beds were mainly for guests who came from a distance. Most Mountsberg people went home to sleep. Members of families took turns in attending meetings and staying home to care for the stock and do other necessary chores.

In 1954, on the occasion of the church centennial, Mr. Charles Laking (1869-1962), of Nassagaweya, and brother of Sarah, wrote the following account of a camp meeting of the late 1870's, held during the ministry of the Rev. Burness Bristol. *(Loaned by Lena Gunby).*

> "A large tent tabernacle, larger than the present church, was erected, in which the services were held three times daily for two weeks.
>
> There were about ten tents, in which the families of the church would take their eatables and bedding, and live in for the whole two weeks. This made quite a little village in the bush.
>
> People would come in democrat loads from all the surrounding districts and villages, any time of the day, tie their horses in the bush and attend the services.
>
> Preachers would be there from all over the whole Church Conference district, and stay for several days at a time. Half a dozen might be there at one time, and would board and sleep in the tents with the families.
>
> Swings for the children were tied among the trees, some at a very great height.
>
> The tabernacle was seated by cutting two tall trees and placing the logs about eight feet apart and laying planks, 12 feet long, across the logs. This would make a row of seats the length of the logs. There were three rows of seats with two aisles between the rows. These seats were not planed, and the slivers were not too friendly to the clothing of the people.
>
> For a carpet, the ground was covered with a few inches of straw. A plank platform was erected at the end of the tabernacle.
>
> At the end of the meetings, after the last service, the people would stand in a circle around

about an acre; possibly 500 persons. One would turn and shake hands down the row, then the next in the row would follow suit, until the whole circle had gone the rounds. Then all the people would be back where they started.

The tents and tabernacle were owned by the General Conference and would be rented out to congregations, where wanted, for a small sum."

Revival Meetings

Camp meetings had their day and passed into history. For about 20 years, revival services flourished as a replacement for camp meetings. Revivals were held inside the church every two or three years, or whenever a travelling evangelist was available. Every night, at such times, a meeting was held at one of the circuit churches. These were rousing evenings of loud preaching and exhortation, interspersed with enthusiastic singing of gospel songs by the congregation.

Invariably, meetings ended with a plea for all who were saved to walk up to the altar and declare themselves. The weakness of these assemblies seemed to be the word "saved" as defined by the individual. It must have been frustrating for the resident minister to see persons saved and re-saved as often as a new evangelist appeared. For obvious reasons, ministers began to favour a less sensational and more thoughtful approach to religion.

Other Customs Change

There are still a few grandparents around who can remember when their grandparents came to church and grandmother moved sedately to the right, while grandfather found a seat on the left. My Laking grandparents and Mr. and Mrs. Page were the last hold-outs for this archaic custom, a custom that must have begun to change, about 1870. That was the year my paternal grandparents were married and, when I knew them, they sat together in the centre of the church.

The early 1900's were the last years of the loud amens and "experience" sessions which, occasionally, followed the regular service. At such times, members were prone to relate personal experiences, with emphasis on their faith which upheld them in trying times.

To children, dangling their legs from the hard, straight-backed pews, these moments were, alternately, entertaining and embarrassing; entertaining, because the many but vague references to sin left broad scope for the imagination. But, when Grandfather John Laking stood up to "testify", I held my breath. Grandfather was a pillar of the church, a holy man and kind. Then, why, oh why, did he have to tell everyone how "grieviously" he had sinned. It was most humiliating. They would never catch me telling on myself, like that, in public. Besides, I was worried. I had heard about the sins of the father being visited upon the children, even unto the third and fourth generation. And, there I was, trapped in the vulnerable second spot.

Picnics and Garden Parties

Every year, about June, the Sunday School had a picnic. From our parents, we heard about early excursions to Puslinch Lake, where rowboats could be rented and people could swim. Four picnics come to my mind; the earliest one at the Emmons home (later Leslies, and still later, Shanks), where we played games on the spacious lawn; another in the woods, near the Mountsberg Road, opposite the (former Paul McCarthy) Orosz farm, where there were swings in the tall trees. One time we travelled as far afield as Oaklands, a public park on the bay, west of the present La Salle Park.

Thursday, June 22, 1911, was a school holiday for the Coronation of King George V and Queen Mary. That date was chosen for our annual picnic, which turned into a neighbourhood celebration in the Revell orchard and the flats between the two Revell houses on the 13th Concession.

Often, but not every year, the church would have a Garden Party. Most of them were held on someone's lawn, where supper would be served at long trestle tables, followed by an evening concert. Performers, local or imported, did their act on a temporary platform, set up outside a door that provided a stage entrance or exit.

The last Garden Party that I recall was at the Woolsey home, early in the summer of 1912. Entertainment was provided by Jack Stevenson and Bert Phoenix of Hamilton. Mr. Stevenson sang. He pranced and posed his way through songs, both old and new. Mr. Phoenix gave readings.

The previous fall, Mr. Phoenix had entertained at a church tea-meeting, and there met our school teacher, Mollie Cluff of Clinton. The friendship that followed soon became courtship. And so, after the outdoor supper, the two strolled about the Woolsey lawn.

Only workers were welcome inside the house. But by carrying piles of dirty dishes, three of us got by unchallenged. Then we quickly disappeared, not outside, but to the front rooms. There we peeked from behind curtained windows to spy on the couple who were married the next year.

Christmas Concerts

Those old enough to remember the Methodist era, probably recall best the Sunday School entertainment which came once a year, as surely as did Christmas; the rehearsals after school, when we walked home in the early dark, so crisp and cold and snowy; the final night when the church looked unreal with a curtained dressing room on the right of the platform, and on the left, a ceiling-high tree loaded with unwrapped presents, one for each child.

Lamplight added fantasy to the church we knew by daylight. At front and back were bracket lamps. Near the centre, suspended from the ceiling and marking the corners of the large imaginary square were four round-wick, brass lamps. To light these, Mrs. John Wingrove had to stand on a chair.

Sleigh ride, 1926. Bill McFarlane, Roy Hewins, Mary H. Spring and John Hewins. *G.A. Hewins.*

Dialogues, drills and carols were not too bad. Companions lent moral support. But, when called upon for a recitation or any solo performance, devastating shyness consumed some of the artists. Boys withdrew as far as possible into their Sunday collars, and girls examined their shiny, new shoes.

From year to year there was little change in the pattern of these concerts. The Sunday School superintendent was the chairman. After he had successfully subdued the babble and welcomed the guests, the minister was asked to "say a few words". To do the reverend gentlemen justice, he did make his words few, well aware that the excited children were in no mood to listen. Slowly, the chairman made his way down the long list of the program, as he announced one number after the next. Finally, just as the last amateur entertainer bowed to acknowledge the applause, Santa Claus jangled in, bend double under a heavy pack.

With a big bag of candy and an orange from Santa Claus, and a gift from the tree, each happy child was bundled up warmly for the trip home. We rode in a sleigh box, drawn by a team of Percherons eager for their warm stalls. The sleigh was cozy. The floor of the box had been well insulated with a thick layer of straw, covered with a horse blanket. Snuggled under a buffalo robe, we stared at a star-packed sky that seemed to barely clear the tree tops; stared until the music of the sleigh bells became a lullaby.

At that moment, life was beautiful. And this was only the beginning. No more practicing. No more school. All we had to do now was wait for Christmas Day.

Weddings

In the history of the church, only five marriages took place within its walls. In early times, weddings were held at home, or quiet marriages were performed at the parsonage. Little is known of the first church ceremony. It took place no later than 1889, when Mounts-berg had a manse. A house-cleaning upheaval was in progress when the couple called at the minister's home to be married. With no suitable space available, the minister walked the couple and their two witnesses down the hill to the church.

The second wedding was in July 1924, when Merle Hewins and William Cust were married. Later, the three daughters of Flossie and Earl Dougherty chose to honour the old church with their weddings: Doreen to Lloyd McGeachy in April 1943; Grace to Jack Bell in June 1943; and Betty to William Payne in September 1949.

The Old Methodist Parsonage

On March 4, 1861, six acres at the north corner of Lot 6, south-east, Conc. 12, were sold by Solomon Dawson to Charles Revel. This became the new parsonage property. But not immediately. A minor mystery is why, nine days later, another document transferred the same property to Joseph Page, whose land abutted. In November of the same year, Joseph Page sold it to J.K. Crooker et al., the trustees of the Methodist Church. Apparently, the frame parsonage had been built in the meantime.

In the following three decades, it became the home of eleven ministers. Very little is known of these gentlemen. Mr. McLean, the first one, was the uncle of Mrs. Roger Maynard, and encouraged Mr. Maynard to move from Listowel and teach in the old log school. The Rev. Burness Bristol was popular enough to have had two babies named for him. The Cohoe children, Margaret, who later became Mrs. Harry Weaver of Toronto, and her brother, Benson, attended Mounts-berg School, and there made lifelong friends. Mr. Cohoe's assistant, Mr. Lucy, rode a horse to Nassagaweya to preach. He was young and handsome. But, maybe that was not the reason why at that time, most of the young ladies chalked up a near-perfect attendance at church.

It was a disappointment to Mountsberg Methodists when, in 1889, the Rev. Charles Deacon moved from the local parsonage into the new larger and more imposing manse in Freelton. The Mountsberg property reverted, by sale, to Joseph Page, all except one-third acre on which the house stood. In October 1889, this was sold to Margaret Dawson (not related closely, if at all, to Solomon). She was a widow who went there from her farm, south of Duff's Church, on the Brock Road.

Methodist Parsonage, 1913, Mr. and Mrs. Peter Page on porch. *Miss Christine Hanson.*

Jessie Dawson, born in 1878, fourth of six daughters in the family of eight, and, after 1918, Mrs. Warren of Lucky Lake, Saskatchewan, told of the time her family lived in the former parsonage.

Mrs. Dawson, who became caretaker of the church, found herself among good neighbours. She was barely settled when Mr. Joseph Page, without ceremony, dropped off a bag of potatoes. Peter Page made a gift of an entire winter's supply of apples; apples not perfect enough for packing, but still good and gratefully received.

Many times, Mrs. Dawson walked to Dundas and carried home her purchases. She thought nothing of a walk to Freelton or Carlisle for items she could not get at the Mountsberg store. Mrs. Warren remembered well her mother scrubbing the plain, board floor of the church. And, on Sunday afternoons, little Jessie liked to slip down the hill to the quiet church and read from the "library", a modest collection of books kept in a cupboard.

And still the aura of Methodism clung to the one-time parsonage. There after 1897, Mr. and Mrs. Peter Page, stalwart Methodists, lived out their retirement years; and there in June 1920, they celebrated their diamond wedding. Sixty years! Sixty good years that began with an elopement in the time-honoured way, where the bride-to-be scrambled down a ladder placed at an upstairs window.

This diamond celebration was no small family affair. The family was there, to be sure, and so was just about everyone in the neighbourhood. A day to remember; the memory touched with sadness just four months later, by the death of Mrs. Page.

Diamond Wedding Anniversary of Peter and Susannah Page, June 1920.   *Mrs. W.C. Cust.*

Schools

In 1816, the Statutes of Upper Canada provided grants for Common Schools where twenty, or more, students would attend; so, 1836 seems a likely date for the erection of the log school, presumed to have stood across the road and slightly north of the 1866 brick school. This was a small, crude structure with two rows of long desks with benches, and very little else except a teacher's desk and a stove. In the thirty years of its existence, the names of only two teachers remain: John McClinton, 1861, and Roger Maynard, 1862-1864. The Statutes of 1816 also encouraged the use of schools on Sunday for religious services, so the Baptists made good use of the log school before they had a church in Freelton in 1844, and, later, their local church of 1852.

Dating from the late 1840's to the turn of the century, a Roman Catholic Academy stood on the east corner of the intersection of the Centre Road and the 11th Concession. This was mainly for the use of two groups of Irish settlers, who came in the 1840's, during the potato famine in Ireland. A Miss Freel is the only known teacher of the school.

Until 1864, when the Beechgrove school was built, there had been a frame school on the Brock Road, at Purnell's Corner, northwest of the Purnell buildings. While it was in use, it is assumed that nearby families, later attending the Mountsberg school, had attended that school.

It was probably in 1866, when the new, brick school was built, that school boundaries for S.S. No. 6, East Flamborough, were defined, to last until 1966:

Concession 11, Northwest lots 1 to 10
Concession 12, All, lots 1 to 10
Concession 13, All 12 lots
Concession 14, All 12 lots

From the beginning up to 1900, or even later, school attendance was prone to be haphazard, especially for boys old enough to help on the farm. They attended mainly in the winter months, when farm work was slack. Teachers accepted the problem of fitting these irregular students into classes, and dealing with the discipline required to cope with a few disinterested non-students who came just to relieve the winter boredom. Some of these young men were twenty or more, often older than the teacher who, before 1897 at Mountsberg, was always a man.

These older winter students did not crowd the class room too greatly. During the blustery weeks of winter, the youngest children, unless they lived near the school, could not struggle through a mile or two of deep snow. For this reason, first graders enrolled after the Easter vacation.

Until about 1908, school re-opened in mid-August after a six week vacation. Before that time, and for many years thereafter, Mountsberg students of the Entrance Class (then Sr. IV, now Grade 8), spent three days at the end of June at the Strabane School sweating over the Entrance Examination. The certificate, so achieved, was the "open sesame" to High Schools and Collegiate Institutes.

Secondary Education

It is unlikely that any students from the log school went on to higher education, although Grammar Schools were becoming more numerous. They were boarding schools that covered the work of Common Schools (later called Public Schools) and went on to advanced studies. Hamilton had a Grammar School in 1821, Ancaster in 1837, Guelph in 1842, and Waterdown about the same time.

Secondary education, as we know it, began in Hamilton when a day school for graduates of Common Schools opened in 1866. Both Guelph Collegiate Institute and Waterdown High School were established in 1879.

In the latter part of the 1800's and into the 1900's, a few local students, mostly young men, went to Waterdown High School and boarded in private homes. For many years, a choice of High School depended much upon transportation and a town where one might live with friends or relatives. Waterdown has always been the school supported by East Flamborough tax payers, but, over the years, Mountsberg has had high school graduates from Hamilton, Guelph, Dundas, Galt, Milton and London, and perhaps other schools, as well as Waterdown.

Ontario's Adolescent School Attendance Act in 1919 required attendance up to 16 years of age, and meant a gradual but decided change in the pattern of education. A Continuation School, offering Grades 9 and 10, opened in the old Baptist Church in Freelton and continued a decade or longer, but students had to attend the new Waterdown High School for the higher grades, and that meant staying in town between weekends.

Finally, secondary education became readily available to all, when a school bus service to Waterdown began operating early in the 1950's.

Mountsberg School (S.S. No. 6, East Flamborough)

Quite a few families in the community were building new homes in the 1860's because they needed larger houses and could afford them. A new school was built in 1866 for the same reasons. There are no records to tell us who built the school, how much it cost, and how much came as a grant from the government. Some of the houses in the community appear to be built of the same buff coloured brick. The size was 40' x 45' of solid brick wall and the school had a high ceiling which made it difficult to heat in cold winter weather. The ink bottles would be frozen solid every morning. There were boxstoves at opposite corners, north and south, and

—110—

Mountsberg School (S.S. No. 6 East Flam borough) as it looked in 1909. *Mrs. VC C. Cust.*

Mountsberg School, June 24, 1896, Mr. Vanderburg, teacher. Fourth row—Warren Dawson, Alex Campbell, Osborne Wingrove, Herbert Wingrove, Aubrey Emmons and Clarke Redpath. Third row—Laura Mount, Jennie Wingrove, not known, Ethel Campbell, Maggie Redpath, Mina Redpath and Mina Campbell. Second row—Dave Stewart, James Campbell, Ethel Haines, Eliza McCurdy, not known, Clara Wingrove, Maud Marshall, Marshall Revell, Gordon Wingrove and Stanley Vanderburg. First row—Minnie Cartwright, not known, Olive Hewins, Beatrice Ford, Laura Vanderburg, Eva Vanderburg, George McCurdy and George Stewart. *The late Miss Eba Haines.*

Mountsberg School, February 14, 1965, Mr. Brydges, teacher. Fourth row—Judy Thibodeau, Evelyn Korb, Susannah Pasuta, Kathie Wingrove, Janet Law, Nancy McCarthy, Karen Korb and Marilyn Dredge. Third row—Ron Page, Peter Grove, Paul Wigood, Richard Grove, Erwin Laking, Dave Coverdale, Bruce Ballantine and Alexander Dryden. Second row—Debbie Mac-Dougall, Debbie Arnold, Bob Law, Diane McCarthy, Heather MacDougall, John Sims, Donna Ballantine and Diane Edmar. First row—Charles Thibodeau, Glenn Dryden, Heinz Korb, Bradley Wingrove, Larry Wigood and Brian McKenna. *Mrs. C. Dryden.*

four rows of double wooden seats and desks on stationary iron frames.

Each year brought change, whether much or little. For example, porches were added in 1911, the basement was excavated and furnace installed in 1926, the school was wired for electricity in 1939, and new toilets and a new front entrance to the school were built in 19561957. By the time ceiling, walls and floor were renewed in the early sixties, there was little left in 1966 to identify the classroom of a century ago.

The school opened in 1866 for the Fall term, and it continued without interruption until the end of June, 1966, a full 100 years. The school was administered by a Board of three trustees. One trustee was elected for a three-year term at the Annual Ratepayers' meeting held at the end of the year. The duties of the Board were to hire a teacher and maintain and operate the school property. In 1964 the school enrollment increased sharply and it became necessary to bus grades 6, 7 and 8 to other schools in the area. A Township Board took over administration of Township schools in 1965.

A centennial reunion of Mountsberg School was held on Saturday July 23, 1966, at 2:30 p.m. Using the

Students in Centennial costume for the 1966 Reunion. Dawn Hewins, Donna Page, Marilyn Coverdale and Brenda Elliott. *Mrs. A. Elliott.*

Speakers at Centennial Reunion of Mountsberg School, July 23, 1966. *Mrs. C. Bryant.*

Rubber collection during W.W. II. Rear—Betty Dougherty, Freda Elliott, Faye Bryant, Alice Revell and Louise Smith. Middle—Elsie Laking, Betty Revell, Margaret McCarthy, Marion Gunby and Audrey Wingrove. Front—Evelyn Laking, Lois Gunby and Patricia Watson. *Mrs. P. Pawlik.*

recently prepared attendance record for 1840-1966, the centennial committee sent out more than 300 invitations and were rewarded with a large attendance at the reunion. Those arriving passed the huge banner which stretched from side to side of Centre Road. Highlights of the day included an oldtimers softball game, Badenoch vs. Mountsberg, horseshoe pitching and races, supper served at the school grounds, and a dance. During the official ceremony at 4:30 p.m., the Hon. Ray Connell, **MPP** for Wentworth, spoke and greetings were made or read from former pupils and teachers.

A school picnic. Rear—Jonathan Scott, Ivan Laking, Morley Hewins, Bill Revell, Charles Roberts, Archie Gunby, Jeffrey Haines, Bob Wingrove and Jim Scott. Middle—Isabel Gunby, unknown, Nellie Scott, Olive Campbell, Lena Revell, Martha Gunby, Jennie Scott, Annie Hewins, Phoebe Jane Revell, Harriet Gunby and Elizabeth Hewins. Front—unknown, Alma Laking, unknown, Fanny Mount, Grace Gunby, Stella Gunby, John Campbell, Reg Hewins, Irene Campbell, Margaret Hewins and Gordon Hewins. Kneeling—unknown and Bruce Patton. *Wm. Revell.*

The school buildings, through the efforts of members of the community, were acquired by the Township in 1966 and have been administered by a Recreation Committee as a Community Centre. Because of renovations previously made to the inside of the school, Mountsberg now has a community centre of which it can be proud.

During the hundred years it operated as a school, many people received a good, basic education. Here is a comment about a one-room school with one teacher teaching all the grades. The pupils were exposed to hearing the grades above and below them being taught. This gave them a preview of what they were to be taught later on, and a review of what they had been taught previously.

Joseph H. Smith, who taught in 1866 and 1867, became a school inspector in 1871, the first year there were school inspectors in Ontario. He made regular visits to the Mountsberg School until his retirement in 1912. Mr. Smith became widely known as a scholar and historian.

Here are lists of the teachers from 1866 to 1966. The following list is incomplete and uncertain as to time and order, but is all we have been able to find out regarding teachers, 1866-1900.

Teachers-1866-1900

1866, 1867-	Joseph H. Smith, became an inspector in 1871
1868, 1869-	James McLean
1880—	(perhaps earlier), Walter Evans, who in 1923 was appointed Judge of Wentworth County Court
After 1881—	Mr. Campbell, who boarded at Fosters
About 1884—	David Bickell, remembered for his severity
? —	George Lamb of Puslinch
? —	John McCuen, who became an M.D. in Michigan
About 1887—	John Irvine (or Irving) of Halton
? —	Ed. Shepherd, who became a preacher
? — 1889	R.H. Cowan, who became a dentist in Hamilton
or later-	J.E. Littlejohn
1895, 1896-	Mr. Vanderburgh; he and his family lived in part of George Johnson's house
1897-1900-	Lily Reid. During this time a brother and sister, Mr. and Miss Henderson, substituted a few times

Teachers, 1900-1966

1900-1905-	Bertha Nixon, later Mrs. Tansley of Carlisle
1905-1907-	Edgar Hamilton of Strabane, who went to Olds, Alberta Ethel
1907-1909-	Chapman of Campbellville, later editor of Farmers' Magazine and a writer
1909-Easter 1910—	Mollie E. Cluff of Clinton
Easter 1910-June 1910-	Mrs. Jacob Mount
1910-1911-	Mary M. Barberree of Corwhin
1911-1912-	Mollie E. Cluff, later Mrs. N.A. Phoenix of Hamilton
1912-1913-	Ruth Benn
1913-1914-	Zetta Bousfield of Carlisle
1914-1915-	Miss Finn
1915-1916—Sept.—	Eliza Norris
Dec. 1916—	Mariana McCann
January 1, 1917—	J.B. Morrow
September 1, 1917—February 1, 1918—	Erle W. Glennie
April 1, 1918—	Geo. W. Williamson
April 22, 1918—September 1, 1918—	Erle E. Glennie
September 1, 1919—April 1, 1920—	Miss Edna Wasman
	Miss Ruby Stickney
	Miss Elizabeth Chowen
	Miss Pearl Hanna
January 1, 1921—	Miss Nina M. Leslie

February 1, 1928-	Miss Verna J. McLaughlin
April 1, 1928-	Miss Nina M. Leslie
September 1, 1928-	Miss Bessie Walker
September 1, 1929-	Miss Doris Binkley
September 1, 1934-	Gordon Mann
September 1, 1935-	Miss Marjorie Harbottle
September 1, 1936-	Miss Anna McPhail
September 1, 1939-	Miss Ethel Schrader
January 1, 1941-	Miss Berenice Taylor
September 1, 1941-	Wm. Roseborough
September 1, 1941	Mary (Hanning) Elliott, music teacher to end of year
December 1, 1941-	Mrs. Nina M. (Leslie) Parker
April, 1942-	Mrs. Alice Brock
September 1, 1942-	Miss Hazel Day
September 1, 1945-	Miss Bessie Alderson
September 1, 1947-	Miss Bernita Attridge
September 1, 1947-	Ed. Watson, music teacher
September 1, 1948-	Miss Verna Banting
September 1, 1949-	Mrs. Doris E. Moffatt
February, 1950-	Mrs. Lorna K. Taylor
March 1, 1950-	Mrs. Jean Potter
September 1, 1951-	Mrs. Lorna K. Taylor
September 1, 1953-	Mrs. Mary K. Greerson
September 1, 1953-	Mrs. Hilbert, music teacher
September 1, 1955-	Miss Donna J. MacDonald
September 1, 1957-	Donald W. Pyper
September 1, 1957-	Mrs. Doreen Mariette, music teacher
September 1, 1959-	Donald Martin
January 1, 1960-	Mrs. Gladys McCrea
September 1, 1961-	Donald R. Olan
September 1, 1964-	Lynn Edward Brydges
September 1, 1965-	Mrs. Doris Montgomery

Council Members

1881-82	William Dougherty	1928-30	Mark Leslie
1884-89	William Laking	1932-38	Alex Campbell
1891-92	Donald Cameron	1940-51	Charles McCarthy
1896	Ralph Hewins	1952-61	William Wingrove*
1899-1903, 1908	William Emmons	1952-67	John Easterbrook
1904-07	Marshall Haines	1968-69	Paul McCarthy
1908-11, 1913	George Dougherty	1969	Frank Hunter
1913-15	Burdge Gunby		
1916-19	Richard Taafe		
1924-27	Charles Mount		

Mr. Wingrove became Deputy Reeve in 1956, Reeve in 1958 and County Warden in 1960.

The Credit Valley Railway

Transportation was a problem to the early settlers, horses and oxen being the only means of travel. From Mountsberg, situated midway between Hamilton, Guelph and Galt (Cambridge), it required a full day to a make a round trip to any one of these cities.

Farmers hauled barley to Sleemans brewery in Guelph or to Brown's Wharf (now known as La Salle Park, Aldershot) for shipment by boat. A common market for beef was Hamilton, necessitating a 2 a.m. start to obtain a favourable location.

In 1871 the Credit Valley Railway obtained a charter to built a railroad from Toronto to St. Thomas to connect up with the Michigan Central Railroad, and, in 1873, surveyors reached Milton, on the route to St. Thomas.

Arrival of Mrs. Osborne Wingrove at McRae. Station, 1916. Looking westward. *Mrs. H. Rennick.*

The news of this railroad was received with much favour from a standpoint of travel and the shipping of produce. No venture of this magnitude progresses without some dissention from the affected citizens. Railways crossed the country via the most direct and economic route, resulting in farms being crossed at any location or angle cutting them into two portions. In such cases the railway provided level crossings and fences, but the farmer had to open and close two gates to reach the other section of the farm. The big problem was driving cattle across the tracks, which required several people to help.

Farmers had to be constantly on the alert for fires caused by sparks from the train locomotives, steam being the energy required and wood the main source of fuel; coal was available in Toronto but not along the line. When fires started, railway employees were required to help fight the flames. Around the turn of the century, one railway fire burned the trestle across the 12 Mile Creek on Lot 5, Concession 13.

The surveyed line passed through the farmyard of Duncan Cameron on Lot 2 separating the barn and sheds from the house. The barn was moved to the southeast side and placed on a foundation. For this inconvenience Mr. Cameron was paid $200.

On Lot 2 an extra 34 feet in width by 500 feet in length was purchased for a siding which never was used. Presumably it was intended as a passing area.

The line continued through Lot 3 owned by Archibald Cameron, Lot 4 owned by Archibald Campbell and into Lot 5 owned by David McCrae. Mr. McCrae was an enterprising Scotsman who visioned great progress from the advent of the railway and made a deal with them to install a siding, stock yards, and flag station, to be maintained for 99 years.

Still visible are traces of a siding extending back from McCrae's siding into a quarry on Lot 4.

The original station was named McCrae but unfortunately the family name was misspelled. It was a three sided structure that was burned about 1910 and replaced by a station that was moved from Dixie Road, near Cooksville.

When James Scott purchased Lot 6 in 1874, negotiations with the C.V.R. had already taken place; but it was in 1880, when trains already were running, that the order for the land went through and there is no record of James Scott ever receiving any money.

The line continues through Lots 7 and 8, just touching the northeast corner of Lot 9 and into Puslinch Township to Brock Road (Highway 6) at Shaw (Schaw) station, later renamed Puslinch.

Aside from the local problems, the railroad proved to be a boon to the residents. Cattle could be shipped from Campbellville, McRae or Shaw stations where stockyards and ramps were available. It was convenient for passenger traffic to Toronto and London or for transfer at Shaw for stagecoach to Guelph or Hamilton.

During the winter seasons of 1914-15 and 1915-16, Murray Crawford of Campbellville cut logs from McCrae's property and shipped the elm logs to the basket factory in Burlington, via the railway, loading the logs on flat cars at McCrae siding.

In the 1920's and early 1930's, McRae station was the terminus for local residents, whose children attended either Milton High School or Galt Collegiate Institute. The McCrae farm was sold to Archibald Scott on January 27, 1931, and, after the death of Dr. Thomas McCrae of Philadelphia, the siding and station were eventually removed. The building is slowly rotting away at its present location on Lot 29, Concession 10 of Puslinch Township. The name still remains visible on each end of the building as a reminder of better days.

The Credit Valley Railway went into regular passenger train operation December 24, 1879 and was purchased by the Canadian Pacific Railway on November 20, 1883.

C.P.R. train, westbound, near Lot 6, Concession 13. *Tom Jordan.*

Barn Raising

Most of the barns in Mountsberg were built between 1880 and 1910, a few later ones being replacements after fires. They are two storey structures with stone wall foundations containing a stable and surmounted by a timber-frame barn. There are two types, known as side drive and end drive. A side drive barn had one or two large doors on the side to drive into the barn with a load of hay. End drive barns had a large door in one end. They were also known as bank barns. If possible, one side or end of the stable wall was built into a slope, giving easier access to the barn.

Some of these barns were built with an 'over-shot'; one wall of the stable built back in from the side of the barn 8 or 10 feet. This provided a loafing area for cattle in the summer and protection from cold fall rain. However, they made the stable smaller and darker.

Not much is known about the barns they replaced. Some of the timbers salvaged were quite long, indicating the former barns were a fair size, perhaps 60 x 36 feet. There were generally one or two of these on each farm, built over the years. Most of them were built at ground level with the stabling inside. As time went on, and farms were producing more crops and supporting more livestock, the old buildings were quite inadequate and it became necessary to build a more modern structure with labour saving rack-lifters and hay fork tracks.

Hay rack-lifter, before hay was baled. *Wm. Wingrove*.

Building a new barn was a major undertaking, and the decision had to be made at least a year or two in advance. It not only meant a lot of work for the farmer, but his wife had to board a lot of extra help for weeks. If there were no sons or daughters old enough to help, a man and girl had to be hired. An extra hog or two had to be butchered that spring.

First the farmer went to see a barn carpenter, generally known as a barn framer, or framer for short. The framer would visit to find out what kind and size of barn was wanted. He also decided how much of the old barn or barns could be used, as generally it, or they, went a long way towards the new one. The framer would make a list of all the material needed. That was quite a list indeed!

A stone-mason had to be found to build the stable walls, and probably more work went into the foundation than into the barn. Many loads of stone had to be brought to the building site, sand hauled and lime brought from the nearest lime-kiln. The stone-mason and framer had to coordinate their work, as for instance the stable posts and sleepers, which had to be put in place before the walls were finished.

To accumulate the materal for the new barn, the farmer would probably buy most of the lumber, for it was as cheap to buy as to cut trees and have them sawed. He wouldn't have decided to build in the first place unless he had enough money. For the timber for posts, beams and girts, he would cut trees, which had to be tall and straight. Pine was the first choice; ash was also used, especially for the small girts. Elm was a poor third.

In the late winter or early spring, the framer would send two of his men to square the logs. The logs were

Bring In the hay. *Wm. Wingrove*.

Raising the Hewins Barn, 1909. Assembling the first bent on the barn floor.. *A.R. Hewins.*

Raising the first bent. *A.R. Hewins.*

Raising the second bent. *A.R. Hewins*

Installing the main plate. . *A.R. Hewins.*

Installing the lower rafters. *A.R. Hewins.*

placed on skids a foot or two off the ground. A log was marked with a chalk line for a guide, then one of the men would stand on the log and chop into the side down to the line. This was known as score-hacking. The other axe-man would trim the chips off and leave a flat face. The log was given a quarter turn and another face was put on it. Two more turns and the log was squared. The faces were then smoothed with a broad-axe.

In the spring, with help from his neighbours, the building site was graded, the foundation built, joists placed and the floor laid but not nailed. The old barns could not be demolished until the weather was fit to turn livestock out to pasture, while the new barn had to be sided and roofed for the haycrop early in July.

About the middle of May, the framer and his crew would arrive with a wagon load of equipment: axes, adzes, a boring machine, chisels, commanders, ropes, ladders, and countless odd tools. A commander was an over-grown wooden mallet. Anyone attending a few raisings soon learned the terms. The gang would soon tear down the old barn and in a few days all the timbers were ready. The framer used a ten foot pole marked in inches and feet, a square and a scribe to mark where the timbers were to be cut, and mortises and tenons made. The rest of the crew used these marks to make the mortises and tenons. The boring machine, a portable, self-feeding drill press, was used to bore out the mortises. They were then finished with chisels. The framer would probably have several barns on the go so they had to work from early in the morning until dark.

Then came the day of the 'Raising'. The farmer would invite about fifty men to come and help. Several women would come too, to help the farmer's wife prepare a hot evening farm meal. There would also be a few older people invited with some children, so there could easily be a hundred people to feed.

The crowd would arrive about noon and get to work. The first job was to carry the timbers onto the barn floor. The framer and one of his crew would send the timbers up in their proper order to see that they were laid in the right places. Then the bents were all framed. The plates and purlins were left until later.

The next procedure was to upend the No. .1 bent. A man would stand at the bottom of each post with a sharp crowbar to keep the whole bent from skidding out of control. Long ropes were tied to the top end to hold the bent in place when it was raised. About fifty men would position themselves to the bent, and at the sound of "Yo-Heave!", everybody would lift the bent to a vertical position. Actually it wasn't particularly heavy and the main reason for having lots of men was for safety. The first lift would get the cap-beam (the top beam of the bent) about ten feet up. The bent was propped and the short pike-poles were brought into play. These were cedar poles with a sharp piece of iron in one end. A few floor boards were removed for the ends of the pike-poles. The other ends were jabbed into the timbers and with another "Yo-Heave!" and men lifting on the poles, the bent went up another step. Then longer pike-poles were used and with another "Yo-Heave!" the bent was lifted and pushed into its vertical position.

The ropes were tied, the bent braced with planks and then the second bent was raised. The girts were then placed in readiness. First the lower girts were lifted into position with ropes by men standing on the cap beam and others helping from the barn floor. The tenons were pushed into the mortises of the first bent, and when the pin holes lined up, the pins were started in. The other end of the girts were started into the mortises on bent No. 2. One mustn't forget to put in the braces and frame in the ladders. Then the top girts were raised, the top of the second bent pushed and pulled into position until all the pin holes lined up. The pins were then driven into place with the commander.

The same procedure was followed for the next bents, but the last bent had to be raised in a slightly different manner. The height of the bent was greater than the distance between them, so the last one was put together with the ends of the posts extending over the foundation. This bent had to be dragged forward as it was being lifted. By the time the cap beam was ten feet off the floor, the ends of the posts were in position. With the last bent raised and girted, it was then necessary to get the plates and purlins in place and to put up the lower run of rafters. Sometimes teams were chosen and they had a race to put up these timbers. Some framers would not permit this frivolity, however.

By this time the afternoon was over and it was time for supper. To feed a crowd like this there would be three 'sittings'. Preparation of the meal by the women is a story in itself. A 'Barn Raising' was a long day and a day long to be remembered.

In a few days the siding and roof were on and the barn was ready for hay. Then the framer and his gang moved on to another place. Later, they would come back to put in a granary and finish the barn and stabling. It would probably be long into the winter before the carpenter could consider his job was done.

Telephones

Mountsberg's first telephone was installed in the store about 1905-06. It was looked upon as a remarkable innovation, not only for the storekeeper, but for the community at large; to be used with discretion, of course. Unfortunately, most of the incoming messages, for people other than the storekeeper, concerned the death of a relative living at some distance; "distance" meaning anything over ten miles.

And, too, the telephone lent prestige to the neighbourhood. There was Freelton that had had a telephone since 1899!

The Mountsberg telephone connected with Puslinch store and, in Freelton, with the store, the doctor, the hotel, and Hilborn's mill. In early times, one could, with patience, get Hamilton or Guelph, but longer distances were attempted only in dire emergencies, as it might take all day to complete a call.

In 1909, installation of telephones in homes was begun in our neighbourhood, by the North Wentworth Telephone Company, organized by Albert Morley Shaver of Ancaster, and F. Reinke. Then came a delay of nearly a year, while the families of Charles Hewins, Albert Hewins and Sandy McKenzie enjoyed what amounted to a private inter-com. Work resumed in 1910, under Mr. Shaver only, and we were connected to Freelton Central, which had been in existence since 1907.

With the increasing number of subscribers, efforts were made to give a more satisfactory long distance service, but it still meant teaming up with the Bell System and perhaps one or more private telephone companies, just for one call. No one, then, even in his most fanciful day dreams, conjured up a time when we could, in one minute and without human aid, call three and four thousand miles away with eleven flips of the finger tip.

Mr. Shaver sold to the Bell Telephone Company in 1912.

The Community Park

The tightly knit community spirit of Mountsberg went hand-in-hand with the need for recreation. It was once the custom for the neighbourhood young people to hold impromptu ball games whenever and wherever a freshly cut hay field was available. The fall of the year was also the occasion for a corn roast and sing-songs around a fire—usually of old fence rails or pine stumps.

The need for a central public field for sport and other social gatherings was recognized following World

Mountsberg Hockey Club at Dam, Lot 9, Concession 13, 1930's. Lyle Dougherty, Lloyd Wingrove, Ivan Wingrove, Lyle Wigood, Allan Stewart, Sid Shanks and Earl Wingrove. *Tom Jordan.*

War I. It was decided to provide such a facility as a memorial to four young men from the community who had paid the supreme sacrifice in that war. In November 1920, three acres facing Centre Road were bought from Charles Hewins by the newly appointed trustees, Burdge Gunby, Albert Hewins and Albert Campbell. Later, Matthew Mount and Charles Hewins were added to the Parks Board.

"Bees" were held to grade and terrace the land, to plant trees and lay out a ball diamond. An official dedication ceremony on a bright summer Sunday afternoon was held, when Reeve Peter Ray and Reverend Robb, a former army chaplain, were the speakers. Olive Hewins, a former organist of the Methodist Church, returned from Toronto to play the piano and brought with her a quartet to provide special music.

The memorial monument was unveiled in 1924. The special service took place on August 31, with Rev.

Privates Leland and Nathan Dougherty. *Mrs. Wm. Payne.*

R.H. Smith of the Methodist Church and the Rev. Sydney Laurence of the Baptist Church taking part. The names inscribed on the monument are as follows:

> Sergeant Roy Wheeler Mount
> Private Leland Hilbert Dougherty
> Private Walter Henry Emmons
> Private Nathan Austin Dougherty
> "Lest We Forget"

One of the first attempts at organized sport was a Tennis Club on a grass court. Unfortunately, there were few of the younger people who seemed to catch the tennis "bug", and after one or two years it passed into a not-too-successful part of our history.

The formation of a Girls Softball Team proved

Memorial Monument unveiled on August 31, 1924. *Mrs. W.C. Cust.*

Softball Team, 1952. Rear—Paul McCarthy, Bernie McCarthy, Bill Revell, Jr. and Ed McCarthy. Middle—Allan Wingrove, Calvin Wigood, Raymond Bryant, Roy Harris—manager, Laverne Gunby, Walter Stewart, Lloyd Wingrove and Sid Shanks. Front—Tom Jordan—treasurer, Archie Gunby, Hugh Wigood and Ted Filtness—team assistants, Cecil Gunby, bat boy. Absent; Bert Campbell and Jack Laking. *Mrs. C. Wigrood.*

much more successful. While they did not compete in a formal league, they were very successful and much in demand to play at garden parties and other occasions. The opposition came from Freelton, Badenoch, Aberfoyle, Carlisle, Crieff, and Strabane.

The team was managed by Albert Emmons and later, by Jim Scott. In the line-up were Margaret Stewart, pitcher, and Lena Revell, catcher. The other players were Catherine Stewart, Merle Hewins, Bessie Leslie, Flossie Dougherty, Bertha Woolsey, Isabel Gunby, Isabel Leslie, Marie McGuire, Pearl Leslie, Marjorie Wetherelt, Agnes Watson and Birdie Hood.

In the face of inevitable change, this team which was formed in 1921, disbanded in 1924, their last game being at a garden party in Strabane.

From the formation of the park until the early 1940's, the young men of the community also were engaged in playing softball with varying degrees of success. Like the girls, they did not compete in a formal league, but on occasion did uphold the good name of Mountsberg at garden parties and tournaments.

An amusing incident occurred during this era, when the minister of the Baptist Church, an outstanding athlete, was the catcher of the team. Face masks were thought to be for sissies in those days and a foul ball connected rather forcefully with the minister's right eye. The game was on a Saturday evening. Some of the rather staid members of the congregation of that time were completely shocked to see their minister in the pulpit of the Baptist Church with a beautiful black eye on Sunday afternoon.

In the mid-40's an excellent softball team was formed consisting exclusively of local boys and which played in the Puslinch Softball League. The opposition was provided by teams from Badenoch, Morriston, Puslinch, Aberfoyle, Arkell, Crieff, Corwhin and Brock Road.

This team was by far the most noteworthy sports organization ever assembled in Mountsberg, winning many awards, the most important being the championship of the League in 1950, 1951 and 1952.

The pitchers of the team were Lloyd Wingrove and Bertram Campbell and the catchers were Sidney Shanks and Ed McCarthy. Team members were Laverne Gun-by, Bernie McCarthy, Bill Revell, Ivan Wingrove, Calvin Wigood, Raymond Bryant, Everly Bryant, Ken Gunby, Jack Laking, Paul McCarthy, Walter Stewart and Allan Wingrove.

Frequent attempts to attain laurels equal to those

of this team have been made since the team passed out of existence. Despite much better equipment and a better maintained playing field, these endeavours have fallen by the wayside one by one. The one missing ingredient is a cohesive community spirit coupled with the presence of many winter attractions of today's world which compete with that spirit.

Literary Society

A further example of how our forefathers made their own entertainment in the winter months was the formation of a Literary Society which met every two weeks. The membership at one time numbered 39 and the meetings were held in the school. The membership fee was 10 cents per member for the season.

In order to provide light for the meetings, records indicate that a gasoline chandelier lamp was purchased from the Lowville Church of England for $5.00. The accounts for one meeting included two mantles for this lamp at 10 cents each and one gallon of white gasoline for 26 cents.

The year ended with a social and the purchases of the Committee included: 3 tins of salmon, 69 cents; 1 pound of coffee, 45 cents; 3 large loaves of bread, 30 cents; and five pounds of sugar, 35 cents. Three people donated half a pound of butter and were credited with a donation of 15 cents each.

The format of the programs was basically a debate, although musical selections and the occasional play were presented for the enjoyment of the members. Of interest are the titles of some of the debates—"Resolved that a clean, cranky woman will make a better wife than a lazy, good-natured one", "Resolved that women should never have been given the franchise", "Resolved that the Canadian farmer is of greater importance to our country than the Canadian manufacturer" and "Resolved that the press had more influence on modern life than the pulpit".

Was all of this better than watching television, I wonder? It held a community together!

Mountsberg Women's Institute

The Mountsberg Branch of the North Wentworth Women's Institute was organized after a motion at a Ladies Aid meeting that Mrs. A. Elliott and Mrs. A. Page contact someone to find out about the work of the Women's Institute. Mrs. Russell Wise was contacted and she, along with the District President, Mrs. M.S. Shellard, arranged a meeting for May 16, 1952.

On that evening 35 ladies assembled in the Mountsberg School. Mrs. C. Bryant favoured us with a piano solo, and Miss Lois Gunby and Miss Betty Revell sang a duet. Mrs. M. Shellard explained the beginning and the work of the Institute. After some discussion it was moved by Mrs. A. Page, and seconded by Mrs. A. Elliott, that we organize.

The first officers were: President—Mrs. A. Page; Vice-Presidents—Mrs. H. Parry, Mrs. T. Wetherelt, Mrs. W. Lacey; Secretary—Miss Lois Gunby; Assistant Secretary—Mrs. H. Wigood; Treasurer—Mrs. A. Gunby; District Director—Mrs. A. Elliott; Directors—Mrs. T. Prowse, Mrs. W. Wingrove, Mrs. W. Revell and Mrs. P. Gray; Conveners of standing committees—Mrs. C. Warner, Mrs. R. Cochrane, Mrs. W. Lacey, Mrs. J. Gunby, Mrs. A. Hulme and Mrs. W. Revell; Flower and Cheer—Mrs. J. Mitchell and Mrs. I. Laking; Pianist—Mrs. C. Bryant.

Institute members have taken part in leader training schools and short courses put on by the Ontario Ministry of Agriculture and Food, Home Economics Branch; gone on informative and enjoyable tours; had many interesting speakers; exhibited at local fairs; and held an annual euchre and quilt draw. In the early days, money was made by bake sales at the Waterdown Market and by a travelling basket. We did work for the Red Cross, the Sanitorium, Cancer Society, and Wentworth Lodge in Dundas, sponsored school contests and also contributed financially to many worthwhile causes. We have supplied picnic tables and washrooms to Mountsberg Park, as well as various improvements to the Centre, and sponsored 4-H Homemaking Clubs.

We celebrated our 10th anniversary with former members, present members and District Officers. Honoured at our 25th anniversary were Charter members: Mrs. A. Hulme, Mrs. C. Warner, Mrs. J. Bell, Mrs. A. Page, Mrs. W. Revell, Mrs. A. Elliott and Mrs. P. McCarthy, who joined the first year. Mrs. D. Heddle, President, introduced Mrs. R. Mills, District President and Mrs. R. Wise, who helped with our

25th Anniversary, May 17, 1977. Charter members of the Mountsberg W.I.—Mrs. A. Hulme, Mrs. C. Warner, Mrs. J. Bell, Mrs. A. Page, Mrs. W. Revell and Mrs. A. Elliott. *Mrs. D. Croft.*

10th Anniversary, May 15, 1962. Front-1st 5 Presidents; Mrs. A. Gunby, Mrs. A. Page, Mrs. P. Gray, Mrs. T. Wetherelt, Mrs. W. Lacey. Middle—Mrs. R. Cochrane, Mrs. L Henwood, Mrs. G. Bowman, Mrs. A. Taylor, Mrs. J. Gunby, Mrs. A. Hulme and Mrs. R. Coiling. Rear—Mrs. C. McCarthy, Mrs. J. Bell, Mrs. D. Stewart, Mrs. C. Wigood, unknown, Mrs. A. Elliott, Mrs. W. Wingrove, Mrs. H. Wigood, Mrs. C. Warner, Mrs. W. Revell, Mrs. L. Wigood and unknown. *Mrs. A. Page.*

organization. We enjoyed entertainment by former members and a barbershop quartet from the Oakville group.

Although Mountsberg is changing, its institute is very active, thanks to continued participation by long-time members and the willingness to participate by those new to the area.

Mountsberg 4-H

The first homemaker's club in Mountsberg was in the fall of 1958, led by Mrs. A. Taylor and Mrs. L. Henwood, "The Club Girl Entertains." The next spring Mrs. L. Henwood and Mrs. R. Rintoul led the girls in "Clothes Closet Up-to-Date." After a break of 13 years, a homemaker's club was again formed and has been active since Spring 1972. Mrs. P. Pawlik has led or assisted in 21 clubs, with the assistance of Mrs. S. Jones, Mrs. L. Stevens, Mrs. S. Gillespie, Mrs. J. Brelsford, Mrs. H. McKenna, Mrs. B. Cottrell, Mrs. E. Devereaux, Mrs. A. Kempenaar, Miss K. Pawlik, Miss J. Bell and Mrs. T. Priest.

4-H Club "World of Food in Canada", 1974. Members of the "Kooky Kooks" were Rosemarie Urban, Margaret Urban, Janice Bell, Karen Pawlik, Kathy McKenna, Sandy Harris and Kerry Pawlik. *Mits Sonoda.*

County Honours, which include a certificate and pin, after completion of six clubs, have been won by

Janice Bell, Kathy McKenna, Karen Pawlik, Rosemarie Urban, Kerry Pawlik, Gina Urban and Gloria Urban.

Provincial Honours of a certificate for completion of 12 clubs have been won by Dianne McCarthy, Janice Bell, Kathy McKenna, Karen Pawlik, Rosemarie Urban and Kerry Pawlik. These girls have also received the Wentworth Women's Institute Silver Tray award (formerly cream and sugar) presented by the W.I. for completion of 12 Homemaking Clubs. This award is presented in the Fall at an Annual Banquet and Dance (sponsored by the Ministry of Agriculture) for all 4-H Clubs.

Advanced Honours, a certificate and silver pie server for the completion of 18 clubs, have been won by Karen Pawlik and Kathy McKenna.

Mrs. P. Pawlik has received a leader's certificate for 5 years.

Conservation Authority

The Twelve Mile Creek Conservation Authority was established by Order in Council on June 12, 1958, when it became apparent that flood control was desirable. In 1963, the Twelve Mile and Sixteen Mile Creek Conservation Authorities amalgamated with Esquesing, Nassagaweya and Town of Milton to form the Halton Region Conservation Authority (H.R.C.A.).

Several reservoir sites were considered, and in 1966, a dam 12 feet high and 1300 feet long was built across a tributary of the Twelve Mile Creek, which rises in Badenoch F. Lot 29, Concession 10, goes through the section and enters East Flamborough Township. The dam is in East Flamborough, although some of the 1,100 acre area is in Puslinch Township and some is in what was Nassagaweya. The conservation area thus formed was called Mountsberg Game Farm and is now known as the Mountsberg Wildlife Centre.

The Wildlife Centre, whose main purpose is to control water in the Bronte Creek watershed, offers the residents of the watershed a unique opportunity for environmental awareness. It provides a series of Environmental Resource programs for schools and groups during the school year and Resource sessions during the summer. There are programs on weekends open to the general public. The Wildlife Centre is recognized for its contributions in bird banding and in the study of bird migration.

Mountsberg Lake and Dam, 1977. *Mrs. D. Croft.*

IV

Folklore and Personalities

Folklore

Perhaps people were more superstitious a few generations ago than they are today. These two yarns will illustrate what can happen when superstitions and fundamental religious beliefs come into play. Both stories are about Susannah Hurren Page, wife of Peter Page. The Pages lived where Elliotts live today and after they sold the farm they lived in the Methodist Parsonage.

One night Susannah saw what she supposed to be a fire flickering in the Methodist Church, on the altar no less. She became rather hysterical.

The explanation: Emanuel "Manny" Mciunt had been burning brush that afternoon. The fire was still burning fitfully after dark. The line of vision between Susannah and the fire was through the two rear side windows of the church.

One quiet evening Susannah heard a most peculiar noise, a sort of moaning and snoring, down in the cemetery. This conjured up ideas of the Devil and ghosts. The reason for the noise was rather simple. A farmer was taking a cow to the neighbour's bull. He met someone he knew when he was passing the cemetery and stopped to chat. He was leading the cow with a "humbug", a gadget that fastened in the cow's nose. Whether it was the condition the cow was in or her dislike of the method in which she was being led, she was straining on this leading device and making the noises that frightened Susannah.

George Johnson and Holy Ann

George Johnson could be called a religious crackpot. He claimed that he had the Devil shackled to a tree on the back fifty with a logging chain. One day George heard Tommy Revell working in the bush. He went over and told Tommy to cease and desist his labours. The world was coming to an end and Tommy was to make the necessary preparations. This evoked a rather witty and crushing rejoinder from Tommy.

When the railways were built they had quite an impact on the rural communities. They brought people like singer-comedian Jimmy Fax and his troupe of entertainers. They also brought Holy Ann.

Holy Ann was a 'Religious Mystic' who lived in Thornhill, north of Toronto. She travelled over Ontario as guest artist at Prayer and Revival meetings. When she was in this area she stayed with George and Carrie Johnson. Ann was a small woman, inclined to 'plumpishness'

As part of her routine, she would go into a dance and trance. Whether it was tap, acrobatic or Salomie's Dance of the Seven Veils it's not known. As a result of her gyrations at one Prayer meeting she knocked a leg off the parlour stove. If this act didn't bring down the house, it at least brought the stove down.

To provide seating space at these meetings, boards were placed on blocks of wood. Perhaps to recover her breath from her exertions and exhortations, Holy Ann sat down on the end of one of these make-shift benches on which some young men were sitting. We have no

George and Carrie Johnson. *Mrs. H. Rennick.*

reason to suspect malice aforethought and collusion, but for some reason these young men all got to their feet in unison. Ann went down, her heels went up, and the voluminous skirts of her dress and petticoats got tangled around her head.

George Johnson had a covered vehicle with seats and a small stove, to take neighbours and Holy Ann to nearby communities. It is distressing to record, even at this date, that some depraved person or persons unknown, while a Prayer meeting was taking place, put a generous application of fresh cow manure on the floor of George's vehicle.

Levity aside, George was a decent fellow who never harmed anyone. He was one of those people whose religious fervor and emotions were dominant over his intellect.

Holy Ann was a Godly woman who firmly believed she was an instrument of God and had a Divine Mission. With her strong beliefs, natural talents and a magnetic personality it was easy for her to project an hypnotic effect on impressionable minds.

She brought religious comfort, hope, cheer, excitement and colour to many people who lived drab and toil-filled lives.

Her old home in Thornhill is said to be haunted, probably with Holy Ann's ghost.

Politics

Politics, like most actions in the lives of our pioneer forefathers, was not taken lightly. In those early years of our history one followed, without fail, the political persuasion of one's father and grandfather. This meant that one was either a Grit or a Tory—Liberal or Conservative, to the more sophisticated.

Mountsberg, for a host of different reasons, was settled by a great majority of those who were proud to be known as Grits. While no one will ever know for sure, because some would sooner confess adultery than reveal their political affiliation, a fairly accurate estimation at one time suggested there were not more than seven or eight Tory families in the entire school section.

Feelings ran high at election time, as is indicated in the following true story of a winter election. The snow was deep and the only way to go to the polling station was by team and sleigh, or on foot. One of the staunch Grits and his hired man had started down the road with the team and sleigh when he noticed two men on foot wading through the knee deep snow. A closer look revealed that the men on foot were brothers who were members of the dreaded Tory party and there was no way the driver of the team would assist them in getting to vote by offering them a ride. This great loyalty to the Liberal Party fell somewhat short of providing enough nerve to pass the walkers, so, for a little over a mile, the lively team pranced and danced under a tight rein as they followed the "Opposition" down the road. While the snow was deep some have suggested, but without proof, that those Conservative gentlemen moved especially slowly on that election day.

Politics in those early days was very interesting.

Romance

Romance in the early years of Mountsberg moved surely and sometimes slowly. More surely and more slowly for some than for others.

The Sunday evening service at the little Methodist Church was drawing to a close. All through the evening a rather chubby young man with a twinkle in his eye, sitting in the back seat, was having difficulty keeping his mind on the sermon. Earlier, as they rose to sing the first hymn, a rather attractive young lady had cast a glance his way, and for the next hour his mind was in a daze. Fanciful thoughts raced through his mind: "She lived one and one-half miles from church and she would be walking home alone. The moon was full and the tall trees and woods beside the road cast eerie shadows across the gravel. She would appreciate a strong young man beside her."

After the service, as the men pulled up to the front of the church with their horses and buggies to pick up their wives or girl friends, this activity provided an excellent setting for the beginning of our hero's love affair. No one really noticed the young lady start away from the church for the walk home, nor the young man, who after a respectable interval, began to follow her.

However, this wasn't as easy as his dreams in church had led him to believe. "What would he say when he caught up to her?" He had never walked a girl home before and didn't know how to act. "He'd hang back for a while," he thought, "until he had the courage to make the move." He began to sweat. "Why was she walking so slow?" All of a sudden the grim realization hit him. "We've covered almost the whole mile and one-half." Finally, just as she was within a few feet of her front gate he broke into a half run and with a shaky voice blurted out, "I thought I would never catch up to you."

Chariot of Fire

Grandfather John Laking smoked a pipe. I remember family members fretting about his smoking habits, and predicting that disaster would overtake him if he didn't take more care. I didn't give it much thought, but then I was only five or six when their forebodings became fact.

My older brother, Roy, and I often packed overnight necessities in a 6-quart basket and happily trudged the two miles to visit, and perhaps, exhaust, our grandparents. From past experience, we could count on a ride home in a day or two, in Grandpa's buggy, drawn by his bay driving horse. And so it was on this particular occasion.

Homeward bound, we mosied along the 13th Concession, facing a hot, strong, southwest wind, Grandfather smoking, as usual. As we were going down the hill at Sandy Campbell's (now Watson's), I thought I heard a crackling sound behind me. I was sitting, slightly forward, in the centre of the crowded seat, and had a better chance to look around. I looked. And what I saw were flames streaming out behind the buggy, in a stiff breeze.

I had been mortally afraid of fire ever since John Revell's barn had been struck by lightning and burned early one morning. That dawn I awakened in terror at the shattering blast of sound. And fire became the anathema of my life.

So, at the sight of fire, and before Grandfather or Roy grasped the situation, I panicked and leaped over the wheel to the ground. No rat ever left a sinking ship faster than I ran home crying. It was only a short distance, and I shortened it further by cutting diagonally across a field to the farm buildings.

At the crest of the hill, I became aware of my father and Uncle Jim Laking standing near the gate to the field. I could tell that they were puzzled at the sight of me. Suddenly, at that moment, I saw myself as a heroine in a tragedy, so I turned up the emotion a few degrees, and sobbed out my story. Their reaction seemed a little less than my dramatic account merited. In fact, I caught a trace of amusement. Whether at me, or a philosophic acceptance of the inevitable, I couldn't tell.

However, they took off immediately, using the short cut across the field. By then, I had recovered my composure enough to tag along. And, as I thought less about myself, I became curious about what was happening at the disaster scene. But it was all over. The fire was out. The horse was tied to a roadside tree. The buggy stood in the middle of the creek, the bare bones of its top arched above the scorched seat. Beside it was Grandfather holding a soggy felt hat he had used for bailing. Roy was in the creek, too. He had found something that would hold water, and had played a much more heroic role than I.

Fortunately, the fire occurred quite near the creek, and there was a fairly good track through the shallow water south east of the old wooden bridge. People often drove that way in order to let their horses have a drink.

Even yet, relatives sometimes speak vaguely of the time Grandpa Laking's pipe set fire to his buggy. They have forgotten details; so, with barely a hint of the old theatrics, I say, in all modesty, "Oh, yes, I was there."

Mr. Sachs, Peddler

Present-day women can, at their convenience, rush off to Guelph, Hamilton or Burlington for a few hours around the stores. It is quite impossible, now, to appreciate the isolation felt by long-ago housewives who were lucky to get to town once or twice a year, and so were thankful for peddlers. Country stores sprang up four, five, or six miles apart. But still, peddlers were welcome and offered wares not to be found in local stores. Some peddlers were casual drop-ins, whose calls were one-time events. Dependable regulars, like Morris Sachs, called every few months and brightened a day for a family. He knew his customers so well that he bought his stock with certain individuals in mind, and he saved special things for the people most likely to appreciate them.

At first, Mr. Sachs travelled with one horse and a small democrat with the back seat removed. In back were bundles, usually three huge, canvas-wrapped mounds, about three feet across. Each bundle was held securely by a broad, leather strap, with at least two feet beyond the buckle to use as a handle. Later, Mr. Sachs' horse pulled a closed wagon, and its faded red panels became a familiar sight on Mountsberg roads.

I usually received the announcement of his arrival in the neighbourhood, when the news hummed along the schoolroom grapevine, "Old Sachs just went by." No disrespect was intended by the title. It was more a term of affection. We were all very fond of Mr. Sachs and could hardly wait to get home to see if he would be at our place, or if we would have to wait for another day. Each visit often took an entire day. He seldom made more than two calls in one day, and he ate at the home where he happened to be at meal time, and slept when bedtime overtook him.

A visit seemed to be as much a social event as a business enterprise. At our place, we waited, not patiently, while Mr. Sachs and my father, whom he called "Chollie", had long discussions about things that, to us, were unutterably dull.

Eventually, the great moment arrived, when Mr. Sachs went out to get a bundle. He backed up to the open wagon, pulled a strap end over his shoulder and hoisted the bundle to his back. Then, bent double under the load, he plodded in to the kitchen, plumped his burden onto the floor and pulled up a chair. With the family gathered around him, he very deliberately unbuckled the strap and peeled back the canvas cover with a flourish. He seemed so slow. I suspect now that he took a moment to savour his position in the spotlight and to tease the wide-eyed children.

The first bundle was yard goods: lengths of woolen material, plaid, plain, check or salt and pepper; shimmering silks in beautiful colours; fancy brocades and embroidered cloth; cotton prints and ginghams. Mr. Sachs held up each piece, stroked it tenderly, arranged the folds with care, and placed it on the pile of things seen. Slowly, hoping someone would want a longer look.

Then came time to replace the stack, and we got a second, quick glance. Mr. Sachs had kept his eyes open. He knew that in that pile was a piece of material that had been admired in silence and self-denial. When he came to it, he measured off a dress length and tossed it into the lap of his hostess. That was his thank-you for food and lodging. Money was never offered nor expected.

Another bundle held underwear, overalls, jackets and pants. A third had household linens and cottons, and, occasionally, a few ready-made dresses that were seldom the right size. In the rare instance where the lady of the house had shown no special interest in dress goods, something from later bundles was tendered, gratis.

Mr. Sachs saved the best till last. After replacing the final bundle in the wagon, he reached under the seat and brought forth a medium-sized box. It was a real treasure chest of lace, ribbons, buttons, braid and jewelry, as well as mundane things like pencils, thread and shoe laces. This was the grand finale.

Mr. Sachs watched children grow from infants, through school age, to adults. And, when they married, he brought, on his next round, a little gift to wish them well. For me, an "Old Colony" meat fork can conjure up a vision of a kindly, stocky, middle-aged man, struggling under a bundle much larger than himself.

There were peddlers before Mr. Sachs. Later, Louis Fine came along, offered competition and remained to be the last of the regular peddlers. He, finally, had to bow out to the automobile and the increasing mobility of his clientele.

But I knew only Old Sachs.

Sports

Sports had an important place in Ontario rural life, especially in the later part of the 19th century and well into the 20th.

Most villages had a good baseball team and football was also popular. Even track and field had its devotees.

Target shooting was quite popular; the Winchester

38-55 was a favourite gun for this sport. Team contests were held and the best 4 or 5 shooters would have a match with a team from a neighbouring community.

This yarn is about a shooting match between a Badenoch team that beat a team from Morriston rather badly. The Badenoch team used a gun owned by Jim Laking, a Stevens 38-55. After the match, Geordie Hanning of the Morriston team asked to have a shot out of Jim Laking's gun. This privilege was readily granted and Tom Beaton carefully loaded the gun. In loading Jim Laking's gun, a shell filled with powder and paper wad was placed in the chamber, then the bullet was inserted in the muzzle, and pushed down the barrel to the shell.

Geordie Hanning took a good long aim at the target from a prone position and then squeezed the trigger. He didn't even hit the target although he claimed he was dead on the bull's-eye. He couldn't understand it.

It was a long time before Tom Beaton admitted that he hadn't put the bullet in the gun.

The Farmer's Cast Iron Kettle

The axe and plow are symbols of pioneer farming. Let us add another, to wit: the farmer's big cast iron kettle. They came in different sizes and were used to make potash, boil down sap for maple syrup and sugar, to boil water to scald hogs at butchering time and to cook potatoes for the pigs.

Potash was an early source of cash income. Hardwood ashes were saved, the end of a barrel knocked out and holes bored in the bottom. The barrel was filled with ashes, water poured in and the leachate caught in a container under the bottom. The liquid was boiled down into a crude potassium carbonate used in making soap.

William Laking
October 11, 1845-March 30, 1931

East Flamborough was the land that lured William, youngest of the large Laking family, away from his native Lincolnshire, about 1863. He scarcely remembered his sister, Sarah (Mrs. Solomon Dawson), who left for Canada when he was four; nor his brother, John, who followed about a year later. But he did remember his parting promise to John, that he would go to him as soon as he was old enough.

So, the lad of 17 set out alone on the long Atlantic crossing. And, what a crossing! Six weary weeks on a sailing vessel, the *Norwegian,* followed by shipwreck in the Gulf of St. Lawrence. He finally reached John who, then, was renting the 200 acres of the John Page farm and living in a frame house (site of Gordon Hewins home). William's assets were the clothes he wore and 25 cents. And he owed John for his passage.

He worked for John about three years. In his second winter in Canada, during the slack season on the farm, he took a job in the bush in Norfolk County. There, he learned to use the axe and saw, and how to square timber. Meanwhile, he became familiar with the sawmill business.

John bought a farm in Nassagaweya in the spring of 1865, and that year, William, debt-free, was hired by George Green who, since about 1860, operated a shingle mill on Centre Road, northwest of the village. William drove a team, and a lifetime career in lumber began in earnest.

Early in 1866, with plenty of optimism but little money, William, at age 20, and Oron Thompson, mill manager, bought the mill and stock for $2,000. According to a Directory of 1868, the mill was 60 feet square, had a 15 horse power steam engine, manufactured shingles and flour barrel headings, and employed 10 hands.

The partners bought up white pine from many area farmers, even going as far afield as the "Scotch Settlement" where they bought a stand of about 600 white pine trees for $600, this without security, and paid for as they sold shingles.

William Laking. *Mrs. W.C. Cust.*

To make shingles, white pine logs were cut to the required length with a cross-cut saw. The blocks were then steamed before being transferred to a Lockport shingle slicer, an up-and-down device which cut them into shingles; a crude, old-fashioned machine, if seen today, but then, modern and adequate. Shingles were put up in half "squares" (720 shingles to the square). Most were shipped from Dundas, many going to the United States.

This was in the decade before the Credit Valley Railway went through the northwest end of East Flamborough. No doubt, in the mill's later years, Shaw Station (Puslinch) was convenient for certain shipments.

Thompson and Laking installed a circular saw and produced lumber for construction, some for local use, but much going to the Robert Stewart Company of Guelph. About this time, good mill-run lumber was selling at $8 to $10 per M. and a teamster and his horses could be hired for $2 a day, without board. The mill was a success, due mainly to hard work. William Laking, himself, often drove a team of oxen for skidding pine logs, in deep snow with the temperature below 0° F. Mr. Thompson sold his interest to William Laking in 1874. By this time, Mr. Laking had married a local girl, Martha Revell, and had two daughters, Elizabeth and Mary Jane (Minnie). John was born three years later.

As lumbering in Mountsberg eased off, William Laking broadened his range. He owned the grist mill at Freelton from 1884 to 1902, and hired a man to run it, while he took over the management of three saw mills, one at Freelton near the grist mill, the others at Carlisle and Strabane, until they, too, ceased to operate. This was a slow period in saw mill business. Mr. Laking was a Councillor for East Flamborough for six years from 1884 to 1889, with one year as Deputy Reeve.

As good trees became scarce in the Flamboroughs, Mr. Laking tried out areas farther north, and bought a mill at Uhthoff, north of Orillia. He operated it for two years before trading for a mill on North River, which burned after one winter's work. Next, he bought a mill at Fesserton, also in the Georgian Bay area. There, he sawed ten million feet of lumber, as well as making shingles and lath, before that mill also burned.

There seemed to be no way of storing or disposing of 8 million feet of timber, ready for sawing, still at Fesserton. A plan was worked out to have it sent to Toronto, but it was cancelled due to the death of the lumberman concerned. To solve the emergency, the William Laking Lumber Company of Toronto was formed. It was a wholesale business, soon complemented by the Riverdale Lumber Company, for the retail trade; also in Toronto. Mr. Laking was president of both companies. He moved some of the surplus stock to Hamilton and, in partnership with James Thompson, opened a retail yard on York Street. The partners made a further move, joining Patterson Brothers who had a planing mill. The combined firms operated under the name Laking, Thompson and Patterson.

About this time, 1891, Mr. Laking moved to Hamilton. For a few years, the family had been living in Freelton, across the road from the grist mill, in a large, red brick house, no longer there. Martha Laking died the following year. The partnership with Thompson and Patterson lasted six or seven years, and when Laking and Thompson left, the new firm became Patterson-Tilley. Mr. Laking later married Jessie Patterson, a sister of his former partner.

In the meantime, his career took an unexpected turn. About 1900, he had loaned money on a mill in Haliburton village. Later, he found himself to be the reluctant owner. However, with his expertise, the unfortunate situation became a profitable project; so profitable that he sold his Hamilton home and moved to Haliburton where he was well received. He was elected to the village council and became warden of Haliburton County.

About 1906, his nephew, William (Will, son of Joseph) moved his family from Mountsberg to Haliburton to help with the work there. The mill operated by water power and turned out about 25,000 feet of lumber a day, along with ties, shingles, and basket bottoms.

As he grew older, he decided to relocate in Hamilton and, in 1915, built a home at 126 Emerald Street South. His son, John, remained with the Haliburton mill until he drowned in Drag Lake in 1917. John's wife, Lila, of Haliburton remained there with their daughter, Evelyn. The Haliburton mill, lasting into the 1920s, was burned after being idle several years.

William Laking never retired, although, in his late years, he took life more leisurely. Weekly, his chauffeur drove him to Toronto to visit his companies, managed by his great-nephew, Ernie Laking. He died in Florida, early in 1931. He was 85.

Much of the milling information was taken from an article about William Laking in the "Canada Lumberman" of October 1922, courtesy of C.C. Laking of Willowdale (grandson of John) who owned and operated the Danforth Lumber Co. of Toronto until he retired.

The Chivaree

The tradition of holding a chivaree began in early times and has continued to the present. The earliest one on record here was to celebrate the marriage of John and Phoebe Maddaugh in the 1870s. Shortly after they were married, Thomas and Anne Revell invited them to a party. There was a small stream of spring run-off water in Revell's lane. John quite gallantly picked up Phoebe to carry her across. At this point in time and place, we are told, the neighbours let loose with a chivaree. John was startled and lost his hold on Phoebe, who fell in the water!

The chivaree consists of a group of neighbours paying a late night surprise visit to newlyweds, sneaking up to the house and letting loose a volley of noise: horns, cymbals, saucepan lids, cowbells and shotguns. The blushing bridegroom would finally emerge from the house, paying the ringleaders of the group in order to be left in peace. Other tricks included slipping into the house and scattering cornflakes and rice, dismantling the marital bed and knotting ropes of undies and hanging them from the light fixture.

In modern form the chivaree occurs after weddings and also on 25th wedding anniversaries. The noise continues, but the ending is more civilized; neighbours, arriving just after dusk, come laden with sandwiches and cake, and serve an improvised lunch to the host and hostess. The noisemakers have taken on new (and louder) forms, with the addition of car sirens and firecrackers but noise and surprise remain the two startling elements of the chivaree.

Roger Maynard

The new teacher for the log school, with his young wife beside him, first saw Mountsberg under circumstances that would have defeated a less intrepid man. It took Roger and Elizabeth Maynard three days to move from Listowel; a two-hour drive today, but, in 1862, roads were rough, even treacherous in places, wagon seats were not upholstered and horses had to be rested. They reached Mountsberg on a Saturday night, accepted the only living quarters available (see Lot 9, Concession 12), and prepared for school on Monday. By Wednesday, Roger was too ill to teach and typhoid fever kept him bedfast for seven weeks. To save the situation from total disaster, they had, near by, Elizabeth's uncle, the Rev. J. McLean, minister of the Methodist Church, who had encouraged them to come to Mountsberg, and they soon found new and sympathetic friends. For the seven, critical weeks, two neighbours waited on him at night.

Roger Maynard spent his first 16 years on farms north of Lake Ontario, near Newcastle. He was born near Darlington on April 24, 1838. His parents, Dixon and Ann Maynard, left Yorkshire, England, for Canada in 1829, with five children. Four more were born in Upper Canada and Roger was youngest of the nine.

When he was four, the family moved to Orono and there he started school at age six. At age eight, another move took them farther north to a bush farm where he continued his education until he was 12. From then until he was 16, he was his father's sole help on the farm, as the older brothers were married and on land of their own.

They were plagued with misfortune. One year they lost five horses and 17 cattle to disease. Another year, their house burned with everything in it. Finally, the father and a son, William, who lived near, decided to try farming in the Queen's Bush. This vast, forested area, north and west of Guelph was what the Canada Company called the Huron Tract. Already, a Maynard daughter was living there at Millbank, and a son, Thomas, some distance north of her. The land was not yet on the market, but, as squatters, they would have first chance to buy.

So, William and his father set out to select a location for new homes. They went by boat to Toronto. From there, partly by stage coach but mostly on foot, they looked over various newly-surveyed townships. Their choice was adjoining lots, not far from where Thomas was living. On the return trip they walked to Hamilton, then on, by boat, to Newcastle.

They spent the summer of 1854 preparing for the long move, a formidable undertaking that required careful planning. It took five days to reach the sister at Millbank. The mother and a sister were left there to rest, along with part of their load, as travelling became more arduous the farther they went. They were 18 impenetrable miles from their destination and had to take a roundabout of 50 miles. Even so, swamps were many and well-defined trails few. At one marshy spot on the trail, with water above the axles, a horse fell, and a man had to stand waist-deep in the brown bog and hold the horse's head above water, lest it drown. The horse, unhurt, regained its footing and on they went. The last 10 miles were the worst. They faced untracked forest, but their way was made less miserable by meeting up with two other squatter families, and they were able to help each other through the difficult places.

Their new cabin had an upstairs and was made entirely of logs; even the roof was made of split and hollowed-out logs, arranged like half-round tile. It was a way of using the timber from the first 10 acres they cleared, and besides, there was no sawmill anywhere. The only lumber used was for doors and windows, made from the wagon box that had carried their household goods from their former home.

When the Maynards settled in the Queen's bush, it was a four-day round trip to the nearest grist mill, so, a year later, there was much rejoicing when a Mr. Hall came along and set up a grist mill and a sawmill, less than a mile away. They named the place Listowel.

Two years later, the first school was built. Roger and another young man competed for the position as teacher. He studied hard, then walked the 45 miles to Stratford to be examined for a Third-Class certificate. He passed the test and won the position.

Because of eye strain, he gave up teaching a year later. He was 20 that year when he and Elizabeth McLean were married by her uncle. The Rev. J. McLean, as well as preaching, was working his farm north of London. Roger and Elizabeth rented that farm a few months and, when it was sold, they returned to Listowel and bought the family farm. During their three years there, Roger worked the thirty arable acres and resumed teaching at $250 per year. Then, in 1862, they sold out and went to Mountsberg.

Roger Maynard described our log school as being "old and dilapidated, with long benches and a passage a foot and a half wide on each side." The discipline was the worst he had known. That was his impression after two days. Then came the illness that kept him from teaching for three months. When he returned, he was happy to find that his substitute, a Scotsman, had successfully subdued the riotous element.

He came to Mountsberg with a Second-Class teaching certificate, at $300 per annum, on the understanding that he would obtain First-Class standing, which he did as soon as he was well enough. He stayed at the log school two years. The new stone school house at Beechgrove, near Freelton, built in 1864, looked attractive to him and, in a field of nine applicants, he won the distinction of being its first teacher, and he stayed 12 years.

It was during his first year at Beechgrove that Elizabeth died, and he was left with three little girls, the youngest, one month old. Relatives from Listowel took the baby home and Roger never saw her again as she died four months later.

Two years after Elizabeth died, Roger married Martha Wheeler of the neighbourhood, and, in August

1916, they celebrated their golden wedding. Roger was the father of six. Elizabeth's daughter, Sarah, married Omar Gidney and Avalina (or Evelina), married Charles Vansickle. Martha's children were: Orpha (Mrs. Robert Flatt of Millgrove); Wesley, who married Harriet Ryckman; Albert, who married Lillian Hill, of Guelph, and Bella (Mrs. Robert Allison).

While at the Beechgrove school, Roger Maynard bought a general store in Freelton. It was not a successful venture. He had to depend too much on hired help and was forced to give it up.

He was a deeply religious man, brought up in a home that had daily, family worship, and, at an early age, he took part in church meetings. However, he told of a year in his early teens, when he rebelled, and refused to participate in any way. It was a phase that passed and, when they lived at Listowel, he opened the first Sunday School in an abandoned shanty. When he came to Mountsberg, he was active in the Methodist Church which seems to have remained his home church, although he preached in countless pulpits during a lifetime devoted to religion and teaching, the two careers often coinciding.

When he left the school at Beechgrove, his aim was to be ordained as a Methodist minister, and, in preparing for that, he had acted as class leader, as "exhorter" or as lay preacher, wherever he was needed. His ordination was delayed because there was a surplus of ministers at that time and he accepted a teaching position at Lynden. While there, his young daughter, Orpha, reached a point in her studies where she could assist him. Later, as a qualified teacher, she and her father worked together at Millgrove in the 1890-1895 period, as they did during a return interval at Beechgrove.

In the meantime, he had been ordained some time before the Methodist Union of 1884, and was given a circuit of six churches. Besides this enormous responsibility, he spoke at revival meetings and at camp meetings, both of which assemblies were highly approved by Methodists of that period.

Mr. Maynard died June 13, 1917, and was buried in the Mountsberg Methodist Cemetery. Terse lettering on a tombstone sums up a long life:

    Roger Maynard   1838-1917
    Elizabeth McLean 1840-1864
    Martha Wheeler   1846-1919

Epilogue

The original purpose in publishing this history of Mountsberg was to have a printed record of the families who settled this area. We trust you have found it interesting, informative and, perhaps, entertaining.

"They came to Canada"; four little words for high adventure. Here, too, is bitter tragedy and shattered dreams. Their story is quite similar to the thousands and thousands of families who came to this country in the first half of the 1800s to form settlements all across Ontario.

Never before in human history did so many people migrate so far, and do so much, in so little time.

Abbott, Norman and Ann	....	15
Adamson, Mr.	....	103
Agro Brothers	....	16, 17, 20, 21
Aiken (Atkins, Adkins, Aitken), Thomas	....	55
Aiken, Mr.	....	69
Alexander, Errol and Roslyn, Family	....	28
Alger, Joe and Isabella, Family	....	85
Allison, Jacob	....	102
Allison, Joshua and Phoebe, Family	....	53
Allison, Thomas	....	16
Ament, Wallace	....	88
Anderson, David	....	91
Appleton, Thomas and Heather, Family	....	54
Armstrong, Dr. A. Riley, Family	....	31
Arnold, Calvin and Doreen, Family	....	92
Ashton, Henrietta	....	15
Ashton, Henry	....	15
Aston, Geoffrey and Brenda, Family	....	30
Attridge, Richard	....	88
Bailey, Edward and Marjorie, Family	....	64
Baker, Percy and Daphne	....	16
Ballantine, George, Family	....	35
Bannatyne, Alexander, Family	....	81
Barlow, William and Inga, Family	....	83
Barnes, John, Family	....	**26**, 102
Barnes, William and Jane, Family	....	5, **26**, 28, 102
Barrow, James R.	....	85
Bates, A., Mrs.	....	11
Bates, Asahel	....	44
Bates, Maria (Mrs. J. C. McNiven)	....	51
Battjes, Hermano and Marie	....	76
Baxter, James and Ellen, Family	....	26
Bayer, Tony and Judith, Family	....	34
Beaton, Thomas and Mary, Family	....	**62**, 88, 130
Beaton, William L.	....	24
Beaty (Beatty, Batie), Joseph	....	6, 22
Beaudoin, Paul and Elizabeth, Family	....	58
Bebluk, William	....	64, 74
Beeforth, Fred and Margaret	....	27
Bell, Frank and Clara	....	60
Bell, James and Jane	....	26
Bell, Janice	....	123, 124

Bell, John and Grace	....	98, 100, 122, 123
Bellingham, John and Eileen, Family	....	**22**, 61
Bennett, William J.	....	16, 17
Bernard, James W., Family	....	86
Bertsch, Waine and Wendy	....	19
Best, George and Arlene	....	31
Biegerl, George and Anna	....	74
Binkley, Gerald	....	12
Blundell, Rev. R.G.	....	96, 99
Bodnar; Joseph and Beverly	....	54
Boehm, Eugen and Maria	....	18
Bogle, George and Annie, Family	....	**44**, 45, 103
Bojeski, Thomas and Mary	....	23
Boka, John and Theresa	....	21
Bolingbroke, Frederick, Family	....	22
Bonham, Kenneth and Lynda	....	15
Bonney, Rubin	....	98, 99
Borer, John, Sr.	....	71
Borthwick, Albert and Lillian	....	21
Bosma Family	....	85
Bowman, George and Daisy	....	20, 103
Bowman, Mrs. G.	....	123
Boyle, Neil and Joan	....	20
Bracken, James	....	96, 99
Brandes, Dieter and Katherine, Family	....	29
Brandstater, Murray and Karen, Family	....	64
Brelsford, Mrs. J.	....	123
Brelsford, Thomas	....	98, 99
Bridle, Edwin and Georgina	....	20, 58
Brillinger Family	....	88
Bristol, Emerson	....	51
Bristol, Rev. Burness	....	106,108
Brock heirs	....	6, 7
Brock, George	....	7
Brock, Sophie	....	7
Brown, Allan	....	21
Brown, David	....	23
Brown, David and Rosalie, Family	....	60
Brown, Edward	....	16
Brown, Edward	....	23, 88
Brown, Harvey and Donna	....	61
Brown, John	....	23
Brown, Thomas and Lorraine	....	49
Browning, Phyllis	....	83

Bryant, Charles and Myrna, Family	....	**45-46**, 99, 100, 105, 122
Bryant, Everly	....	46, 121
Bryant, Raymond	....	45, 121
Bryce, Janette (Mrs. M. Haines), Family	....	27
Buchan, Charles and Agnes, Family	....	6, 92
Burbridge, Mrs., Family	....	47
Burge, Roger	....	49
Burger, Peter and Gerda, Family	....	29, 30
Burness, William	....	87
Burns, Matthew	....	72
Buttenham, Cecil and Elizabeth	....	20
Buttenham, Glen and Marilyn, Family	....	31
Byrne, John	....	16
Cairns, Archie	....	62
Cairns, Roy	....	62
Cairns, William	....	15
Caldwell, Thomas	....	98, 99
Calloway, David L., Family	....	55
Cameron, Archibald	....	**65**, 66, 87
Cameron, Archibald, Sr. and Janet Family	....	5, 64, 65
Cameron, Donald, Family	....	**64**, 65, 66
Cameron, Duncan and Janet, Family	....	**65**, 66, 67, 116
Cameron, Duncan, Sr. and Isabella	....	5, **65**
Cameron, John Hillyard, Judge	....	7, 46, 67, 88, 90
Campbell Family	....	5
Campbell, Albert E. and Harriet, Family	....	59, **75**, 89, 90, 97, 99, 120
Campbell, Alex and Edith, Family	....	53, 54
Campbell, Alexander and Jane, Family	....	6, **25**, 66
Campbell, Alexander and Margaret Family	....	**66**, 128
Campbell, Archibald and Martha, Family	....	25, **66**, 96, 116
Campbell, Archibald, Jr., Family	....	32, 47, 48, **53**, 66, 75, 77
Campbell, Bertram	....	**75**, 121
Campbell, Catherine (Mrs. Donald Cameron)	....	**25**, 64
Campbell, Colin	....	25
Campbell, Colin D. and Lois, Family	....	**76**, 99
Campbell, David and Ellen, Family	....	**66**, 67
Campbell, Francis	....	87
Campbell, George and Nadine	....	12, **54**
Campbell, James and Isabella	....	25
Campbell, Janet (Mrs. Duncan Cameron)	....	25, **65**
Campbell, John and Ann, Family	....	25
Campbell, John D. and Ina, Family	....	76
Campbell, Lena Revell, Family	....	74, **75**, 100

Campbell, Peter	....	*25*
Campbell, R. D.	....	*97, 99*
Campbell, William C. and Maria	....	*19*
Carlisle, Schools, Balaclava	....	*15, 21*
Carpenter, Stanley and Louise, Family	....	*43*
Carr, Robert and Elsie	....	*23*
Carrol, Edward	....	*18*
Carton, Emerson and Ellen, Family	....	***40**, 47, 48, 103, 104*
Cartwright, Edmund and Margaret, Family	....	*85*
Cartwright, George and Minnie, Family	....	*48*
Cartwright, John and Matilda	....	***85**, 96*
Case, Elder William	....	*101*
Castleton, William and Margaret	....	*60*
Caswell, Barbara	....	*55*
Caswell, Lyle	....	*12*
Caswell, Pansy	....	*55*
Cemeteries, Carlisle	....	*24*
Cemeteries, Mountsberg Baptist	....	*53, 54*
Cemeteries, Mountsberg Methodist	....	*24, 36, 38, 43, 49, 54, 55,*
	....	*75, 101, 102, 133*
Challinor, Roger, Family	....	*22*
Chambers, Daniel	....	*80*
Chambers, George Henry	....	*102*
Chandler, Fred	....	*47*
Chapman, George and Elizabeth	....	*66*
Chechalk, Edward and Ruth, Family	....	*76*
Chester, Edward and Grace, Family	....	*25, **26***
Chettle, John and Kathleen	....	*16*
Christensen, Stanley and Dianne	....	*16*
Chysik, Julia	....	*61*
Clark, Annie (Mrs. George Stewart)	....	*65*
Clark, George	....	*67*
Cleghorn, Mrs. Douglas (Flora McCrae)	....	***68**, 69*
Clement, Rev. E. L.	....	*102*
Cluff, Mollie	....	*107*
Clutton, Elder Joseph	....	*95, 99*
Cochrane, Robert and Flora	....	***55**, 122, 123*
Cockburn, Margaret	....	*87*
Cohen, Esther	....	*88*
Cohoe, Rev. B. L., Family	....	*102, **108***
Cohrs, Fritz	....	*22*
Collier, Frederick and Drusilla	....	*16*
Collier, Thomas	....	*19*
Coiling, Russell and Ruth, Family	....	***57**, 98, 123*

Collingridge, Raymond and Pauline	....	61
Comin Brothers Farms	....	28
Connell, Hon. Ray	....	113
Connell, John and Mary, Family	....	43, 44, **46**
Connor, Thomas and Mary, Family	....	42
Cook, Edward and Elizabeth	....	22
Cooke, Donald and Judith, Family	....	29
Cooke, Hamilton and Helen	....	20
Cooke, Llewelyn	....	24
Cooper, Elizabeth	....	28
Cooper, Gilbert and Joan, Family	....	31, 34
Cormack, Donald and Marilyn, Family	....	29
Corman, Robert and Elizabeth, Family	....	28
Cottrell, John and Brenda, Family	....	**30**, 123
Coulson, Sarah (Mrs. Frank)	....	**61,** 105, 106
Coulson, Sherwood	....	15
Coulter, Frank	....	55
Coupland, Ron F.	....	98, 99
Coverdale, Lloyd and Faye, Family	....	**31**, 45
Coverdale, Margaret (Mrs. Corn. Hewins)	....	47
Crawford, Murray	....	70, 116
Credit Valley Railway	....	65, 69, 72, 75, 89, 90, 91, 115, 116, 131
Croall, Kenneth and Myrna	....	15
Croft, David and Jane, Family	....	64
Crooker, J. C.	....	44
Crooker, J. K.	....	102, 108
Crooker, M. M.	....	45
Cuculich, Walter and Mary	....	20
Cumming, Vera	....	23
Curry, John B., Family	....	59
Cust, L. S.	....	105
Cust, William and Merle	....	72, 108
Cuvaj, Francis and Susan	....	20
Cyopik, Charles and Linda	....	81
Dal Bello, L.	....	64
Daley, George, Sr., Family	....	15
Darling, Adam	....	6, 83, 91
Davidson, Peter	....	25
Davidson, Peter and Agnes	....	83
Davies, Anthony and Marjorie, Family	....	29, 30
Davis, Dr.	....	61
Davis, William	....	16
Davis, William and Joan	....	61

Daw, Jeffrey	....	*43*
Dawson, Francis	....	*44*
Dawson, Margaret, Family	....	*36, 108,* ***109***
Dawson, Sarah	....	***37****, 130*
Dawson, Solomon, Family	....	*32, 36,* ***37****, 49, 66, 102, 108*
Day, Richard	....	*16*
Deacon, Rev. Charles	....	*108*
DeBlauw, Ralph and Barbara	....	*61*
DeGroot, R.	....	*63, 64*
Dempsey, Terry	....	*98, 99*
Dent, Douglas and Opal, Family	....	*35, 36*
Dent, Paul and Merejean, Family	....	*35, 36*
Desender, Remi and Blanche, Family	....	*40, 47,* ***66***
Devereaux, Mrs. E.	....	*123*
DeVries, Foppe and Glenda, Family	....	*46*
DeVries, John	....	*26, 28, 35*
Devries, U. J. and T.	....	*61*
Dickson, Anna	....	*100*
Didero, Silverine	....	*20, 21*
DiRado, Vincenzo	....	*64*
Dixon, Joseph	....	*6, 64*
Dolynuk, H.	....	*60*
Domenico, Errol and Sylvia	....	*20*
Donelly, Hiram	....	*16*
Donovan, Henry, Family	....	*66*
Dougherty, Earl and Flossie, Family	....	***31****, 58, 100, 108, 121*
Dougherty, George, Family	....	***31****, 45, 103*
Dougherty, James and Joanna, Family	....	***58****, 80, 81, 86, 102*
Dougherty, Leland Hilbert	....	*31, 120*
Dougherty, Lyle and Florence, Family	....	***58****, 120*
Dougherty, Nathan Austin	....	*31, 120*
Dougherty, William, Family	....	***30****, 31, 80*
Doveika, Anthony	....	*86*
Dowling, Thomas and Barbara	....	*61*
Doxey, David and Bonnie	....	*21*
Draper, William Henry	....	*6, 7, 49*
Dredge, Douglas and Menedora, Family	....	***26****, 64, 98*
Dredge, Edward and Helen, Family	....	*64*
Dredge, Elmer and Barbara, Family	....	*64*
Drown, Donald and Nadja, Family	....	*58*
Drumm, Roscoe	....	*88*
Drummond Family	....	*23*
Dryden, Clifford and Theresa, Family	....	***83****, 100*
Dulic, Nikola and Margit	....	*22*

Duncan, Gerald and Melba, Family	....	64
Dunham, James F. and Linda, Family	....	**53**, 54
Dunham, Lynda	....	21
Dunk, Victor and Evelyn	....	19
Durrant, Bruce and Susan, Family	....	85
Dutton, William	....	47, 48, 77
Dziepak, Stanley and Dorothy	....	47
East Flamborough, maps	....	4
Easterbrook, Brock and Debbie, Family	....	75
Easterbrook, John and Edythe, Family	....	**75**, 89, 90
Easterbrook, Mrs., Family	....	77
Easterbrook, William and Mary	....	87
Eaton, Allan	....	66, 88
Eaton, Archibald T.	....	88
Eaton, Fawcett	....	67
Eaton, Mr. and Mrs. George, Family	....	32, **66**
Edmar, Edward and Patricia, Family	....	40
Edwards, Geoffrey and Rosemarie	....	76
Elder, George C. and Eva A.	....	19
Elliot, Patricia, Family	....	74
Elliott, Allan and Isabel, Family	....	26, **38**, 122, 123
Elliott, Charles and Isabella, Family	....	**38**, 40
Elliott, David	....	98, 99
Elliott, Wayne and Wendy	....	20
Elms, Sharon	....	22
Elvin, Harry and Sarah, Family	....	40
Emmert, Judith A.	....	70
Emmons, Albert	....	43, **56,** 121
Emmons, Henry and Hannah, Family	....	**60**, 103
Emmons, John and Maybelle	....	56
Emmons, Walter and Elizabeth, Family	....	42, **43**, 56, 120
Emmons, William, Family	....	18, 43, 44, 47, **56**, 57, 60,
	....	103, 104, 107
Empey, O. G.	....	22
English, James and Elizabeth, Family	....	60
Evans, John	....	23
Everton, G.	....	96, 99
Farley, Edward H.	....	88
Fearnley, Charles and Phoebe, Family	....	**60,** 77
Fearnley, Fred	....	46
Fearnley, George and Ann, Family	....	6, **53**, 55, 60, 95, 98
Fearnley, Joseph	....	**53**, 55

Fenrock Ltd.	…………………………	*40, 47, 48*
Ferrier, John	…………………………	*18*
Ferrier, Oliver and Elizabeth, Family	…………………………	**28**, *58, 102*
Fiddler, Edward J.	…………………………	*61*
Field, Francis and Tomasina, Family	…………………………	*29*
Figsbee, Esther (Mrs. J. Wheeler, Jr.)	…………………………	*24*
Filtness, Ted	…………………………	*12, 121*
Finkbeiner, Alvin and Verlie	…………………………	*23*
Finlay, William and Elizabeth	…………………………	*28*
Fisher, William	…………………………	*69*
Flamborough Centre Properties	…………………………	*35, 46*
Flatt, W. D.	…………………………	*10*
Flatt, Wm. D.	…………………………	*23*
Fletcher, James and Gertrude, Family	…………………………	*57*
Flowers, John	…………………………	*59, 102*
Flowers, Sarah Whitehead	…………………………	*57*
Flynn Family	…………………………	*84*
Foley, Michael, Family	…………………………	*16,* **17**, *18*
Foley, Thomas, Family	…………………………	**17**, *118*
Ford, James and Hannah, Family	…………………………	*46,* **54**
Forest, Abraham	…………………………	*90*
Forsyth, Amelia	…………………………	*91*
Forsyth, Rev. William and Mary, Family	…………………………	*57, 82,* **91**, *96, 99*
Forsyth, Wrn. A. and Sarah, Family	…………………………	**81,** *91*
Foster, William and Mary Ann, Family	…………………………	*45*
Four Seasons Nature Park	…………………………	*58*
Fox, Kenneth and Theresa, Family	…………………………	*26*
Fraser, Zebina	…………………………	*15*
Freed, Edmund	…………………………	*19*
Freel, Miss	…………………………	*110*
Freestone Family	…………………………	*28*
Frost, Rev. T. A. P.	…………………………	*96, 99*
Gaetan, B.	…………………………	*64*
Gage, Andrew	…………………………	*87*
Gage, James, Family	…………………………	**16**, *66*
Gallagher, John	…………………………	*88*
Galloway, Charles E.	…………………………	*24, 57*
Gant, John and Elizabeth	…………………………	*71*
Gartley, Edward	…………………………	*24*
Gavin, Patrick and Mary Ann, Family	…………………………	*16,* **17**, *18*
Gavin (Garvin), Thomas, Sr., Family	…………………………	*16,* **17**, *18*
Gay, Rev. Alexander, Family	…………………………	**46**, *96, 99*
George, Donald and Barbara, Family	…………………………	*58*

Gerre, Rev. John	....	96
Gilbertson, Mr.	....	64
Gillespie, Thomas and Stella, Family	....	20, **35**, 123
Gilmore, Ira and Violet	....	21
Gilmour, Andrew and Effie, Family	....	88, **89**
Glasgow, John	....	66
Glendinning, Roland	....	98, 99
Golden Family	....	75
Gonder, Rev. R. K.	....	97, 88
Gonnsen, Karl and Donna	....	22
Goodbrand, Bruce and Carol	....	18
Gordon, James	....	46
Graham Family	....	52
Gramme, George and Mary	....	20
Grant, James	....	16
Grant, Kenneth, Family	....	22
Grant, Mrs. (Mrs. Dan Wingrove)	....	57
Grant, William	....	96, 99
Gray, John, Family	....	22
Gray, Percy, Family	....	19, **21**, 122, 123
Green, George	....	46
Gregory, A. R.	....	96, 99
Griffin, Catherine (Mrs. Tho. Wingrove)	....	30
Griffin, Joseph	....	30
Groves, Marvin and Ruth	....	83
Gruenberg, Werner and Lucy	....	21
Gunby, Archibald and Lena, Family	....	12, **52**, 70, 100, 121, 122, 123
Gunby, Burdge and Martha	....	12, 43, 51, **52**, 53, 54, 59, 70, 89, 90, 120
Gunby, Burdge, Sr.	....	19
Gunby, Cecil and Teresa	....	52, **70**, 121
Gunby, Isabel	....	52, 121
Gunby, John and Vera, Family	....	11, **43**, 46, 52, 100, 122, 123
Gunby, John, Sr.	....	52
Gunby, Ken	....	52, 121
Gunby, Laverne	....	52, 121
Gunby, Lois	....	43, 122
Gurney, H. G.	....	96, 99
Gyrpstra, Betty Jean	....	22
Haggerty, John, Sr., Family	....	15
Haggis, Craig	....	95
Haines, Eba	....	96, 99
Haines, John, Sr., Family	....	3, 5, 15, 25, **26**, 27, 68, 101, 102

Haines, Marshall and Lucinda, Family	....	25, 26, **27**, 28, 92
Haines, Rev. E. J.	....	96, 97, 99
Haines, Thomas and Margaret, Family	....	25, 26, **77**, 91, 92, 102, 104
Hall, Barry and Eimar, Family	....	47
Hall, Frederick and Constance, Family	....	26
Hall, John and Sue, Family	....	66
Hall, Vernon and Loretta, Family	....	36
Halton Region Conservation Authority	....	63-67, 69, 87, 88, 124
Hambleton, George and Frances	....	76
Hambsch, Reinhold and Gerlinde	....	61
Hand, Greig and Mary, Family	....	74, **75**
Hanning, Geordie	....	130
Happy, Dennis and Lesley	....	20
Hardie, Philip W.	....	17
Harper, Charles and Elizabeth	....	61
Harris, Edwin	....	47
Harris, Gordon and Mary, Family	....	36
Harris, John, Family	....	37
Harris, Matthew, Family	....	25, 26, **27**
Harris, Morley	....	25, 26, 27, 28
Harris, Ronald and Bertha	....	47, 48
Harris, Roy	....	27, 121
Harris, Roy A.	....	24
Harris, Sandy	....	123
Harrison, Mervin and Marion	....	88
Hart, John	....	102
Haskell, Percy and Edith, Family	....	32, 46, **84**
Hazelton, Rev. W. P.	....	96, 99
Head, Charles and Joyce, Family	....	64
Hearn, Mary I.	....	16, 17, 18, 19
Heaton, Susannah	....	77
Hebert, Arthur and Cheryl	....	22
Heddle, Dunbar and Flora	....	32, 122
Hellenbroich, Karl and Rosemarie	....	22
Henwood, Lorne and Joan	....	19, 123
Hewins, Aaron and Christine, Family	....	39, 46, **71,** 103
Hewins, Albert and Elizabeth, Family	....	11, 46, **51**, 53, 100, 105, 106, 119, 120
Hewins, Charles and Annie, Family	....	40, 47, 49, 52, 69, 71, **72**, 103, 119, 120
Hewins, Cornelius and Ann, Family	....	5, 6, 7, 36, 38, **39**, 46, 47, 72, 102
Hewins, Gordon	....	12, 49, 51, 130
Hewins, John	....	51, 108
Hewins, John and Margaret, Family	....	9, **39,** 40, 43, 46, 47, 48, 49, 71, 108
Hewins, Merle	....	72, 121
Hewins, Olive	....	51, 104, 120

Hewins, Ralph and Janet, Family	....	39, 46, **51**, 71
Hewins, Reginald and Violet, Family	....	12, 39, **72**
Hewins, Richard and Mary Ann, Family	....	39, 40, **44**, 45, 48, 51
Hewins, Roy	....	72, 108, 128
Hicks, Dale and Diane	....	61
Hillyard, Thomas and Mary Ann	....	47
Hinton, George and Catherine	....	44, 45, 48
Hogg, Shirley	....	98
Hole, Michael and Sally	....	22
Hollander, Pieter and Hendrika	....	24
Holmes, William and Catherine, Family	....	64
Hood, Birdie	....	121
Hood, Cecil	....	58
Hood, John, Family	....	23
Hood, Oscar and Betsy, Family	....	82
Hopkins, Grace	....	24
Hopkins, Robert	....	96, 99
Hopkins, Ruth	....	55
Hopkinson, George	....	31, 32
Hopkinson, Thomas	....	15, 102
Horyn, Edward	....	60
Houston, Alfred and Dorothy	....	31
Houston, Brian and Dianne, Family	....	28
Howard, Brock and Irene, Family	....	31
Howard, John	....	77
Howlett, Ezra	....	86
Hoyle, Elder	....	96, 99
Hughes, John, Family	....	22
Hughes, Stanley	....	74
Huiskamp, William	....	63
Hulme, Albert, Family	....	**18**, 122, 123
Hunt, Jeremiah, Family	....	31, **33**
Hunt, Marshall, Family	....	31, **33**, 103
Hunter, Daniel and Anne, Family	....	22
Hunter, Dennis and Helen, Family	....	22
Hunter, Dennis, Family	....	21
Hunter, Edna P.	....	88
Hunter, James and Jane, Family	....	22
Hunter, James and Lina, Family	....	21, **22**, 23
Hunter, Ursula	....	16
Hunter, William	....	80
Hurren, Charity (Mrs. Wm. Wingrove)	....	78
Hurren, Edmund and Jane, Family	....	**77**, 96
Hurren, Francis and Harriet, Family	....	90, **91**

Hurren, James and Ruth, Family	....	71, **77**, 90, 92
Hurren, James, Jr. and Annie	....	45
Hurren, Philip, Family	....	76, **77**
Hurren, Robert and Olive	....	28, **75**
Hurren, William and Charlotte, Family	....	37, 80,81, **90**, 91
Hurst (Mrs. Dan Wingrove)	....	57
Hurst, Benjamin	....	86
Hutchison, J.	....	19
Hutchison, James and Marianne	....	61
Hutt, Wayne and Gayle	....	29
Hysert, William, Family	....	40
Indians	....	3, 5
Inglis, James, Mr. and Mrs.	....	15
Jablonowski, Frank and Geraldine, Family	....	54
Jacques (Jones), Nicholas	....	57
Jensen, Aage and Anna	....	18
Johnson, Benjamin and Ann, Family	....	36, 44, **47,** 48, 62, 102
Johnson, Philip, Family	....	5, 6, 7, **36**, 38, 49, 58, 101
Johnson, Trueman and Emma	....	15, 47, 62, 120, 103, 104
Johnson, William and Charlotte, Family	....	36, **75**, 102
Johnstone, John R.	....	24
Johnstone, William and Mary	....	23
Jones, David and Shirley, Family	....	**34,** 123
Jones, Dr. Arthur	....	37
Jones, G.	....	20
Jones, Robert and June	....	61
Jordan, Tom	....	121
Juraschka, Elfriede	....	20
Kallman, Hans J.	....	88
Kane, John and Ann	....	19
Kangas, Yngve and Tuulikki, Family	....	64
Kearns, Dr. J. R.	....	23, 57
Kelk, Harness	....	40, 102
Kellington, Dr. Win. and Ena, Family	....	75
Kempenaar, Gary and Allie, Family	....	**32**, 123
Kendrick, Alexander and Helen, Family	....	92
Kennedy, Donald	....	69
Kennedy, John	....	80
Kennedy, John and Janet, Family	....	67
Kent, John and Dorothy	....	15
Kerr, Francis	....	71, 72

Kerr, John R. and Annie, Family	....	**59**, 102
Kerr, Robert and Isabella, Family	....	6, 24 58, **59**, 102
Kerr, William H. and Jane, Family	....	**59**, 102, 103
Kierstead, Prof.	....	97
Kilmer, G.	....	106
King, John	....	61, 64, 65, 88
Kirk, Andre and Dora	....	22
Kitchen, Billy	....	53, 59
Kitchen, James, Family	....	60, **62**
Kitchen, Lorrie (Mrs. John Peacock)	....	60
Kloepfer, Christian	....	23
Kopp, Fritz and Ursula, Family	....	35
Korb, Karl and Wiltrant	....	48
Korb, Willy, Family	....	48
Kort, Cornelius W. D.	....	19
Kraus, Vratislav	....	34
Lacey, William and Patricia	....	16, 17, 19, 122, 123
Laking, Charles and Margaret, Family	....	52, **92**, 105
Laking, Charles and Rachel, Family	....	**61**, 106
Laking, Ernie	....	52, 131
Laking, Frank and Donna, Family	....	90, **92**
Laking, Fred and Mary Jane, Family	....	24, 52, 55, **81**, 91
Laking, Ivan and Myrtle, Family	....	90, **91**, 92, 122
Laking, Jack	....	121
Laking, James S. and Annie, Family	....	**61**, 128, 130
Laking, John and Lucy, Family	....	49, 52, **61**, 102, 104, 128, 130
Laking, Joseph and Charlotte, Family	....	47, **52**
Laking, Robert and Gertrude, Family	....	**61**, 105
Laking, Ross and Camilla, Family	....	31
Laking, Will	....	52, 131
Laking, William and Martha, Family	....	36, 39, 44, **46-47**, 51, 52, 54, 55, 55, 56, 103, 104, 130, 131
Lamm, Herbert and Renate	....	60
Lapp, Frederick and Eleanor	....	21
Lassaline, Jerome and Teresa, Family	....	30
Laurence, Rev. Sydney	....	120
Law, Hector and Flora, Family	....	**76**, 89
Law, J. Garnet and Ida, Family	....	88, **89**
Lawrence, Sidney	....	97, 99
Legg Family	....	76
Leith, James	....	68
Leith, William	....	68
Leslie, Bessie	....	56, 121

Name	Page
Leslie, Isabel	56, *121*
Leslie, Mark and Myrtle, Family	*23*, **56**
Leslie, Pearl	*121*
Lewis, George, Family	*5*, **28**
Lewis, John and Mary, Family	**90**, *102*
Lewis, Lyn Crawford	*47*
Lewis, Robert and Thelma	*88*
Lickers	*64*
Linn, Hugh and Jane, Family	*62*
Linn, Joseph	*6, 7*
Linn, William and Charity, Family	*44*, **62**
Linten, John	*96*
Lisson, Allen and Loretta	*15*
Livingston, Thomas D. and Marion	*83*
London, Eleanor	*40*, **47**
Lostrocco, Mimmo and Julianne	*20*
Lucy, Mr.	*108*
Lumsden, Catherine	*66*
Lynn, Hugh and Agnes, Family	*63*
Lynn, Joseph and Margaret, Family	**63**, *64*
Lytle, Stanley and Carolyn	*30*
Maby, Christopher and Margaret, Family	*28*
MacAulay, Muriel	*100*
MacCallum, Rev. J.H.	*106*
Macdonnell, William	*19*
MacEdward, James and Mary, Family	*86*
MacEdward, William and Beatrice, Family	*86*
MacIntyre, Alexander, Family	*82*
MacIntyre, Margaret (Mrs. Wm. Wingrove)	*78*
MacKay, Harry and Margaret	*21*
Mackie, Elder	*96, 99*
Mackie, Rev. J.	*96, 99*
MacLaren, James H.	*66*
MacLaren, William	*66*
MacPherson, John and Ann, Family	*55, 88*, **89**
MacPherson, Peter and Catherine, Family	**89**, *90*
Maddaugh, Jake	*44*
Maddaugh, John and Catherine, Family	*11*, **86**
Maher, Ruby, Family	*47*
Maitland Family	*67*
Manary, Elizabeth (Mrs. Jos. Laking)	*52*
Mancini, Elio and Thelma, Family	*74*
Manger, Richard and Marie	*26*

Manto, Edwin and Nellie	....	19, 23, 24
Marinucci, Giacoma and Liberata	....	30
Marshall, George W. and Margaret, Family	....	90, **91**
Marshall, John and Jody, Family	....	55
Marshall, Robert and Margaret, Family	....	26, 90, **91**, 102
Martin, James	....	72
Martin, Joseph B. and Maryetta	....	86
Martin, Margaret M.	....	88
Martin, Peter and Anne, Family	....	47
Mason, Job	....	64
Mast, William and Rosine, Family	....	92
Maszaros, Leslie	....	24
Matthews, Norman and Beverly, Family	....	29
May, Peter and Sylvia	....	61
Mayhew, John, Family	....	87
Maynard, Dixon and Ann	....	132
Maynard, Martha Wheeler, Family	....	132, **133**
Maynard, Roger and Elizabeth, Family	....	55, 102, 108, 110, **132**
Mazzucco, L. and P.	....	74
Mazzucco, S. and M.	....	74
McAllister, John A.	....	70
McArthur, Amos	....	15
McCarthy, Bernard and Lorraine, Family	....	31, **34**, 121
McCarthy, Charles	....	23
McCarthy, Charles and Mary, Family	....	19, 20, 21, 27, 31, 33, **34**, 36, 54, 76, 123
McCarthy, Dennis (4th)	....	23
McCarthy, Dennis and Annie	....	17, 23
McCarthy, Dennis and Margaret	....	17, 20, 23
McCarthy, Dennis, Sr., Family	....	**17**, 18, 22
McCarthy, Dianne	....	54, 124
McCarthy, Edward and Joyce, Family	....	**54**, 121
McCarthy, John (Jack)	....	36
McCarthy, Ned	....	83, 91
McCarthy, Patrick and Annie, Family	....	17, 20, **37-38**, 46, 75
McCarthy, Patrick and Dorothy, Family	....	19, **54**
McCarthy, Paul and Rose, Family	....	**54**, 107, 121, 122
McCartney, Theophilus, Family	....	15
McClinton, John	....	110
McComb, Gordon, Family	....	16
McComb, Roy, Family	....	16
McConnell, H. A.	....	96, 99
McCormack, James, Families	....	43
McCrae, Col. David and Janet, Family	....	**67**, 68, 72, 116
McCrae, David and Jessie, Family	....	**68**, 70, 88

McCrae, David, Sr. and Mareon	....	*67*
McCrae, John	....	*67, 68, 70*
McCrae, Thomas and Jane, Family	....	*10, 25,* ***67****, 69*
McCrae, Thomas, M.D.	....	*67, 69, 116*
McCrae, William and Jessie, Family	....	***68****, 69*
McCuen, Wesley	....	*24*
McCurdy, Adam	....	*68, 83*
McCurdy, Daniel and Maud	....	*81, 83*
McCurdy, James (3) and Elizabeth, Family	....	*68,* ***83***
McCurdy, James and Rose, Family	....	*83*
McCurdy, James, Sr., Family	....	*83*
McDermand, Rev. W. S.	....	*96, 99*
McDermid, Henry and Georgette, Family	....	***40****, 47*
McDonald, James	....	*88*
McDonald, Robert	....	*88*
McDonald, Wm, and Isabella, Family	....	*88*
McDonnell, William and Eileen	....	*40*
McDougall Family	....	*34*
McDougall, Duncan, Family	....	*16*
McDougall, John, Family	....	*16,* ***18****, 19*
McDowell, Arthur, G.	....	*98, 99*
McElroy, A.	....	*19*
McFarlane, Bill	....	*51, 108*
McGroty, Francis and Rena, Family	....	*36,* ***64***
McGuire, Bill	....	*38*
McGuire, Dan, Family	....	*34*
McGuire, Elmer (Al), Family	....	*38*
McGuire, Marie	....	*121*
McIntosh, Donald	....	*46*
McIntosh, George	....	*69*
McIntosh, James and Margaret, Family	....	*89*
McIntyre, Joseph	....	*40*
McKay, Cliff, Family	....	*74*
McKenna, Dennis and Frances, Family	....	*19, 24,* ***86***
McKenna, John and Bridget	....	*19*
McKenna, John and Doreen, Family	....	***60****, 86*
McKenna, John, Sr., Family	....	***18****, 19*
McKenna, Kathy	....	*58, 123, 124*
McKenna, Michael and Helen, Family	....	***58****, 123*
McKenna, Thomas, Family	....	*17, 18,* ***19***
McKenzie, Alexander and Isabella, Family	....	*25,* ***26****, 119*
McKenzie, Annie	....	*64*
McLaren, Henry	....	*28*
McLaren, John	....	*44*

McLaren, Peter		51
McLean, Alexander and Penelope, Family		89
McLean, J.		102
McLean, James		43
McLean, John		87
McLean, Mr.		108, 132
McLeod, Donald		92
McLeod, Kenneth		68
McMonies, James		87
McMurdo, James and Ruth, Family		49
McNeil, Gordon and Margaret Boyd, Family		35
McNiven, Daniel		15
McNiven, John C. and Rachel, Family		15, 49, **51**, 102, 103
McPhail, John, Family		59
McPherson, John (Sandy), Family		55
Menzies, Mr.		61
Millman, John, Family		**30**, 102
Mills, Mrs. R.		122
Milne, Alexander		28
Misener, Donald G.		98, 99
Misner, Merlin and Margaret, Family		54
Mitchell, Charles N.		96, 99
Mitchell, George, Family		15, 16
Mitchell, Joseph and Mabel		23, 122
Mitchell, Lois		28
Moffat, William		68
Moggack Family		16
Monas, George and Jean		29
Monkhouse, Isaac		102
Monkhouse, Thomas		86
Moon, Stewart and Cheryl		89
Mooney, Mr.		71
Moore, Richard Nelson		81, 91
Moore, William and Katie, Family		75
Moskalyk, William		34
Mount, Alpheus and Hulda, Family		**35**, 96, 99
Mount, Charles and Rachel, Family		35, 40, 41, **43**, 102
Mount, Charles R.		35, 90, 91, 97, 98
Mount, Emanuel and Jane, Family		40, 41, **42**, 43, 45, 127
Mount, Jacob and Annie, Family		42
Mount, John and Mary Ann, Family		35, 41, **42**, 45, 46
Mount, Josiah and Mary, Family		3, 5, 34, **35**, 38, 40, 41, 43, 102
Mount, Matthew and Rachel, Family		40, 41, 43, 44, **45,** 46, 120
Mount, Minerva		42, 57

Mount, Page and Elizabeth, Family	....	**38**, 106
Mount, Roy Wheeler	....	42, 120
Mount, William	....	42, 46
Mount, Wm. Leonard, Family	....	**38**, 91, 102, 104
Mountsberg Community Park	....	49, 119-122
Mountsberg 4-H Club	....	123, 124
Mountsberg Hydro Station	....	24
Mountsberg School	....	15, 16, 17, 19, 21, 22, 28, 37, 38,
	....	44, 46, 48, 49, 52, 53, 55, 62,
	....	75, 86, 87, 89, 95, 108, 110-115, 122
Mountsberg Wildlife Centre	....	124
Mountsberg, Agricultural Census	....	9, 10, 11, 75, 82
Mountsberg, Agriculture	....	9, 10, 11, 12, 91
Mountsberg, Barnraising	....	71, 82, 117-119
Mountsberg, Brock Grants	....	6, 7, 15, 17, 21, 23, 25, 28, 31, 36,
	....	40, 49, 53, 58, 59, 63, 66, 67, 73, 75,
	....	82, 83, 87, 88, 90, 91, 92
Mountsberg, Bronte Creek	....	8, 61
Mountsberg, Canada Land Company	....	6, 16, 19, 23, 32, 64, 78
Mountsberg, Churches, Anglican	....	16
Mountsberg, Churches, Baptist	....	35, 46, 76, 77, 95-100, 120, 121
Mountsberg, Churches, Methodist	....	36, 48, 59, 61, 95, 101-109, 120,
	....	127, 132
Mountsberg, Clergy Reserves	....	6, 7, 16, 19, 26, 55, 65, 71, 86, 88, 91
Mountsberg, Concession 11, Lot 1	....	15, 16
Mountsberg, Concession 11, Lot 2	....	16
Mountsberg, Concession 11, Lot 3	....	16, 17
Mountsberg, Concession 11, Lot 4	....	17
Mountsberg, Concession 11, Lot 5	....	17, 18, 19, 23
Mountsberg, Concession 11, Lot 6	....	5, 19
Mountsberg, Concession 11, Lot 7	....	6, 20, 21, 23
Mountsberg, Concession 11, Lot 8	....	6, 21
Mountsberg, Concession 11, Lot 9	....	6, 23
Mountsberg, Concession 11, Lot 10	....	23
Mountsberg, Concession 11, Lot 11	....	23, 24
Mountsberg, Concession 11, Lot 12	....	24
Mountsberg, Concession 12, Lot 1	....	6, 25
Mountsberg, Concession 12, Lot 2	....	3, 5, 15, 26
Mountsberg, Concession 12, Lot 3	....	5, 28
Mountsberg, Concession 12, Lot 4	....	31
Mountsberg, Concession 12, Lot 5	....	32
Mountsberg, Concession 12, Lot 6	....	6, 7, 9, 22, 36
Mountsberg, Concession 12, Lot 7	....	3, 6, 7, 9. 40

Mountsberg, Concession 12, Lot 8	....	*5, 49*
Mountsberg, Concession 12, Lot 9	....	*6, 53, 132*
Mountsberg, Concession 12, Lot 10	....	*5, 55*
Mountsberg, Concession 12, Lot 11	....	*5, 6, 24, 58*
Mountsberg, Concession 12, Lot 12	....	*22, 59*
Mountsberg, Concession 13, Lot 1	....	*6, 7, 63*
Mountsberg, Concession 13, Lot 2	....	*6, 64*
Mountsberg, Concession 13, Lot 3	....	*5, 65*
Mountsberg, Concession 13, Lot 4	....	*5, 66*
Mountsberg, Concession 13, Lot 5	....	*67*
Mountsberg, Concession 13, Lot 6	....	*71*
Mountsberg, Concession 13, Lot 7	....	*6, 9, 12, 73*
Mountsberg, Concession 13, Lot 8	....	*3, 6, 24, 75*
Mountsberg, Concession 13, Lot 9	....	*5, 24, 78*
Mountsberg, Concession 13, Lot 10	....	*5, 82*
Mountsberg, Concession 13, Lot 11	....	*24, 83*
Mountsberg, Concession 13, Lot 12	....	*86*
Mountsberg, Concession 14, Lot 1	....	*87*
Mountsberg, Concession 14, Lot 2	....	*87*
Mountsberg, Concession 14, Lot 3	....	*87*
Mountsberg, Concession 14, Lot 4	....	*87*
Mountsberg, Concession 14, Lot 5	....	*88*
Mountsberg, Concession 14, Lot 6	....	*88*
Mountsberg, Concession 14, Lot 7	....	*88*
Mountsberg, Concession 14, Lot 8	....	*90*
Mountsberg, Concession 14, Lot 9	....	*91*
Mountsberg, Concession 14, Lot 10	....	*6, 91*
Mountsberg, Concession 14, Lot 11	....	*6, 92*
Mountsberg, Concession 14, Lot 12	....	*6, 92*
Mountsberg, Concessions 1-14	....	*6, 7, 110*
Mountsberg, Indian Artifacts	....	*35*
Mountsberg, Indians	....	*3, 5*
Mountsberg, Lime Kiln	....	*21, 32*
Mountsberg, Literary Society	....	*122*
Mountsberg, Post Office	....	*45*
Mountsberg, Sawmills	....	*16, 18, 19, 25, 67, 68*
Mountsberg, Schools, Roman Catholic	....	*15, 20, 110*
Mountsberg, Shingle Mill	....	*36, 46, 49, 52*
Mountsberg, Squatters	....	*5, 47*
Mountsberg, Store	....	*44, 45, 49, 55*
Mountsberg, Timber rights	....	*15, 23, 25, 32 , 66, 67, 68, 70*

Mountsberg, Twelve-Mile Creek	....	3, 8, 35, 67, 88, 102, 124
Mountsberg, Village Map	....	41
Mountsberg, Women's Institute	....	123, 124
Moxom, Elder Job	....	95, 96, 99
Muller, Vivian	....	15
Mullins, James and Sheila	....	86
Mundy, Ronald and Ruth, Family	....	48
Murray, Anna	....	16
Murray, Bernard, Family	....	23
Murray, Edith, Miss	....	19
Murray, William	....	102
Mykytiuk, Joseph and Alice	....	86
Nantais, Peter	....	76
Nassagaweya Township of Halton	....	61, 62
Nassagaweya Twp. Schools, S.S. No. 1	....	15
Neil, Elizabeth I.	....	70
Nelson Township, Agriculture, Exports	....	9
Newell, Samuel	....	15
Nicholson, George, Family	....	40, **85-86**
Nicoll, William	....	87
Novak, John and Helga, Family	....	32
O'Donnell, Dennis, Sr., Family	....	**19**, 20
O'Neil, Pat and Martha, Family	....	92
Orosz, William and Patricia	....	54
Osler, Briton B.	....	19
Page, Albert and Evelyn, Family	....	**43**, 51, 98, 105, 122, 123
Page, Burnice and Hannah, Family	....	33, **56**, 103, 105, 106
Page, Dr. John H., Family	....	31, **33**, 36, 103
Page, J. Albert and Mary Ann, Family	....	**33**, 36, 43
Page, John and Catherine, Family	....	5, 22, 32, 37, **49**, 54, 61, 75, 76, 102, 130
Page, Joseph and Ann, Family	....	5, 31, 32, **33**, 36, 58, 102, 108, 109
Page, Matthew, Family	....	33
Page, Mervyn and Bonnie, Family	....	51
Page, Peter and Susannah, Family	....	36, **37,** 49, 90, 103, 108, 109, 127
Paine, James	....	41, 44, 45
Palmer Family	....	52
Parks, Stanley and Dorothy	....	88
Parnell, George and Elizabeth, Family	....	55
Parry, J. K. Hall, Family	....	**21,** 122
Partridge, Arthur	....	62
Pasuta, Michael and Stella, Family	....	12, 66, **67**, 69, 100

Pasuta, Robert and Elaine, Family	....	48, **67**
Patterson Brothers	....	*131*
Patterson, Jessie	....	*131*
Patton, Matthew and Amy, Family	....	40, **47**
Pawlik, Karen	....	*46, 123, 124*
Pawlik, Kerry	....	*46, 123, 124*
Pawlik, Peter and Marion, Family	....	*3, 43,* **46***, 52, 98, 105, 123, 124*
Pearson, Roy D.	....	*23*
Peer, Arthur and Sarah	....	44
Peer, Arthur, Family	....	37
Peer, Rev. William	....	96, 99
Pegg, Oscar and Louise, Family	....	**44**, 45, 48
Pennings, Garry and Corrie, Family	....	54
Pentecost, Cecil and Myrtle	....	60
Perilli Family	....	60
Perry, John, Family	....	5, **19**
Petch, Robert and Lynne, Family	....	47
Peters, Donald, Family	....	22
Pett, Harry S.	....	28, 48
Pettingill, Peter and Jane, Family	....	65
Phillips, Wilfred and Linda	....	49, 72
Phoenix, Bert	....	107
Plouffe, Donald	....	29
Pook, Alfred and Doris, Family	....	60
Poole, Robert	....	98, 99
Porter, Robert	....	68
Priest, Mrs. T.	....	123
Prowse, Thomas and Minnie	....	22, 122
Prudham, Charles and Jessie	....	*19*
Prudham, Harvey and Jessie	....	27
Pudney, Rev. E. J.	....	97, 99
Pudwill, Arthur	....	21
Purdy, Ronald G.	....	29
Purnell, Abraham, Family	....	24
Purnell, Abraham, Sr., Family	....	5, 24, **58**, 102,
Purnell, Alfred, Family	....	24
Purnell, Joseph and Hannah, Family	....	58
Purnell, Robert L., Family	....	58
Purnell, Thomas and Mary, Family	....	24, **58**
Rasberry, Douglas and Joyce	....	58
Rasmussen, Kaj and Freida	....	20
Rath, H. George	....	98, 99
Ray, Peter	....	120

Rayner, Gordon and Edith, Family	....	*87*
Rayner, Wayne and Jane, Family	....	*65*
Readman, Beatrice, Mrs.	....	*16*
Reding, Bishop Paul	....	*19*
Redpath, Peter, Family	....	*43*
Reinke, F.	....	*119*
Restivo, Joseph and Suzanne	....	*21*
Revell, Alice	....	*11, 74*
Revell, Barbara	....	*11, 74*
Revell, Betty	....	*74, 122*
Revell, Charles and Delilah, Family	....	*36, 38, 43, 44, 45, 55,* **_56_** *, 102, 108*
Revell, Charles and Jean, Family	....	*38*
Revell, Charles and Phoebe, Family	....	*73,* **_74_** *, 96, 97, 99, 100*
Revell, Job and Margaret, Family	....	**_73, 74_** *, 96, 104*
Revell, Lena	....	*74 , 75, 121*
Revell, Levi and Agnes, Family	....	*44,* **_56_**
Revell (Revel), John and Mary, Family	....	*5, 6, 7, 36,* **_38,_** *39, 49, 58, 60, 77, 101, 128*
Revell, Thomas and Anne, Family	....	*6, 9, 38, 39, 46,* **_73,_** *76, 127, 131*
Revell, William and Mildred, Family	....	*12, 19,* **_74_** *, 98, 100, 121, 122, 123*
Rice, Frank	....	*97, 98, 99*
Rice, Rev. I. J.	....	*96*
Rintoul, Roy and Dorothy, Family	....	*73,* **_74,_** *98, 123.*
Roadhammer Family	....	*57*
Roads	....	
12th Concession Road	....	*3 , 6, 15, 17, 19, 23*
13th Concession Road	....	*3 , 6, 35*
Brock Road	....	*5*
Centre Road	....	*3, 6, 15, 17, 20, 23, 40, 46, 49, 77, 90*
Cross Road	....	*6, 40, 101*
Glenron Road	....	*29*
Mountsberg Road	....	*3, 6, 25, 29, 36*
Robb, Rev.	....	*120*
Roberts, Jim and Etta, Family	....	*46*
Roberts, Morris, Family	....	*18*
Robertson, Ann	....	*98*
Robertson, Arch., Jr. and Isabel, Family	....	*77,* **_87,_** *88, 98*
Robertson, Archibald, Sr. Family	....	**_87_** *, 95, 98*
Robertson, Henry and Shirley, Family	....	*49*
Robertson, Margaret	....	*98*
Robinson, Eva	....	*100*
Roblin, A. S.	....	*97, 99*
Roediger, Reinhold and Gillian	....	*15*
Rollins, George and Olive	....	*62, 100*
Ross, Alexander	....	*20*

Roth, Mr.	....	*105*
Rousseau(x), George B.	....	*23, 88*
Rudge, Stanley and Anne	....	*49*
Runciman, James and Margaret	....	*20*
Rutherford, James and Alice, Family	....	*59,* ***60-61***
Ryerson, Egerton	....	*101*
Sachs, Morris	....	*129*
Samis, Elder James	....	*96, 99*
Sanderson, John, Family	....	*19*
Satelmeyer, George	....	*63*
Sauer, Kirk and Christine, Family	....	*54*
Savage, John, Sr., Family	....	*18,* ***23***
Savage, Thomas, Family	....	*23*
Savage, William, Sr., Family	....	*6, 18, 22,* ***23***
Sayers, Edna (Mrs. Richard Hewins)	....	*51*
Schalme, Nicholas	....	*61*
Schmitz, Paul, Mr. and Mrs.	....	*76*
Schnepf, Louis, Family	....	*22*
Schofield, Thomas and Faith	....	*22*
Scholey, Harold, Family	....	*19*
Schwab, Arthur and Susan	....	*20*
Scott, Andrew and Mary, Family	....	***73****, 88*
Scott, Archie and Mary	....	*69, 70, 73, 88, 116*
Scott, James and Mary, Family	....	*72,* ***73****, 75 , 76, 116*
Scott, Jim	....	*76, 121*
Scott, John and Pauline, Family	....	*58*
Scott, Jonathan and Janet (jennie), Family	....	*28, 73,* ***76***
Scott, Morris and Muriel	....	*40, 47*
Scully, Jack and Lyda	....	*61*
Seggie, Alexander and Joanne	....	*24*
Senier, James and Barbara	....	*49*
Shanks, David	....	*57*
Shanks, Samuel, Family	....	*23, 32, 36, 56,* ***57***
Shanks, Sidney	....	*23, 56, 57, 57, 120, 121*
Shanks, William	....	*57*
Sharp, Bryan and Susan, Family	....	*48*
Sharp, Elaine, Mrs.	....	*19*
Sharp, James and Margaret, Family	....	*59*
Sharp, Marguerite	....	*22*
Shaver, Albert Morley	....	*119*
Shead, George	....	*24*
Shellard, Mrs. M. S.	....	*122*
Sheppard Family	....	*40*

Simms, John and Isabel	....	22
Simons Family	....	28
Simons, Elsie Mae	....	22
Simpson, Charles	....	55
Simpson, Robert	....	15
Sinclair, Alex	....	68
Sinclair, Alex and Isabella, Family	....	88
Sinclair, Alexander	....	19
Singleton, George and Joan, Family	....	65
Slade, Charles	....	87
Slater, Henry	....	23
Small, Donald and Mary	....	28, 63
Small, Harold and Charlotte, Family	....	7, **63**
Smith, Alexander and Shirley, Family	....	77, **78**
Smith, Alfred, Family	....	44
Smith, Andrew, Sr., Family	....	6, **21**, 22, 23
Smith, Arthur, Family	....	20, 21
Smith, Charles and Gladys	....	88
Smith, Doris	....	86
Smith, Edgar and Phyllis, Family	....	**48**, 49
Smith, Elizabeth	....	30
Smith, Frederick and Dorothy	....	16
Smith, George F.	....	91
Smith, Hugh	....	23
Smith, James and Bridget, Family	....	6, **20**, 21
Smith, James, Sr., Family	....	16
Smith, John	....	88
Smith, John and Ann Eliza, Family	....	57
Smith, John and Isabel, Family	....	57
Smith, John H. and Judith, Family	....	86
Smith, Joseph	....	24
Smith, Joseph H.	....	3, 43, 114
Smith, Murray and Jessie, Family	....	30
Smith, Patrick	....	23
Smith, Percy and Edith	....	73
Smith, Philip	....	23
Smith, Rev. R. H.	....	120
Smith, Wayne and Shannon	....	89
Smutylo, Steve and Mary	....	31
Smye, John and Jane, Family	....	59
Snell, Philip	....	18
Snell, Thomas	....	18
Sole, Rev. John	....	96
Sonnenburg, George and Norma, Family	....	29

Sparks, J. S.	....	*103*
Spencer, Anna, Family	....	*28*
Spencer, Rev. William	....	*96, 99*
Spring, Mary H.	....	*71, 108*
Springer, Darius	....	*23*
Springer, Elmer S.	....	*23*
Springer, Fred and Mary	....	*57*
Steele, John, Family	....	*20*
Stein, Hans and Elizabeth	....	*58*
Stevens, Donald and Brenda, Family	....	*26, 38*
Stevens, Mrs. L.	....	*123*
Stevens, Muriel M.	....	*23*
Stevens, Robert and Marilyn, Family	....	***43***, *47*
Stevenson, Jack	....	*107*
Stewart, Alexander and Catherine, Family	....	*83, 84, 86*
Stewart, Allan	....	*82, 120*
Stewart, Catherine	....	*84, 121*
Stewart, Charles, Jr.	....	*16*
Stewart, David and Jane, Family	....	***82-83***, *100, 123*
Stewart, George and Annie, Family	....	*84*
Stewart, Glenn and Linda, Family	....	*43*
Stewart, John, Sr., Family	....	*83*
Stewart, Margaret	....	*84, 121*
Stewart, Neil	....	*88*
Stewart, Rev. Dr. H. S.	....	*98*
Stewart, Rev. John	....	*103*
Stewart, Walter	....	*82, 121*
Stewart, William	....	*52*
Stewart, William	....	*90, 91*
Stewart, William and Audrey, Family	....	*84*
Stewart, William E. and Mary, Family	....	*82, 83,* ***84***, *86*
Stoeckner, Alfred and Annie, Family	....	*31*
Stone, George H. and Lola	....	*19, 20*
Stony Battery	....	*15*
Stringfellow, Sydney and Margaret	....	*20*
Sullivan Family	....	*16*
Sullivan, Bartholomew, Sr., Family	....	*20, 23*
Sullivan, Bill	....	*21*
Sullivan, James	....	*6, 20*
Sullivan, Patrick, Family	....	*20*
Summerfield, Ernest and Alice, Family	....	*51*
Surerus, Jack and Winnifred	....	*21*
Surveys	....	*6, 15, 20, 36*
Sutherland, Innes	....	*20*

Sutton, John and Ann	....	*39*
Sutton, Laommi	....	*95, 98*
Svab, Frank and Annie	....	*22*
Swim, Mrs. Harriet	....	*75*
Szelei, Anton and Kathleen	....	*74*
Szitas, Andor	....	*76*
Szollosy, Mary	....	*26*
Szponarski, Frank and Frances, Family	....	*55*
Tansley, Robert, Family	....	*49*
Tashan Construction	....	*17*
Taylor, Brian and Leslee	....	*47*
Taylor, Gerald	....	*61*
Taylor, Mrs. A.	....	*123*
Tenbrinke, John W.	....	*15*
Tennant, Jane	....	*43*
Tennigkeit, Kurt and Irmgard	....	*32*
Thatcher, Mr.	....	*15*
Thibeau	....	*64*
Thibodeau, Mr.	....	*66*
Thomas, E. Cartwright	....	*23*
Thomas, John E.	....	*98, 99*
Thompson, Claude	....	*22*
Thompson, John	....	*67*
Thompson, Oron, Family	....	*44, 46, 47,* ***56,*** *130, 131*
Thornborrow, Brian and Jacqueline	....	*22*
Thurston, Samuel, Family	....	*43*
Tief (Taafe), Richard and Margaret	....	*81, 91*
Tigchelaar, John and Claire, Family	....	*26,* ***91***
Titmas, Sarah	....	*98*
Traas, John and Patricia	....	*23*
Trask, George and Emily, Family	....	*45*
Tuinstra, Dorothy	....	*23*
Turner, Albert and Colleen, Family	....	*86*
Uberig, Adolph	....	*15*
Urban, Gina	....	*58, 124*
Urban, Gloria	....	*58, 124*
Urban, Joachim and Walltrant, Family	....	*58*
Urban, Margaret	....	*58, 123*
Urban, Rosemarie	....	*58, 123, 124*
Uttermarck, John De Haviland	....	*7, 23, 31, 87, 90*
Van Damme, Joan, Family	....	*74*

Van der Meulen, Ryck	....	76
Vanderburgh, Mr. and Mrs., Family	....	75
VanderSchaaf, David and Sylvia	....	26
Vanderstar, Hermanus and Leona	....	16
Vanfleet	....	64
Vegh, Barry and Patricia	....	34
Velke, William and Renee, Family	....	74
Vince, Gordon and Rene	....	86
Vowels, Neil and Robin, Family	....	86
Waggood (Wigood), James and Rhoda, Family	....	32, **89**
Walker Family	....	40
Walker, John and Lynne	....	15
Walker, William and Ann, Family	....	33
Waller, Arnold and Eileen	....	22
Ward, Everett G.	....	97, 98, 99
Ward, John	....	97, 99
Warford, Arthur and Bridget	....	15
Warner, Clarence and Lillian, Family	....	**73**, 122, 123
Warren, Ernest and Marjorie	....	22
Warren, Gary and Susan, Family	....	47
Warren, Rev. Archibald	....	96, 99
Waterdown Sportsman's Club	....	60
Watson, Agnes	....	121
Watson, Jack and Florence, Family	....	32, **66**, 67, 76
Watson, James	....	19
Watson, Milford and Alice, Family	....	25, 26, **27**, 28
Watson, Richard, Family	....	19
Watson, Ross and Lynn, Family	....	66
Watson, William, Family	....	15
Waygood (Wigood), William, Family	....	23, **24**
Webb, Anthony and Yoskyl	....	47
Weir, Raymon V.	....	24
Weir, Thomas, Family	....	**24**, 57
Weir, Thomas, Sr. and Isabella, Family	....	24, **58**
Weir, William R.	....	24
Welsh, Michael	....	68
Wernaart, Martin and Toni, Family	....	65
Wetherelt, Marjorie	....	121
Wetherelt, Mrs. T.	....	122, 123
Wheeler, James and Sarah, Family	....	6, 24, **75**, 76
Wheeler, James, Jr. and Christiana, Family	....	23, **24**
Wheeler, Peter	....	60
Wheeler, Rose Ann	....	24

Wheelihan, John D.	....	*20, 21*
Whibley, Murray and Sally, Family	....	*74*
Whidden, David	....	*19*
White, John	....	*16, 64, 87*
Whitehead, Henry and Anthea, Family	....	*57*
Wignall, Robert and Ann, Family	....	*64*
Wigood, Calvin and Marjorie, Family	....	*12, **32**, 105, 121, 123*
Wigood, Donald and Lynda	....	*22*
Wigood, Glen, Family	....	*24*
Wigood, Hugh and Annie, Family	....	*12, 26, **28**, 100, 121, 122, 123*
Wigood, James and Martha, Family	....	*57*
Wigood, Lyle and Mary, Family	....	***28**, 120, 123*
Wigood, Murray and Dianne	....	*24*
Wigood, Robert and Martha, Family	....	*28, 31, **32**, 102*
Wigood, Robert, Jr. and Emily, Family	....	***32**, 57*
Wigood, William T. and Alma, Family	....	*24*
Wildeman, Richard and Lorene, Family	....	*49*
Wilkerson, Charles	....	*28*
Wilkerson, David	....	*28*
Williams, Florence	....	*19*
Williams, Rev. Dr. George	....	*104*
Williamson, J. Elmore	....	*97, 99*
Winard (Winer), John, Sr.	....	*92*
Winard, John, Jr., Family	....	*92*
Winder, Edric and Emily, Family	....	***87**, 88*
Wingrove, Allan	....	*78, 121*
Wingrove, Charles and Sarah, Family	....	*5, 54, **55**, 77, 102*
Wingrove, Clarence and Nellie, Family	....	***77**, 81, 100*
Wingrove, Daniel and Elizabeth, Family	....	*57*
Wingrove, Douglas and Evelyn, Family	....	*55, 76, **78**, 79, 80*
Wingrove, Earl and Mary, Family	....	***77**, 98, 120*
Wingrove, George and Ann, Family	....	*5, 54, **57**, 102*
Wingrove, Gordon and Anna	....	*55*
Wingrove, Gordon and Selena, Family	....	***78**, 79, 97, 100*
Wingrove, Ivan	....	*77, 120, 121*
Wingrove, James and Sarah, Family	....	*5, 54, 55, **78**, 79, 98*
Wingrove, John W. and Margaret, Family	....	***45**, **57**, 60, 91, 107*
Wingrove, Jonathan and Janet, Family	....	*82*
Wingrove, Lloyd and Hazel, Family	....	***81**, 120, 121*
Wingrove, Osborne, Mr. and Mrs.	....	*45, 57, 98, 105, 116*
Wingrove, Richard	....	*54*
Wingrove, Thomas and Catherine, Family	....	*5, 31, 54, **82**, 95, 98*
Wingrove, Thomas and Nettie, Family	....	*57, **82***
Wingrove, William	....	*54*

Wingrove, William and Elizabeth, Family	....	28, 55, **78**, 79, 96
Wingrove, Wm. A. and Marjorie, Family	....	**78**, 79, 80, 98, 100, 122, 123
Wise, Mrs. Russell	....	122
Wolverton, Donald and Carol	....	17
Wood, David and Marion, Family	....	26, **65**
Wood, John F.	....	19
Woolsey, Bertha	....	59, 121
Woolsey, Robert Garnet, M.D., Family	....	59
Woolsey, Stanley and Gladys, Family	....	**59**, 75
Woolsey, Thomas and Susan, Family	....	**59**, 107
Woolsey, William and Emma, Family	....	59
Wright, Graham L.	....	86, 87
Wright, Jacob	....	32, 66, 102
Wright, Kenneth, Family	....	**75**, 90
Wright, Rev. Daniel	....	96, 99
Zaborowski, Eugene and Janine	....	31
Zaionz, Bernard	....	16
Zaionz, Charles	....	16
Zieman, Rev. P. P. W.	....	98
Zimmerman, Cramer, Family	....	21
Zimmerman, Margaret (Mrs. G. Dougherty)	....	31
Zimmerman, Samuel	....	24
Zsadanyi, L., L. M., and A. Z.	....	21

www.ingramcontent.com/pod-product-compliance
Lightning Source LLC
Chambersburg PA
CBHW080413170426
43194CB00015B/2797